CHURCHES OF THE
SOUTH ATLANTIC ISLANDS
1502-1991

Edward Cannan joined the Royal Air Force in 1937 as an Aircraft Apprentice. Commissioned as a Signals Officer in 1942, he resigned in 1946 to read Divinity at King's College, London. After a curacy in Dorset, he spent 20 years as a Chaplain in the Royal Air Force, becoming an Assistant Chaplain-in-Chief and Principal of the RAF Chaplains' School. There followed five years as Chaplain of a girls' boarding school. He was Bishop of St Helena from 1979 to 1985. He now lives in the Diocese of Hereford, where he is an Assistant Bishop. Such free time as retirement allows is spent with his wife Eunice in the relaxations of gardening and house maintenance.

Edward Cannan

Churches of the South Atlantic Islands 1502-1991

ANTHONY NELSON

First published in 1992 by Anthony Nelson
PO Box 9, Oswestry, Shropshire sy11 1by, England

isbn 0 904614 48 4

Typeset in Linotype Baskerville
by Nene Phototypesetters Ltd, Northampton
and printed by The Bath Press, Avon, England

cover picture
The Portuguese Church in Chapel Valley, St Helena.
From a sketch by Jan Huyghen van Linschoten, 1589.
(Courtesy Trevor Hearl)

Contents

To Eunice

Foreword *by Canon A. M. Allchin*

I find it impossible to disguise my admiration and enthusiasm for this book. The author has gathered together a mass of information from a great variety of sources about the life both of Church and people on the South Atlantic Islands of St Helena, Ascension, Tristan da Cunha and the Falklands. His researches have gone back as far as the sixteenth century, while his personal experiences as Bishop of St Helena in the years 1979-85 have allowed him to add vivid details to the more recent chapters of the story.

The book takes us to four very distant and very different places. It gives us an impression of the physical conditions of life in the South Atlantic, and a picture of the characters of the people who live in such isolated and inaccessible situations. If the delinquencies of some of the earlier Chaplains on St Helena make depressing reading, few can fail to be impressed by the evident devotion of many of the clergy who have served on these islands during the last two centuries. Many of them were clearly rugged and independent characters like the people that they served. It is good that their lives should be recorded here.

One of the facts which the book reveals is the evident love of the people of the islands for their church buildings, buildings which they have often constructed with their own hands. From Bishop Cannan's writing one gets the sense of places dearly loved, carefully looked after and full of the spirit of prayer and thanksgiving. I shall not soon forget the image of the brightly painted sanctuary on the storm battered island of Tristan da Cunha. 'This is none other than the house of God, this is the gate of heaven.'

Oxford

A. M. Allchin.

List of Maps and Illustrations

Preface and Acknowledgements

The lack of any systematic treatment of the history of the Churches on the South Atlantic Islands of St Helena, Ascension, Tristan da Cunha and the Falklands can probably be explained by the difficulties of collecting together material, which is scattered, not only in a variety of sources in the islands, but also in a number of libraries and archives in the UK.

Six years as Bishop of St Helena, followed by five years' retirement in England, suggested that I was in a favourable position to attempt to repair the omission.

I must first acknowledge my indebtedness to the authors of what has already been written, and who are listed in the bibliography and the references. Two books in particular have been invaluable for the earlier period, providing source material in an easily accessible form: *St Helena 1502-1928* by Philip Gosse and *Extracts from the St Helena Records* by Hudson Ralph Janisch. My gratitude to Miss Jennifer Gosse and Percy Teale and their publishers. For the history of the Diocese of St Helena in the period 1899 to 1951 the *St Helena (Diocesan) Magazine*, edited first by Canon Porter and from 1921 by Canon Walcott, is invaluable. Then to the librarians of the Oriental and India Office Collections, British Library, and the Lambeth Palace library, and especially to Alan Bell, chief librarian of the Rhodes House library, Oxford, a branch of the Bodleian Library, for guiding me through the USPG Archives, which he has in his care. To the Archbishop of Canterbury and the Trustees of Lambeth Palace Library and to USPG for allowing me to quote from their respective archives. To Mrs Janet Williams, Information Services Manager of USPG. To the staff of the Hereford Public Library, for obtaining many books.

My thanks to the many past and present clergy of the islands who have so willingly provided a great deal of material, especially Patrick Helyer, Michael Edwards, Jack Jewell, Michael Houghton, and others too numerous to list, but who will recognize their contributions.

To Allan Crawford, who with his great knowledge of Tristan, kindly commented on those chapters, and to all who have scrutinized relevant extracts. To Jonathan Mané, Lecturer in Art History in the University of Canterbury, New Zealand, to Percy Teale, to the late Dean Ronald Jasper, to the Reverend Gordon Taylor, to Mark Parker of USPG, to Mrs Joan Thomas, to the Reverend Dr D.H.Edwards, for providing material and allowing me to quote.

To Mrs Anne Kotze, Archivist of the Church of the Province of Southern Africa, for permission to quote from her *St Helena Journal*, and to Mrs A.M.Cunningham, Curator of Manuscripts at the University of the Witwatersrand. To the Reverend Edward Rogers for permission to quote from his mother's diary. To Mrs Margaret Banks, Girl Guide Commissioner for Branch Associations. To Owen George, Colin Brooks and the Oxford Branch of the St Helena Association (UK).

To the Right Reverend William Flagg, General Secretary of the South American Missionary Society, and to Mrs Dorothy Welch, Honorary Librarian. To the Right Reverend Cyril Tucker, last Bishop of the Falklands. To my predecessors and successors on St Helena, Bishops Edmund Capper, Kenneth Giggall and James Johnson and to the present Bishop John Ruston for permission to quote from the Diocesan Archives.

To Cecil Maggott, Curator of the St Helena Government Archives, and to past and present Governors of St Helena for use of the Archives and permission to reproduce a picture of the old Country Church now in Plantation House, and to Sister Lilian Hepworth for her photographic copy. To the late Arthur Mawson, and to Nicholas Thorpe, past and present Chairmen of the St Helena Heritage Society.

To Allan Crawford and the Reverend Patrick Helyer for pictures of Tristan. I am also grateful to Mr Michael Flint, nephew of Fr Flint, for kindly giving me his uncle's slides of Tristan, some of which I have reproduced. To Trevor Hearl and Nicholas Thorpe for old pictures, and to David Bentham for recent pictures, of St Helena, and the Reverend Richard Davison for a picture of St Mary's Ascension. To Mrs Martha George of St Helena for a picture of Bishop Welby and his fellow Bishops. To Charles Frater for a picture of the Salvation Army. To Stephen Phillips for help with the maps. To Archbishop Philip Russell and Bishop Leslie Stradling for accounts of their visits.

In my accounts of Churches other than the Anglican Church, I have written with some hesitation, from outside their community. I am grateful to the Reverend D.C.McPhee, Secretary-Depute of the Department of National Mission of the Church of Scotland, the Reverend Professor C.Graham, Principal Clerk of Assembly of the Free Church of Scotland, Miss Brenda Webster for her research, the Reverend Bernard Green, General Secretary of the Baptist Union of Great

Britain, Commissioner Stanley Walters, International Secretary of the Salvation Army and Colonel Dinsdale-Pender. My especial thanks for considerable help and material to the Reverend Michael Longstaff and the Reverend Andrew Coats, past and present Baptist ministers on St Helena, to Lieutenant Leslie Pinner of the Salvation Army, to Pastor Charles Chalmers of the Seventh Day Adventist Church. To Monsignor Anton Agreiter MHM, Apostolic Prefect on the Falklands, for generous co-operation concerning the history of the Roman Catholic Church on the Falklands, for his own historical summary, and for a copy of Brunet's history of the Church in the Spanish period. To the Archivist of the Salesian Fathers in Rome for the history of the Church on the Falklands in the Salesian period and to Mrs Elizabeth Dooley, a missionary of the South American Missionary Society for kindly translating it. To Brother Venantius Roozendaal MHM, for making available his expert knowledge of Falkland postage stamps.

To Trevor Hearl, for so generously making available his wide knowledge of the islands, for much encouragement and provision of a great deal of material, for reading my script and making innumerable suggestions for improvement. Any remaining imperfections are probably due to my not having accepted all his suggestions. To Tony Nelson, one-time itinerant teacher on the Falklands, for all his encouragement and assistance in publishing the book and to Mrs Penny David for her invaluable editorial help.

To Eunice, my wife, for her encouragement and for reading the script over and over again and suggesting amendments. To our sons and daughters-in-law, Jeremy and Sandra, Stephen and Eleanor, Nigel and Sally-Anne for much help, ranging from research and comment to provision of word processors.

Finally my thanks to Canon Donald Allchin for so kindly writing the foreword.

EDWARD CANNAN
January 1992

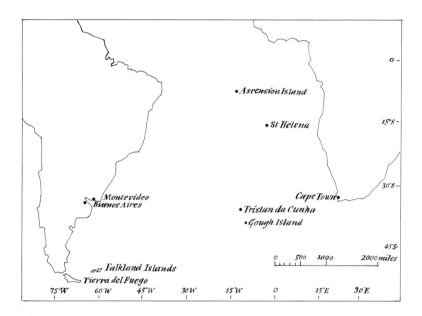

- *Ascension Island*

- *St Helena* — 15°S

Cape Town — 30°S

- *Montevideo*
- *Buenos Aires*

- *Tristan da Cunha*
- *Gough Island*

45°S

| 0 | 500 | 1000 | 2000 *miles* |

_o_ *Falkland Islands*
Tierra del Fuego

75°W | 60°W | 45°W | 30°W | 15°W | 0 | 15°E | 30°E

Introduction

The South Atlantic Islands of St Helena, Ascension, Tristan da Cunha and the Falklands have four things in common. They were all discovered in the sixteenth century; they were all uninhabited when discovered; they are all British Dependencies and they were all at one time in the Anglican Diocese of St Helena, or (in the case of the Falklands), nominally under the pastoral care of the Bishop of St Helena from 1859 to 1869.

In almost every other way, especially topographically and sociologically, they are totally different.

The Falkland Islands are the most southerly, the nearest (250 miles) to a mainland, and by far the largest, being over twenty times the size of the other three put together. Comparatively flat, both East and West Falklands have a range of hills rising to about 2,300 feet. There are many anchorages and a good harbour at Port Stanley.

St Helena, Ascension and Tristan all lie on or near the Central Atlantic Ridge and are volcanic in origin, which the Falklands are not. None has a harbour and getting ashore can be difficult, especially at Tristan. However, I realized how very different the relief of these three islands would be when, in an attempt to understand the topography of St Helena, I made a relief map of the island (now in the Museum on St Helena), based on the contours of the single sheet Ordnance Survey map.

On St Helena, the cliffs rise vertically from the sea to heights of between 450 and 2,000 feet on three sides. From the central ridge, part of the rim of an ancient crater, which rises to 2,700 feet, radiate deep valleys which hinder internal communications. Roads have steep gradients and sharp bends. There is luxuriant vegetation above 1,500 feet, but below that level there is only barren rock. Man cut down the woods which once extended to the cliff edge, goats introduced by the Portuguese to victual their ships prevented regrowth, and the soil eroded. A Victorian writer aptly described the island as 'an emerald set in bronze'. Only 47 square miles in area (a quarter the size of the Isle of Wight), with no airfield, the island lies 1,000 miles from the nearest part of Africa. Cape Town is 1,800 miles to the south-east and 5 days by sea. Ascension is 700 miles away, Tristan 1,500 miles and the Falklands nearly 4,000 miles.

Ascension is comparatively flat, except for Green Mountain which rises to 2,800 feet and whose top is covered with vegetation. The rest of the island is dotted with 44 craters and extensive lava flows, perhaps the nearest on earth to a lunar landscape.

Tristan is a cone, with a base 7½ miles in diameter, and rising to 6,760 feet above sea level. There is one small plateau on the north-west, large enough for a small settlement. There are numerous springs and streams supporting the vegetation.

Even more striking are the differences in population.

The present colony on the Falklands, in number something over 2,000, dates from 1833 when Britain resumed official occupation. The island supports about a hundred sheep farms of various sizes. The population has always been of European origin, save for a few Indians from Tierra del Fuego, brought to a mission on Keppel Island in the 19th century, and the St Helenians who came for employment in the 1980s. The island is self-supporting.

On St Helena the present population of 5,500, save for about 80 expatriates mostly working for the Government on short term contracts, is the result of intermarriage between the different races brought to the island by the East India Company since 1659 – English settlers, soldiers, Company slaves from the East Indies and Madagascar, Chinese indentured labourers, Africans released from captured slave ships in the 1840s, and Boer prisoners (there were 6,000 on the island in 1900). In the 18th and 19th centuries there were two social classes, the English settlers and the rest; today there are no remaining racial groups, all are St Helenians of whatever shade of colour, and decidedly British.

From 1659 St Helena had an important role as a staging post for victualling East India Company ships returning from the Far East, and this relationship with shipping continued into the 19th century. The advent of steam and the opening of the Suez Canal produced a dramatic change. Whereas in the 1850s there were over 1,000 shipping calls a year, by 1910 the number had dropped to about 50. The latter part of the 19th century saw a great increase in poverty on the island and a rise in emigration to South Africa. Bishop Welby wrote in 1872 of:

a small settlement in the midst of the Atlantic without trade, or any source of wealth, composed of a mixed coloured race, the offspring of slaves and others, whom England in former days (the days of slavery) brought together here from

India, China and Africa, and of prize negroes brought since; – England placed them here exposed to all the corrupting influences of a garrison and a seaport, – and now that it seems no longer desirable to expend large sums of money in keeping up a military and civil establishment, she leaves the population which she has formed, in miserable poverty.[1]

In the same year the Government offered free passages to Lagos or Sierra Leone in HMS *Himalaya* to Africans living on St Helena; 260 went, about one third of the Africans of pure blood on the island. Bishop Welby wrote that they were sorry to leave, but were compelled to do so on account of the increasing poverty. At a farewell service at St John's he urged them to continue in the faith and promised to commend them to the Bishops of the Dioceses to which they were going.[2]

Successive Governors endeavoured to find some way to help the economy, but none were successful. St Helena has well been called 'an Island of lost causes'. The export of fibre from large areas planted with New Zealand flax was successful for a time, particularly during the two World Wars, but finally succumbed by 1965 to the advent of man made fibres, and, for example, the British Post Office eventually using rubber bands instead of string.[3] Today the flax mills are silent and the rope-making machinery rusting away. Save for the present attempts to improve the fishing industry, there are virtually no exports. The terrain and other factors make it difficult for the island to be self-supporting in food. The island exists on a subsidy of several million pounds from the British Government, including a subsidy for the RMS *St Helena*, virtually the only ship to call, on its two monthly round trip between Cardiff and Cape Town.

Ascension and Tristan were both first inhabited, save for castaways, in 1815/16, when the British Government put a small garrison on each island to prevent the French using either as a springboard to rescue Napoleon from St Helena. On Ascension the community has remained an artificial one to this day, men and women on contract work, some with their families. There is a hospital and school, but no old people. As the late Vicar of my parish commented, 'You mean nobody's grand-mother lives there?' Today it is a technological, communications island with a BBC relay station, Cable & Wireless, a civilian staffed American base, the South African-staffed South Atlantic Cable Company and, since the Falklands invasion, a Royal Air Force presence. Some 750 St Helenians are employed by the different organizations and this is the financial salvation of most St Helenian families.

On Tristan, when the garrison was withdrawn in 1817, Corporal William Glass elected to remain together with his wife and children.

They were joined by others – British, Dutch, American and Italian – including some shipwrecked mariners and five St Helenian women. By 1939, the tiny and very isolated community had grown to about 200, living in great hardship, sometimes not seeing a ship for a year at a time. They shared seven surnames among them. The only expatriate was, from time to time, an SPG (Society for the Propagation of the Gospel) missionary, sometimes accompanied by his family. The situation changed dramatically in 1948 with the establishment of a crayfish canning factory by a South African company, bringing an influx of expatriates, a British Administrator, improved standards of living, medical care and much more contact with the outside world. Today Tristan is self-supporting.

After his three day visit to Tristan in 1937, Bishop Aylen noted a marked contrast between the little community of 101 men and 81 women on Tristan, and the 5,000 or so people on St Helena. On Tristan

you have a community chaste, contented, honest, polite and industrious. There has been no case of fornication or adultery in Tristan da Cunha within living memory. In St Helena these social sins are all too common.

In Tristan da Cunha the only influences which have been externally introduced are the influences of the men of God whom for 84 years the SPG ... has been sending ... In St Helena every heterogeneous influence has been introduced and has left its heavy nasty fruit.[4]

No doubt the Bishop was seeing things far too starkly in black and white. Only a few years later, David Luard, Royal Naval Chaplain on Tristan (1944-6) was to write:

In some ways they are a very law abiding people, and they are certainly in advance of the average run of people in England. There is e.g. very little stealing in spite of the great temptation offered by great poverty in close neighbourhood with comparative wealth ... Nor do they steal from each another ... Fighting and quarrelling are not common.

If the sixth and eighth commandments are well observed, the seventh perhaps is not so good. This side of their lives is shrouded in mystery ... It is probable that in these matters their standards and practices are much like those of villagers anywhere in Europe. The arrival of a really large number of outsiders to stay in the island complicated things a good deal.[5]

However that may be, Bishop Aylen draws attention to the great contrast in the influences on the two communities. Matters have changed since then. Employment on Ascension has brought cultural changes on St Helena. And life on Tristan today is very different.

Martha Rogers, born in 1896 and interviewed for the *Tristan Times* in December 1983 said that she preferred the old Tristan because 'you had no worries about money or anything like that. Times were hard but they were happy times.'[6] Younger Tristanians may have a different view. But after their evacuation to England following the volcanic eruption of 1961, the decision to return to Tristan in 1962 was virtually unanimous.

By far the earliest Christian presence in the South Atlantic was on St Helena, dating from the Portuguese arrival in 1502. The Anglican Church arrived with the East India Company, the first church being built about 1674 on or near the site of the Portuguese church. Its replacement, St James', built in 1774, is the oldest surviving Anglican church in the Southern Hemisphere. Apart from the Portuguese and Napoleon's chaplains, the Roman Catholic Church dates from 1852 but has always been small in numbers. The Baptists arrived in 1845, the Salvation Army in 1884. Since then a number of sects have established themselves on the island. As with the other islands, the Anglican Church has the greatest proportion of adherents. Apart from the clergy and a handful of expatriates, it is entirely a St Helenian Church. It has always been dependent, for money and manpower, on help from overseas, at first from England, continued today by USPG and the Diocesan Association, and now also, and substantially, by the Church of the Province of Southern Africa.

On the other three islands the Church dates from the middle of the 19th century. On Ascension the Anglican Church has relied primarily on lay leadership, with occasional episcopal visits. The first Vicar was not appointed until 1966. Today it is self-supporting and has an ecumenical role, with many Christian Churches being represented on its Church Council, and with friendly relations with the small Roman Catholic community.

William Glass was a religious man and held daily prayers and a Sunday service on Tristan. Since 1851, SPG have sent a resident priest, when there was a volunteer available. In 1952, Tristan became part of the Diocese of Cape Town and since 1980 the clergy have come from South Africa. There is a small Roman Catholic presence dating from 1908.

On the Falklands, the first Colonial Chaplain was appointed in 1845. Ten years later, the Patagonian Missionary Society established a Mission Station on Keppel Island, for work among the natives of Tierra del Fuego. The Roman Catholics date from about 1857, with their first resident priest in 1875. There was a strong Presbyterian presence from 1872, owing to the numbers of Scottish shepherds introduced by the Falkland Islands Company, and in 1888 the renowned C. H. Spurgeon sent out a Baptist minister.

The history of the Churches on these islands, remote from each other and the rest of the world, yet each with a strong attachment to their motherland, is a fascinating one.

Part I

St Helena

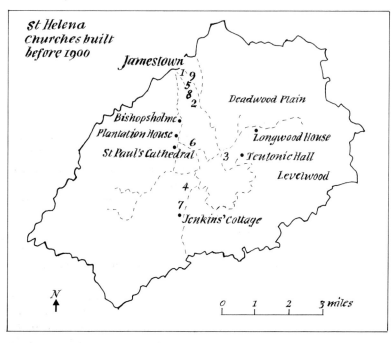

St Helena
Churches built
before 1900

Jamestown

1 9
5
8
2

Deadwood Plain

Bishopsholme
Plantation House
St Paul's Cathedral

6

3 • Teutonic Hall

Longwood House

Levelwood

4

7
• Jenkins' Cottage

N

0   1   2   3 miles

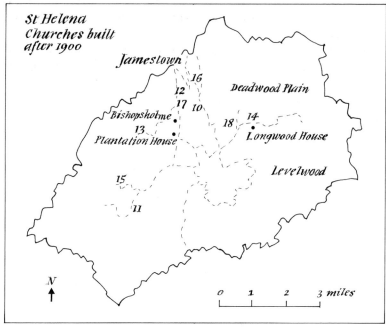

St Helena
Churches built
after 1900

Jamestown

16
12
17 10

Deadwood Plain

Bishopsholme
13
Plantation House

18   14

Longwood House

Levelwood

15

11

N

0   1   2   3 miles

1
Early Days

The Portuguese Church (1502-1659)

'Where the English settle they first build a Punch house, the Dutch a Fort and the Portuguese a Church.' When the Portuguese Admiral Joao da Nova Castella discovered the island on 21 May 1502, he named it after St Helena, whose feast day it was. Tradition also has it that he built a chapel in what is now Jamestown. It is said that he broke up one of his unseaworthy ships and 'drew on shore her weather-beaten sides ... building with the timber a chappell in this valley, from thence is called Chappell Valley'.[1] Sometimes proverbs do give rise to traditions, but we see no reason to doubt that Castella did build a chapel.[2] The Portuguese built one at Mossel Bay in South Africa in 1501, incidentally just pre-empting Jamestown's claim to be the earliest Christian site south of the Equator. We can imagine the sense of thankfulness which the sailors would have felt on sighting this unknown island in the midst of the ocean. In such an age of faith, building a church in which to offer thanks to God, and naming the island after the Saint's Day would have seemed perfectly natural.

However, this raises an intriguing question. It is in the Calendar of the Eastern Orthodox Church that the feast day of St Helena, the

Key to maps opposite

Churches built before 1900

1 St James
2 St John's
3 St Matthew's, Hutts Gate
4 St Peter's
5 Jamestown Baptist Chapel
6 Knollcombe Baptist Chapel
7 Sandy Bay Baptist Chapel
8 Church of the Sacred Heart (RC)
9 Salvation Army HQ
    St Paul's Cathedral

Churches built after 1900

10 St Mary the Briars
11 St Helena and The Cross, Blue Hill
12 St Andrew's, Half Tree Hollow
13 St Martin's-in-the-Hills, High Point
14 St Mark's, Longwood
15 Head 'O Wain Baptist Chapel
16 Seventh Day Adventist Church, Jamestown
17 Salvation Army, Half Tree Hollow
18 Salvation Army, Deadwood

mother of the Roman Emperor Constantine the Great, is 21 May; in the Western Calendar it is 18 August. Why were the Portuguese using an Eastern Calendar? A manuscript note, almost certainly by Bishop Holbech, in the margin of Melliss' *St Helena* in the Bishopsholme library, states: 'May 21st is the Eve of the feast of St Helen, Virgin of Auxerre, who lived in *c*.AD410'. Perhaps Bishop Holbech thought we had the wrong girl! I am indebted to the late Ronald Jasper, when he was Dean of York, for a more convincing explanation. St Helena has always shared a day with the Emperor Constantine, whose traditional date of death is firmly established as 21 May, and is commemorated in the Greek Church on that day. Jasper pointed out that during the late medieval and early Reformation period, the whole of the Iberian Peninsula was heavily influenced by the Greeks.

In particular Greek sailors were used, and it would seem more than likely that even on Portuguese ships at this time there would ... be a share of Greek sailors on board. I think it would therefore be extremely likely that this Greek influence will undoubtedly be the reason why the 21st May is the date observed ... further evidence of the Portuguese being interested in Eastern affairs is clear from their colonization with people in India in the 15th-16th centuries. They were very active with the Christians in Malabar.[3]

This interest in Eastern affairs is shown by the military assistance offered by the Portuguese in the 16th century to Abyssinia, where there was an eastern Monophysite Church. The Patriarch of Abyssinia, Bermudez, who chose to spend a year, apparently in spiritual retreat, in St Helena in 1557 was on his way back to Portugal.[4]

The medieval chroniclers Geoffrey of Monmouth and Henry of Huntingdon, who are notoriously unreliable, believed that Helena was the daughter of Old King Cole of Colchester, which city still proudly claims Helena as its patron Saint. In the splendid set of late 15th century glass of the life of St Helena in the Parish Church of St Michael and All Angels, Ashton-under-Lyne (featured on the Colony's Christmas postage stamps for 1983-5), the window showing her birth has the inscription, '*Hic nascitur Elena Coyle Regis Filia*'. In fact she was born in Asia Minor, possibly at Drepanum (later known as Helenopolis), and St Ambrose, writing about 70 years after her death, in his *Oratio de obitu Theodosii* describes her as a *stabularia*, or innkeeper. She married the Emperor Constantius Chlorus, and her son Constantine, born in AD274 became Emperor in 306. Helena became a Christian in 313. In 326 aged about 75, she made a lengthy pilgrimage to Palestine, where she built churches on holy sites, particularly at Bethlehem and on the Mount of Olives. The cistern where later writers (*c*.AD400) assert that she discovered the Cross is below the Church of the Resurrection in Jerusalem, built by Constantine. St Helena died *c.*AD330.

By 1588, when the English Captain Thomas Cavendish visited St Helena, the early wooden church had been replaced by a stone one:

We went on shore, where we found a marvellous fair and pleasant valley, wherein divers handsome buildings and houses were set up, and especially one which was a Church, which was tiled, and whitened on the outside very fair, and made with a porch, and within the church at the upper end was set an altar, whereon stood a very large table, set in a frame, having on it the picture of our Saviour Christ upon the Cross, and the image of our Lady praying, with divers other histories painted curiously upon the same. The sides of the church were hung round with stained cloths, having many devices drawn upon them.

Nearby was 'a very fair causeway'

and upon the said causeway is a frame erected, whereon hang two bells, wherewith they ring to mass; and near to it a cross is set up, which is squared and framed, and made very artificially of free-stone, whereon is carved in cyphers what time it was built, which was in the year of our Lord 1571.[5]

A drawing of this church and belfry by the Dutch navigator Jan van Linschoten was published shortly afterwards.

Cavendish is reputedly the first Englishman to have visited St Helena, but *The Dictionary of National Biography* states that the famous Elizabethan mathematician, clergyman and astrologer, Dr John Dee 'at some period of his life ... visited St Helena and wrote an account of his voyage.' This, however, seems to be an error which arose because the diary of the Reverend Richard Madox had been filed among Dr Dee's papers in the British Library. Madox was Chaplain aboard the galleon *Leicester* with an expedition, part trading, part buccaneering, led by Captain Edward Fenton along the coast of West Africa to Brazil via the North Atlantic Islands during 1582-3. On several occasions, Madox wrote in his journal – using a confusing code to protect it from prying eyes – that Fenton planned to 'occupy' St Helena, set himself up as 'King' and waylay the homecoming Portuguese East Indies fleet. Fenton's little fleet did not, in fact, make for St Helena, yet it is significant that this English seaman already knew enough about the Island to envisage such a piratical scheme.[6]

If Dee did not visit St Helena, then the first Anglican clergyman to land there was almost certainly John Way, 'preacher' with Cavendish on the *Desire*.[7]

Jan van Linschoten visited in 1589 with the Portuguese East India

The Portuguese Church in Chapel Valley, St Helena. From a sketch by Jan Huyghen van Linschoten, 1589 (courtesy Trevor Hearl)

fleet. He noted the abundance of fresh water, the fruit trees planted by the Portuguese and the animals they had introduced. But

> no man dwelleth therein; but only the sick men ... It is the fashion, that all the sick persons that are in the ships, and cannot sail well in them, are left there in the island; with some provision of rice, biscuit, oil and spices; for fish and flesh, they may have enough ... These sick men stay there till the next year, till other ships come hither, which take them with them. They are commonly soon healed in that island ... and it is very seldom that any of them die there, because they have always a temperate air and cool wind, and always have fruit throughout the whole year. The King will not suffer any man to dwell in it, because they should not destroy and spoil the country and hold it as their own: but will have it common for every man to take what he hath need of. In time past, there dwelt an hermit in the isle, under pretence of doing penance and to uphold the Church. He killed many of the goats and bucks: so that every year, he sold at least 500 or 600 skins, and made great profit thereon; which the King hearing, caused him presently to be brought from thence to Portugal. When the ships come thither, every man maketh his lodging under a tree, setting a tent about it; and the trees are there so thick, that it presently seemeth a little town or an army in the field, every man provideth for himself, flesh, fish, fruit and wood; for there is enough for them all: and every one washeth linen. There, they hold a General Fasting and Prayer with Mass every day: which is done with great devotion, with procession, and thanksgiving, and other hymns; thanking God that He hath preserved them from the danger of the Cape of Good Hope, and brought them to that island in safety.[8]

It is interesting, regarding the discussion on the Eastern Calendar, that Linschoten writes that he left St Helena on 'The 21st of May (N.S.) being Saint Helena's Day and Whitsunday'.

The Dutch began to call at St Helena and disputes between them and the Portuguese led to damage to the church. One Francois Pyrard on a visit in 1601 found the chapel in good condition, adorned with a fair altar and several handsome images and pictures, while in front of it stood a fine cross of free-stone, white as marble and well carved, which the Portuguese had brought from Portugal . On his second visit in a Portuguese ship in 1610, the cross had been broken and the chapel was in a bad condition. The Portuguese, on a nine-day visit, did what they could to repair the chapel. On one occasion the Dutch left a message – 'Portuguese, leave us our inscriptions and letters and we will leave you your crosses and pictures'.[9] However, in 1625, an Icelander, Jon Olafsson, found the Church in good repair,[10] and in 1638 when Peter Mundy, a Cornishman, made his second visit, the chapel had been repaired by the Dutch and 'the names of divers ships, principal men, as also of some women, were fairly written on boards and nailed up in the chapel'.[11]

A French traveller, J.B.Tavernier, visited St Helena in 1649 and wrote:

There is only a little settlement near the sea, where a chapel was once built, and where a Portuguese Franciscan friar lived for fourteen years; but this chapel is now half a ruin. While he lived there the friar was very useful to the ships which put in there, as he provided them with fish caught and dried by himself, and was given in return rice, biscuits and Spanish wine. After having lived there in a very austere manner for some time, he fell ill, luckily just as a Portuguese ship appeared. They did all they could for him, but he died five days after the vessel dropped anchor, and was buried by his compatriots.[12]

East India Company Chaplains (1659-1834)

So far the occupation of the island had been spasmodic, but in 1659 the English East India Company began a permanent settlement to provide a fortified staging post for their ships returning from the East, and to deny St Helena to the Dutch and Spanish. The Company had its own chaplaincy service and recruited Anglican clergy for its stations in India, St Helena and elsewhere. They were not to act as missionaries, but to minister to the members of the Company's settlements, including, at least in the case of St Helena, their own slaves. Indeed it was promised that 'all negroes both men and women living in the Island that shall make profession of the Christian faith and be baptized shall within 7 years after be free planters', but there is no record that any slaves were set free on this account.[13]

The Company's policy on religion is set out in their Laws and Constitution for the Island of Sancta Helena of 1682. The Lord's Day is to be observed by abstinence from all labour and gaming and other unlawful pastimes. Places are to be set aside for the worship of God and the Governor and Council are by their presence to encourage the Minister. 'If there shall happen to be noe Minister upon the said Island, yet they shall in solemn manner assemble together on the Lord's Day and shall cause some part ... of Holy Scripture, and some godly Sermons to be read, with prayer'. The Minister is to catechize the younger people each week and to expound the doctrine of the Christian religion at a time to be 'appointed by our Governor and Council, who are to be present thereat if not hindered by necessary affayrs'. Fines are laid down for all who 'publiquely prophane the Lord's Day', for taking the name of God in vain and for drunkenness, and 'If any person of quality (who should be examples to others) be found guilty they may pay a greater fine than persons of a meaner rank'. Furthermore, 'All fornication, uncleaness and adultery shall be punished in such a way as shall be found most efficacious'. This policy was reiterated by the Court of Directors in a letter of 1701:

Our present Governor's continued care for discountenancing vice and promoting virtue we very well approve and earnestly recommend to all of you to lay your shoulders heartily to so good a work as you expect ye Divine protection and blessing and our Favour. When those in authority sett a good example the reformation of their Inferiors is therefore rendered more facil. Your care for keeping ye Lord's Day we approve but must at the same time remember that works of necessity and mercy are allowed at all times so yt when any ships are in danger of losing their passage or otherwise streightened in want of time, they should not be restrained from fetching water or other refreshments on ye Lord's Day nor on the other hand ought they be allowed to do any servile work on that day which can without prejudice be deffered to the next.[14]

The first Chaplain whose name is recorded was William Noakes, who arrived in 1671. It was not long before the Governor was accusing Noakes of anti-Royalist opinions by introducing books to the soldiers which taught that 'Kings, Princes and Governors may be disempowered by the people', and indeed in 1672 mutineers actually imprisoned the Governor and elected Noakes in his stead![15] The next Governor, Anthony Beale, appointed Noakes to the Council, but he was excluded from succession in the event of the death of the Governor. As it happened, the Dutch captured the island and held it for five months (January to May 1673) before it was retaken by a British force led by Captain Munden. The Company had to recruit another Chaplain for St Helena.

What motivated the clergy to offer themselves to serve with the Company? One reason may well have been the poverty of the majority of the profession in England. There was an excess of clergy and preferment was only for those who had influential patrons. In 1700 over half the parishes were worth less than £50 a year, and some only £30 or even £20 or less.[16] Goldsmith's village parson was 'passing rich with forty pounds a year', whereas in St Helena in 1673 the next Chaplain, William Swindle, was paid £50 a year as Minister, £25 as Schoolmaster and £25 gratuity, and was given his meals at the Governor's table.[17] Nevertheless, St Helena must have been low in the Chaplains' preferences, for although Joseph Church in 1683 managed to acquire 30 acres of land,[18] there were not, in general, the same opportunities of profiting from private trade or regimental chaplaincies as in India; a posting to St Helena merely placed them on the first rung of the ladder of the Company's service, in the hope of future preferment.

It is not perhaps surprising, therefore, that many of the Company's Chaplains on St Helena seem to have had neither a high standard of education nor indeed a high sense of their calling. Thus the Chaplain in 1719 was John Jones, who had previously been a soldier-schoolmaster on St Helena, and had returned to the island after being ordained in England. To improve his conversation and 'draw him off from associating himself with those of too mean a rank for him now as a Clergyman tho his equals when he was in the island before as a private soldier', the Governor thoughtfully invited him to stay at Plantation House, his country residence.[19]

Of the 18 Chaplains recorded between 1671 and 1830, 11 are spoken of as quarrelsome or drunken, or both. No doubt a similar situation existed elsewhere in the Company's overseas stations, although perhaps not to such a serious extent as on St Helena.[20] Not that drunkenness or poor education among the senior officials was confined to the chaplains. Doctor Wignall complained in 1723 that Parson Giles had threatened 'as soon as he was well, to lead him up and down the valley by the nose'.[21] If the Parson was dissatisfied with the Doctor's professional skill, it is perhaps not surprising, since a little over a year later we read: 'Dr Wignall always drunk and nearly killed the Governor by giving unsuitable medicines, his excuse being that he had nothing else to give ... Dr Wignall for drunken disorderly conduct placed in the Stocks for one hour and he sung and swore the whole time'.[22]

But Parson Giles himself could drink two or three quarts of arrack a day, a fact perhaps partly explained by a Board Resolution of 1674:

In the Governor's absence, there shall stand a salt upon the table, which shall be placed below the Council and Chaplain. Those who sit above the salt, shall always drink as they think proper, either wine or punch; but those who sit below the salt shall have to two persons, one common bowl of punch (which contains 3 pints).

Things were no better in 1732:

Mr White our Chaplain and his wife have for a long time led very scandalous and immoral lives, the woman having been drunk almost every day since she has been upon the Island and Mr White himself often in the same condition and always Rude and troublesome. One thing relating to him is very remarkable ... he has been here 16 months and yet ... has never dined or supped with his wife but once, which is a precedent very illtaken and highly resented by all the good Dames of this place ... the woman says that this cold unkind usage is the cause of her giving herself up to Liquor and ill company.[24]

Whatever the shortcomings of the early chaplains, within a few years of

Plantation House, residence of the Governor of St Helena

the repossession of the island from the Dutch, two churches had been built. The first, in Jamestown (where numbers 1, 2 and 3 Main Street now stand),[25] was completed by 1674, and the second, a wooden building in the country, near the Governor's residence, shortly afterwards. By 1678 two Churchwardens had been appointed, one for each church. By 1691 both churches were in bad repair[26] but it is not until 1732 that we read of the Vestry Meeting discussing 'the ruinous condition both of the Chapple in the Country and the Chapple at the Fort'.[27]

Captain Daniel Beeckman, who visited in 1715, described the ceremony when the Governor attended the church in Jamestown:

They use great formality in going to Church, for about nine o'clock in the morning, the Council, the Minister, and their wives, together with such commanders of ships as have a mind to it, do wait on the Governor in the castle. After which a bell being ordered to ring, a company of soldiers, with a serjeant, in good liveries, are drawn up in the castle, where they make a lane (resting on their arms) as a passage to the gate, where there is another serjeant and a company, which march with beat of drum before the Governor into Church. After follow the gentlemen and their ladies in their respective order. As soon as the soldiers get into the churchyard, they fall off to the right and left, making a lane to the church-door. The Governor has a handsome large seat, with books, where he generally desires the commanders of ships to sit, the ladies being seated by themselves.[28]

The Governors and their Chaplains seem to have been, more often than not, at loggerheads. In attempting to account for this situation, we must remember that our sources for this period are the Company records and are likely to be biased in favour of the Governors.[29] There was a great deal of petty bickering between island officials, and it may be that the Chaplains in particular felt themselves to be in an anomalous position when their role as the moral conscience of the community brought them into conflict with their social superiors. Some examples will illustrate these tensions. Thus in 1684,

Mr Sault the Minister immediately after dinner propounded something to the Gov. relating to a small parcel of land. Disliking the answer in some disgust and disturbance of mind he threw upon the table a paper folded up and departed. The paper complains of his discouragements, particularly the Governor's resentment of Mr Bowyers marriage which I will prove was strictly according to the canon law of the Church of England. The Gov. and his man both of them striking me (who am a priest in holy orders) on board Capt. Lane's ship because I told the Govr. I laughed to hear him say I was his domestic Chaplain whereas we both serve the same Hon'ble masters.[30]

This may give a clue to one source of trouble. The Chaplain, being appointed by the Honourable East India Company, did not consider that he was answerable to the Governor. But in fact he was appointed at least partly as Domestic Chaplain, as the Court of Directors made clear in 1683 concerning Sault's predecessor:

We find by Mr Church's proceedings he is an encroaching avaricious person and therefore we would have no allowance of provision made him hereafter since he has become so great a planter upon 30 acres of land, more than his beare salary and gratuity and diet att the Governor's table when he is there to say grace and do his duty as a Domestic Chaplain.

By 1685 Sault had been in prison for debt for over a year, and advantage had to be taken of the services of Mr Buttler, Chaplain of the ship *London*, to bring up the arrears of marriages. But he soon found himself in trouble:

On 2nd December Mr Buttler was complained of for having married one couple at 9 o'clock at night. He was ordered to give under his hand a catalogue of all the Christennings, Burialls and Mariages by him officiated on the Island since the coming of the said shipp tomorrow morning by nine of the Clock and when so done yt ye said Mr Buttler shall be presently carried on board of ye said shipp and there remain without coming on shore any more at this place.[31]

In the absence of a parson, military personnel were called upon. In 1691 we read: 'Manning the Chirurgeon being unskilled and ignorant disrated to a private sentinell (as formerly he was) but to continue to read the prayers as before and funeral services at 2s a week.' But later that year, 'Manning very sottish and continuing in his old drunken practises dismist and Clifton to read the Prayers.'[32] And in 1692, 'William Clifton soldier and schoolmaster allowed 20s for having drawne out and perfected the Register Books of Christenings, Marriages and Burials.'[33]

There is some evidence that the Company endeavoured to exercise a degree of selection. In 1701:

Mr Humphrey is come here and would fain extenuate ye crimes you charged upon him. We are sorry he proved so contrary to ye character wch first recommended him unto us. If we can hear of another of good report we intend to send him, otherwise we think it far better to send none at all.[34]

Alas in 1703 we read: 'Dr John Kerr the Chaplain a most dangerous man and was always getting people by the ears worse than ever Mr Humphrey was – had boasted that he came here on purpose to ruin the French rogue and refugee – meaning the Governor.' And the Clerk of Council reported that 'drinking Punch with Dr Kerr in company with the Serjeant and Corporal, Dr Kerr abused the Governor saying he stood up in Church in time of Divine Service like a French Hogonot proud fool (and I think Rouge too) when he ought to have kneeled down to make his confession.' The Governor, Captain Poirier, was a French Huguenot refugee.[35]

The fault was not always the Chaplain's, of course. John Jones, the ex-soldier Chaplain whom the Governor had invited to stay at Plantation House took an unfortunate joke by the Governor as a personal reflection. What happened was this:

On the 22nd of Sept at the Plantation House a wedding happened, one of the gentlemen of the Council to a young gentlewoman. The acct. of what fish the fishing boat had taken was brought to the Gov. as usual. The account was 12 fishes called Jacks and 12 fishes called Old Wives which occasioned the Gov. to jocke with Mr Jones by saying Parson you nor I need not despair for the old English proverb a Jack for every Jill is verified even by the fish you see here 12 Jacks to 12 Old Wives – which expression put Mr Jones in mind of the old woman he married when he went from hence to England before and raised his passion which the Gov. took no notice at first but endeavoured to overlook it. But when he grew noisy the Gov. asked him what was the matter who had angered him. He in a surly loud way replied why you have if I had the misfortune to marry an old woman must I always be twitted in the teeth of it.

When the Gov. told him he did not design any reflection on him it was the
Proverb agreeing with the Fish was the occasion, but that answer was not
assuaging his fury, the Gov. told him since he could not be easy he should quit
the house tomorrow, to which he replied Aye that I'll do now I wont be
beholden to you and so went his way.[36]

However, in church two months later, on 29 November as Jones read
the Collect for Advent Sunday, the Governor called out: 'You are
wrong, this is the second Sunday in Advent'. To keep the peace Mr
Jones obediently read the Collect for the second Sunday. Later in the
service he again used the Advent Sunday Collect and was again
interrupted by the Governor. When Jones announced that as the
following day was St Andrew's Day there would be prayers in church,
the Governor called out, 'Not by you Sir; Officer, take him prisoner!'
and the unfortunate Chaplain was put on the next ship to England. Dr
Civil and Sarah Southern wrote home in defence of Jones and were put
in the pillory for one hour for their pains. Yet 29 November must have
been Advent Sunday – the Chaplain was right and the Governor
wrong![37]

Not all Chaplains were unsatisfactory. Charles Masham took the
trouble to obtain tracts worth £5 from the Society for the Propagation
of the Gospel in 1704, only three years after the SPG was founded, and
later received Bibles and Prayer Books from them.[38] When the Town
Church was in need of repair we read that 'The Minister [Parson
Thomlinson] who is a very honest man has been industrious in getting
subscriptions. He is a useful man and since our best Doctor dyed he has
offered to prescribe in Physick for any of the Garrison gratis being
always ready to do any good he can.'[39] Alas, in 1716 Thomlinson also
fell from grace: 'Parson having sold Arrack to a soldier the Governor
says the Parson has engaged himself to him never to sell any more
Arrack and the Governor is resolved he never will look upon him nor
his wife if ever he does.'[40] And the following year: 'Of late our parson
has been more troublesome than usual and has several new notions.
Last Sunday there was a great omission of several parts of the Liturgy,
the Nicene Creed, the prayer for the Company and Shipping and there
was only a Collect and the Lord's prayer before sermon.' Mr Thomlinson being sent for and questioned is told, 'The Governor and Council
are resolved to have no more of these Fopperies nor alterations in the
established forms of the Church prayers and if you go on in these
whimsical methods of altering the established prayers by halving them
you will render yourself incapable of acting as a Minister of the Church
of England here and must expect to be sent home.' One way of dealing
with would-be liturgical reformers![41]

In 1738, 'we had the misfortune to lose our Chaplain Mr Barlow. The most acceptable of his profession of any we have had among us for a great number of years past. We have supplied his place with Archbishop Tillotson, Dr South, Bishop Fleetwood, Dr Calamy and other eminent English Divines from whose discourses we are sure we shall be much more improved than by the crude uncouth compositions we have commonly met with for several years past, and such as were so far from edifying that often times they were not intelligible.'[42] Unfortunately Mr Barlow's successors do not seem to have come up to his standard. In 1790 we read of 'Rev. Mr Wilson's turbulent conduct'[43] and in 1797 'Rev. Mr Wilkinson reproved for litigious conduct and ridiculous ideas of self-importance.'[44]

The fact is that the Company must have found it difficult to recruit professional men of any calibre for St Helena during the early period, whether as Chaplains or even as Governors. Robert Jenkins, of 'The War of Jenkins' Ear' fame, had to be sent to the island in 1740 to uncover and put right financial scandals. But there were able Governors, especially from the middle of the eighteenth century onwards, with resultant reforms in many spheres, such as military, economic and agricultural.

Improvement in the treatment of slaves was required by revised Laws 'for the better government of slaves' laid down by the Company in 1792.[45] While slaves shall 'work diligently ... be obedient ... and in all respects demean themselves as good and faithful servants', masters and mistresses, under pain of a fine of forty shillings, 'shall treat their slaves with kindness, and shall give them protection from injury, and supply them with good and wholesome provision, and with proper cloathing and lodging; and, in sickness, with necessary medicines'. For minor faults 'it shall be lawful for masters and mistresses to give, or cause moderate [!] correction to be given them, for their crimes and faults, not exceeding twelve lashes, with a cat of nine tails'. If the permitted punishments seem harsh, they were a vast improvement on earlier standards. Slaves 'shall be allowed Sundays to themselves, and shall not be required to work thereon', but household servants 'shall be allowed one Sunday out of two to themselves'. However, slaves are to be instructed in the Christian religion and morality for not less than two hours every Sunday, and also to attend Divine Service.

From the turn of the century, the improvement in the quality of Governors was matched, perhaps as a result of the Evangelical Revival in England, by a marked improvement in the calibre of the Chaplains. In 1794 Charles Grant was appointed as Director of the East India Company. Grant was one of the leading members of the 'Clapham

Sect', a group of Evangelical Anglicans, mostly laymen distinguished in their own fields, of whom William Wilberforce is perhaps the best known today. They were concerned with such schemes as the abolition of the slave trade and the extension of missionary endeavour, especially in India. Grant used his considerable influence in the selection of Company Chaplains, certainly for India, and presumably also for St Helena.[46] The appointment of Richard Boys in 1811 may well have been due to Charles Grant.

If the captivity of Napoleon dominates the secular history of St Helena in the early 19th century, it might be said that the religious history is dominated by the Reverend Richard Boys. He was a man of some education, a strong character, self-opinionated and sometimes controversial, fearless in his denunciation of vice, but with a real pastoral sense.

He was appointed Junior Chaplain and Schoolmaster in 1811. At first, some confidence was placed in Boys by the Governor. A small printing press had been privately imported in 1806 and set up as the St Helena Press under Saul Solomon. Governor Beatson, who came in 1808, used it to popularize his views on agriculture by articles in the *St Helena Monthly Register*. However,

1810 Jan 14. Mr Solomon proprietor of St Helena Press is informed that objectionable remarks had appeared in the REGISTER for the month Dec., and is directed to print no more until the sheets have first been submitted to the Secretary.

Aug 23. Mr Boys having undertaken to superintend the printing of the ST HELENA REGISTER the regulation of Jan 14 is annulled in confidence of Mr Boys judgement that personalities and inaccuracies shall not be admitted. Doubtful communication to be first sent to the Governor.[47]

The senior Chaplain, Samuel Jones, in 1812 complained to the Directors of interference by the Governor with the spiritual part of his work, and the following month sent a 28 page letter to the Governor 'defending himself from imaginary attacks'.[48] Jones very reasonably felt insulted when the Easter Vestry elected him 'Inspector of the Common Sheep and Goats'. He suggested that the sheep be taken to their respective owners' farms and the goats be destroyed, which would prevent his appointment from interfering with more important duties. 'Otherwise he had already a very wild herd of goats under his charge, viz. those whose conduct is here reprobated'.[49]

As early as 1682 the Company had laid down rules concerning work on Sundays, and in 1701 Mr Luffkin had been fined 6s for allowing his slave to carry a burden on his back on a Sunday.[50] Perhaps during the

ensuing century, Sunday observance had grown slack, or maybe Jones
had come under Evangelical influence in England, but it seems he had
reasonable cause when in 1813 he complained

of profanation of the Sabbath on 4th April on board the *Armiston* where an
elegant tiffin was given and a splendid dance in the evening. Exhibition of
Conjurers etc. attended by an alarming number of respectable Inhabitants.[51]

Sadly Jones and Boys quarrelled and in January 1815:

the controversy between the two clergymen Jones and Boys, productive of
disgraceful effects – ordered to abstain from any further personal controversy or
circulation of written or printed letters referring to it on pain of suspension.[52]

In April Jones was retired on a pension of 5*s* per diem,[53] and Boys
became Senior Chaplain. He was soon accused of discriminating
between social classes by Governor Mark Wilks, who saw himself as a
protector of the slaves and poorer classes:

April 15. Mr Boys having refused to take to Church the corpse of a deceased
person, alleging it to be a privilege for the upper classes only; is called upon for
an explanation.

May 29. Mr Boys in explanations. Complains of the superstitious habits of
the place, the large concourse at every funeral to parade through the streets.
Their passage up the aisle of the Church round by the altar. Their anxiety to
throw every piece of myrtle into the grave.[54]

It would be interesting to know what the 'superstitious habits' were,
and what the significance of myrtle was. Is there a connection with
today's practice at funerals of the Foresters Friendly Society when
sprigs of greenery are thrown into the grave? As for discriminating
between social classes, Boys proved himself no less critical of the 'upper
classes', as we shall see.

The arrival of HMS *Northumberland* bringing Napoleon Bonaparte in
October 1815 ushered in a new period in the history of St Helena. The
troops drafted in to guard Napoleon caused a sudden and dramatic
increase in the island's population. The concern of the East India
Company for the effect of this on the religious life of the community is
shown in their letter to Sir Hudson Lowe on his appointment by the
British Government as Governor in 1816:

The observance and inculcation of religion, both by precept and example, at St
Helena, has constantly been an object of the Court's unremitting anxiety. In
furtherance of which they have for several years past, maintained the establishment of two Chaplains concerning whose religious principles and moral
character they were well satisfied at the time of their appointment. Their

ordinary duties are the regular performance of Divine Worship on Sundays in the Town and Country Churches, to visit the sick in the hospital, and the inhabitants of the Island, as occasion may require, and otherwise to deport themselves in a manner becoming the clerical character.

We are impressed with a belief that the moral and religious feelings of the inhabitants of the Island have been progressively improving, and that the principles of the established religion of Great Britain successfully inculcated upon the rising generation of St Helena, will be productive of the most solid and beneficial effects both present and in the future.

Considering the subject to be of the highest importance to the well being of the society upon the Island, we cannot but contemplate the great change which is about to take place, both in the number of residents and varieties of religious persuasions, as fraught with the most serious consequence if not specially guarded against by the utmost vigilance and care. The subversion of the Established Church we should consider an evil of incalculable magnitude, and we cannot too strongly recommend that the maintenance of the Established Religion be an object of your special attention and unceasing solicitude.[55]

Perhaps the clause 'at the time of their appointment' was to exonerate the Company from subsequent misdemeanours of the Chaplains, and one notes that they clearly defined the Chaplain's duties. They are concerned, even in 1816, about the possibility of the arrival of members of other Churches, presumably British soldiers or members of Napoleon's entourage.

Boys had no hesitation in denouncing wickedness in high places, including senior members of the Governor's staff. This culminated only a few weeks before Sir Hudson Lowe's departure in a celebrated sermon which Boys preached before him in the Country Church on 8 July 1821 on the text 'Verily I say unto you, that publicans and harlots go into the kingdom of God before you.' The next day the Council asked Boys for a copy of the sermon. Dr Chaplin records that Boys 'asked if they preferred the request as a favour or as a right, and when they answered, as a right, he further requested them to show him a copy of any law or regulation by which he was compelled to give a copy of his sermon.' Since we have no copy, we have to rely on Sir Hudson Lowe's recollection. Boys had emphasized that no matter how serious a crime one had committed, if one sincerely repented one could be sure of salvation. According to Lowe, he was addressing the poor, the slaves, the servants, the black women, the soldiers, in contrast to the upper classes with their hypocrisy. The sermon was probably not directed against Lowe himself, but against those members of his staff – and there were such – who lived lives of questionable morality and failed to set a good example.[56] The following Sunday Boys defended himself in the pulpit, and Thomas Brooke, who became Acting Governor on Lowe's departure, expressed his disgust at 'hearing Mr Boys in an extempore address represent himself as persecuted for righteousness sake and implying that his persecutors were the Government'.[57]

Boys and his wife could exercise a real pastoral care.[58] Among the military personnel drafted to the island for Napoleon's captivity were a number of sincere young Christians. Robert Grant had been a Midshipman on the *Vigo* which sailed to St Helena in 1820. Shortly after joining his ship, he was taken ill with consumption. He was given the Flag Lieutenant's cabin, where he was visited by a fellow midshipman, R. J. Mellish, a Christian who read the Bible to him and brought him to a knowledge of Christ as his Saviour. On arrival at St Helena Grant was transferred to the Naval Hospital at High Peak, where Mellish continued to visit him and introduced him to Lieutenant G. H. Wood[59] of the 20th Regiment of Foot. When Grant was moved to a boarding house in Jamestown, Wood invited him to stay at Mason's Stock House where he was stationed. Miss Mason (who lived at what is now Teutonic Hall) owned this small house, which was on the opposite side of Fisher's Valley to Longwood, from where they could see Longwood House where Napoleon lived in exile. Here a number of young officers, including Lieutenant Armstrong of the St Helena Regiment of Artillery, used to pray each night for Napoleon that 'God would mitigate his severe bodily sufferings during his long illness, and sanctify them to his immortal soul's conversion and salvation.' Grant gradually became weaker but rejoiced in the company of his fellow Christians. One is particularly struck not only by their sincere evangelical Christianity but also by how sensitive was their pastoral care of Grant. Thus Wood wrote to a friend:

If I was reading the Bible, or any good book, or praying, he would frequently interrupt me if he did not clearly comprehend what I read or said … and would say, Oh that's a kind fellow, say that again … and he would often repeat the same request two or three times; particularly when I was praying with him, and for him, when anything was said peculiarly applicable to his state or feelings; for in my prayers I used chiefly to pray in his stead as it were for him, as I thought he would have prayed for himself, as sick, weak, troubled greatly with a cough, and dying; and for those spiritual blessings and comforts which I knew his soul panted for, and richly enjoyed.

When he complained of being unable to concentrate in his prayers, Lieutenant Armstrong advised him to write them down or to dictate them. Robson appends to his book twelve of Grant's prayers. One must suffice to show their quality:

O Merciful Father, again I have to praise thee for multiplied mercies during the night, and raising me up to see the light of another day. I thank thee, O my God, for putting it into my heart to write to my brother on that important subject death, and pray that it may be serviceable to the souls of all my family who read it, to turn them unto righteousness, and to seek the salvation of their own souls. Forgive me, O Lord, all my sins and offences which I have committed, and keep me this night in quietness and peace of soul, that I may receive that holy ordinance of the Lord's Supper, on the morrow, in remembrance of our blessed Lord and Saviour's sufferings and death for poor guilty sinners, and give me additional strength of faith and grace. If I awake, be with me, Oh my blessed Saviour.[60]

Bowater James Vernon, a Chaplain who joined Boys in 1816 wrote of those prayers:

I have several of them, they breathe such a child-like spirit; he throws himself into the arms of his Saviour as a child would yield himself up to a tender nurse, and such a warmth of love pervades throughout, that it brought tears to my eyes when I read them.

Grant was anxious to reach his 21st birthday so that he might legally bequeath to his mother and other relatives his estate of £10,000 which otherwise would have gone to his brother, who was already in good circumstances. His birthday was on 17 December 1820 and on that morning Mr Boys visited him for over an hour and ministered to him. Just after noon he signed the will he had made some days previously. It was his last act – at nine o'clock that night he fell asleep in Christ, surrounded by his friends.

One is struck by the high regard these young officers had for the Sacrament of Holy Communion, and the high esteem in which they held the Chaplains. A few years later, Lieutenant Wood was to write:

Mr Boys was only to be known to be heartily and fully loved; for, for a long time we had been greatly prejudiced against him, by the scandalous reports we were in the habit of hearing from many quarters, and we only regretted that we did not know him before. But, however, we soon became on the strictest terms of brotherly love and intimacy; and he became a Father in Christ to all the young Christians in the Army and Navy, and opened his house and his heart, and all his soul to receive them, and to promote their growth in grace, and knowledge, and love and obedience to the gospel ... We had meetings in his house every week, frequently assembling to the number of twenty; and two days in the week we used to be there for breakfast, and spend the whole day in religious exercises ... And now that a new and amiable Governor commands the island, and is his friend and patron in promoting the cause of Christ, the work of the Lord is flourishing abundantly, particularly among the slaves; who, by the Governor's new regulations, commanding their masters to send them to Church at all regular services, have the gospel preached constantly by Mr Boys and Mr Vernon, and the schools have greatly increased in numbers, so that the rising generation, in this once abandoned and profligate island, is now brought up strictly in the nurture and admonition of the Lord ... He [Mr Boys] made his house a regular hospital for any of the Naval Christians when sick, and both he and dear Mrs Boys (a true mother in Israel) not only attended to their bodily wants, but above all to their souls.

The references to new regulations about slaves attending church, and the increase in schools, suggest that the 'new and amiable Governor' was Alexander Walker (1823-8). Boys was incumbent of the Country Church. He was on furlough in 1818, retired in 1830 and died at Loose, Kent in 1866.

The early decades of the century were a time of much progress in social matters. The Benevolent Society was founded in 1814, with Richard Boys as a founder member, for the diffusion of Moral and Religious Instruction among the lower classes, and both the Society and the Government opened schools in Jamestown and in the country. The Government opened their Head School, a fee-paying school for boys, in 1825, with Boys as the first Headmaster. A public library also was opened.

Considerable improvements were made in agriculture. At some risk to his popularity, Governor Beatson endeavoured, not entirely successfully, to reduce the incidence of drunkenness.

Slavery had been a normal part of the life of the island since the arrival of the East India Company, and accounts of the treatment of slaves in the early days are horrific. Earlier, General Patton had introduced a more humanitarian approach and Sir Hudson Lowe and his Council, at the instigation of Sir George Bingham, the Military Commander, decreed that from Christmas 1818, all children born of a slave woman were to be free. The final abolition of slavery on the island came in 1832, at a cost to the East India Company of £28,000 in compensation for the freedom of the remaining 614 slaves.[61]

Colonial Chaplains and the See of Cape Town (1834-59)

In 1834 the island was transferred from the control of the Honourable East India Company to His Majesty's Government, and St Helena became a Crown Colony. This change posed problems for the general populace and for the Church. A few of the Company's servants were employed by the Government, but most found themselves in straitened circumstances. The new Governor did not arrive for two years. Social

conditions became appalling. Today, one's first impression of Jamestown, with its houses painted in pastel shades, is of an attractive small
town. In the 1840s, as described by G.C. Kitching, quoting contemporary reports, the impression was of squalor and filth. Drunkenness was
rife, church services were interfered with, the Police were powerless to
intervene, and 'it was impossible to pass along the main street without
being molested by drunkards, half naked prostitutes and stripped men
fighting in the gutter'. The stench from overfull privies, pigsties and
slaughter-houses was loathsome. 'The dwellings are not houses; in each
case the occupant resorts for his evening hours to the wine shops, and
he is driven there by the dirt of his home which he only enters to forget
himself in sleep.'[62]

In place of the Company Chaplains, there were now to be Colonial
Chaplains, appointed by the Colonial Office, and licensed by, and
under the general supervision of, the Bishop of London. Richard
Kempthorne was the first Senior Colonial Chaplain to be appointed in
1839. Before his arrival, the last Company Chaplain, Robert Parkinson
Brooke, remained until February 1837, presumably as Acting Colonial
Chaplain.[63] The Reverend W. Helps came in 1836 as a Military
Chaplain, but after Brooke left he was the only priest and so he also
became Acting Colonial Chaplain until Kempthorne's arrival. As well
as his duties with the troops, Helps took responsibility for the crews of
visiting ships; often as many as 26 men-of-war, none with chaplains,
would be at anchor.[64]

Kempthorne and Helps were the only two clergy on the island until
the arrival of William Bousfield in 1847, the first 'missionary' to be sent
to St Helena by the Society for the Propagation of the Gospel (SPG), at
the instigation of Robert Gray, the first Bishop of Cape Town. In fact,
Kempthorne was the only Senior Colonial Chaplain to be appointed by
the Colonial Office, since when Kempthorne left in 1859, the Bishop of
the newly formed Diocese of St Helena was appointed as Colonial
Chaplain. The junior Chaplains were recruited by SPG but served as
Junior Colonial Chaplains, until the formation of the Diocese.

Kempthorne was well regarded for his industry, his zeal and his
kindness. It is said that he kept a separate vegetable garden at
Oakbank to provide for the poor, and even his wife was not allowed to
use it!

The educational background of men offering themselves as missionaries showed a marked improvement in the middle of the 19th
century, according to Canon Max Warren, one-time General Secretary
of the Church Missionary Society.[65] The same may be said of the clergy

coming to St Helena, such as Kempthorne and his successors. But was there a change of Churchmanship from the Evangelical influence of the later Company Chaplains?

A Baptist Minister, James Bertram, arrived in 1845, and this marks the beginning of the Baptist Church on the island. The somewhat chequered relations between the Established Church and the Baptists is treated in Chapter 5. However, an account of Bertram's ministry, written by Pastor Edwin Hatfield, of the New York Presbyterian Church, gives us an outsider's view, although scarcely an impartial one, of the Anglican clergy at this time, and suggests that they had been influenced by the Oxford Movement. His description of Kempthorne and Helps as 'both of the Oxford School, and fully embracing the Romanising doctrines of Dr Pusey and the Tractarians' might have been just ecclesiastical name-calling, especially when in the arrival of William Bousfield he saw, 'another full-fledged Tractarian who knew all the attitudes and gestures, and could display a jewelled finger, and a lily-white hand to admiration, but nothing further in the way of winning souls'. However, more circumstantial, and convincing, evidence is adduced: 'Several of the Oxford Tracts were put into free circulation; particularly the Tract of Archdeacon Wilberforce, on Dissent.'[66]

The introduction of Nonconformity into the island presumably prompted the Government to pass the Religious Worship (Protection) Ordinance of February 1847 (not applicable to places of worship of the Church of England or to its clergy), which made it an offence to disturb any assembly for religious worship or to molest any Preacher. It also prohibited any worship in places with the door locked or bolted so as to prevent anyone from entering. Further legislation in 1849, the Lord's Day (Observance) Ordinance, re-enacted the Company's regulations prohibiting work on Sundays (works of charity or necessity excepted), or the opening of shops except for the sale of fish or milk. The Church was regarded very much as part of the 'establishment', as 'the Church of England in St Helena' and this attitude persisted even when the Church became part of the new Diocese of Cape Town, and later a Diocese in the Province of South Africa. Matters of administration such as the rules for the calling of Vestry meetings and the appointment of Churchwardens was regulated by Government Ordinance. Even as late as 1983, the Diocesan Synod had to ask the Governor to repeal these regulations which were by then in conflict with the Provincial Canon Law.

Helps gave Kempthorne considerable assistance, but even so relations between the Civil and Military Chaplains could sometimes be strained, over apparently minor matters. In 1849 the Bishop of London, replying to an appeal from Kempthorne, regretted the differences which had arisen between the two over marriages and the use of the church by the Military Chaplain. Kempthorne cannot claim the rights and privileges of a Rector in England. He is indeed bound to act in accordance with the general spirit of the Canons, but the letter of the Canons is not binding in St Helena, but only in the Provinces of Canterbury and York. Therefore Helps may use the church at times which do not interfere with its use by the Civil Chaplain, and it is the duty of the Military Chaplain to enter the Register books 'in his own hand'.

It is much to be regretted that such disputes should have arisen upon points of mere etiquette, between two representatives of the English colony in the small community of St Helena, and I trust that for the future they will be prevented by a spirit of mutual accommodation and forebearance.[67]

The See of Cape Town was formed in 1847 and the Letters Patent specifically include St Helena in the new Diocese. Robert Gray was appointed the first Bishop. As a result, St Helena received its very first visit by an Anglican Bishop.[68] No one had ever been confirmed on the island in all the years of settlement since 1659. Bishop Gray was well aware of this and wrote to Kempthorne in December 1848, stressing the need for careful preparation and for especial pastoral consideration for those adults who through no fault of their own had not been confirmed:

I wish you to give notice that I purpose, God willing, shortly after my return to Cape Town, and probably in the month of March, to hold a visitation in the Parish and Island of St Helena, when I shall be prepared to confirm such members of the Church as may be presented to me by yourself or the other clergy holding office in the island.

As I believe a Confirmation has never been held in that part of the Diocese, you will probably find many persons at an advanced period of life who have never partaken of this sacred ordinance. I trust that no false feeling of shame will prevent them from coming forward on this their first opportunity, and confessing Christ before men. There is no season of greater importance to ministers than that which precedes Confirmation. They are then called not only to examine into the faith of those who desire to partake of this holy rite, but to instruct them if needful in that faith. And they have also opportunities not always within their reach of conversing closely with many, and giving much wholesome and earnest exhortation. I trust the clergy of St Helena will not fail to avail themselves of the occasion, to seek to impress upon the hearts and minds of all who may present themselves, the need there is of an entire dedication of themselves to God, and of their holding the true faith of Christ. With a view to this I should recommend that classes be speedily formed of the candidates which should meet from time to time to receive instruction in the faith, and that the clergy should also seek by private exhortation to each separate candidate to impress upon them the solemn nature of the engagement which they are about to enter into with their God ... None should be presented under 14 years of age, except there are peculiar reasons for it.

Kempthorne replied that he had established Sunday Schools under five voluntary teachers, in the country districts, but his attempts to do the same in the town had been frustrated by the dilatoriness of Mr Bousfield, whose district it was. (Happily Bishop Gray after his visit reported to SPG that Kempthorne and Bousfield were both 'excellent and devoted men, and labouring assiduously in their sacred calling'.) Robert Gray's first visit was in 1849. His voyage in HM steam frigate *Geyser* took 14 days. Arriving on 7 March, he declined the honour of a salute being fired, offered by the Governor's ADC, Captain Knipe, but accepted an invitation to stay with the Governor, Sir Patrick Ross, at Plantation House. The Bishop, in a letter to his brother, speaks well of the Governor, 'that most excellent man', and his hospitality. He had put his carriage and horses at the Bishop's disposal and held a levee 'at which the whole of the respectable inhabitants of the island were present'.

The Bishop held two Confirmations, one for 111 people already receiving Communion and one for 250 non-communicants.

Extracts from his letters will give the best account of his visit.[69] He missed his wife. 'I really should have been quite happy during my visit to this sweet island, had dearest Sophy been with me.'

All our places of worship, and there are five, are attended by crowded congregations, and I do hope a great deal may be done for the revival of religion throughout the island. The people are, however, all very poor. [The 5 places of worship were St James' in Jamestown, the Old Country Church, Longwood House and rooms at Sandy Bay and Jamestown.]

Longwood has nothing very interesting about it. I preached yesterday in Napoleon's billiard room – not in the old house where he lived, but in the new one built for him, which is an excellent house.

I have been busily employed every day in visiting the parishioners, assisting the Clergy in preparing candidates for Confirmation, confirming, consecrating the Church and various churchyards, examination of schools, preaching, and in business arising out of the Visitation, such as the repeal of local ordinances, which interfered with the Bishop's office, in the conveyance of the Churches and burial-grounds (all of which were still in the hands of the Government) to the See; in remodelling and placing upon a sounder and more extended footing the Church Society,[70] and I trust also another very important ecclesiastical association called the Benevolent Society.[71]

There are four clergymen now belonging to the island ... the fourth is Mr Frey, whom I had much satisfaction in ordaining to the holy office of Deacon ... He was formerly a German missionary in India ... He is now Master of the Country Government School. He will strictly confine himself to the duties which properly belong to the Diaconate, continuing in his office of teacher, and devoting his days after 2p.m. to visiting the poor, many of whom, especially those who were slaves, are very ignorant ... The island still greatly needs another Clergyman, who should devote much of his time to visiting the poor from house to house. The rugged and mountainous nature of the country, coupled with the very great heat of the climate, renders it impossible for a Clergyman to do as much parochial work here as in England.

Kempthorne entirely agreed! As he later wrote to Bishop Gray:

My parishioners find the services on the Communion Sunday, especially the females, so exhausting that some are no longer equal to it. I may say for myself also, that at this season, after being engaged in my morning duty from 11-2 (and it has sometimes been longer) I come to the Evening Service rather jaded.

At this time the Royal Navy was engaged in the abolition of the slave trade, and captured slave ships were brought to St Helena. A Liberated African Depot was set up in Rupert's Valley, where the human cargoes of men, women and children were temporarily housed. Many were dead when they arrived. Up to 3,000 slaves were brought to St Helena and released each year; most were then taken to the West Indies as free people, but some remained on St Helena. An account of the Liberated African Depot will be found in Chapter 2. Here we consider Bishop Gray's reactions. He was greatly moved when he visited Rupert's Valley and wrote that over half were in hospital from the hardships they had endured. He was

pained to find that no effort is made to instruct these poor things during the time they are in the island; and the more so, because the Superintendent informed me that they show a great aptitude for instruction, and have a strong desire for it ... it is sad to think that our Government should spend £10,000 a year on this institution, and between £300,000 and £400,000 in support of the squadron, and yet not allow the trifling sum which would be needful to supply them with a teacher. Mr Frey, whom I have just ordained, did at one time undertake the work, and with some success; but the Government would not sanction the appropriation of a stipend.

During his visit a captured slave ship was brought in by one of the cruisers. The Bishop went aboard and was appalled by the conditions:

She was a schooner of about 100 tons, and had 560 slaves on board … I crept down between decks to the place where they are usually stowed away, – it might be between three or four feet high, and the atmosphere was most offensive … The condition, however, of a slave ship has been too often described to make it necessary for me to enlarge on it. I shall only say, I never beheld a more piteous sight … never before felt so powerful a call to be a Missionary.[72]

Bishop Gray was concerned about the growth of the Baptists, and his remarks showed, we might think, a sad lack of ecumenical spirit!

Unfortunately for the first time schism began in this island two or three years ago, by an emissary from the Cape, and I find him now in full confidence of success. He has started a church of his own, and is an Anabaptist on principle. His success is chiefly with the poor, and he is a thorn in the side of the Church. But God brings good out of evil, and the members of the Church here have been led to examine the grounds of their own faith, and many have been led to take a deeper interest in religious matters; and I am … calling upon the laity to take a greater part in the work of the Church than they have hitherto done.

Meanwhile, HMS *Geyser* had been cruising off the coast of Africa for slavers. She now returned to St Helena and left with the Bishop on 16 April 1849 for Cape Town.

Kempthorne was responsible for overseeing several Church building projects. The tower of St James' was moved and a spire added in 1843 and the new Country Church built in 1850 (see Chapter 3). He also built two dual-purpose schools in the country, and wrote to Bishop Gray telling him of the progress of the work:

Our schools at Sandy Bay and High Peak are four feet above ground. They are so planned that a small chancel can be subsequently attached. I feel it at the same time so important to have some Church feature to mark these places, which will be used from the first as oratories, that I am very anxious to order them to be framed of wood and sent out from England. Thompson of Limehouse, with whom I have corresponded had done work of this kind and, as far as I can judge, acceptably. There is much poverty, even among our Proprietors, and though such a mode of attaining the object is in one sense cheap, it is the only one within our power for many years.[73]

One matter which had concerned the Bishop during his first visit was the question of marriage regulations. There was an Island Ordinance which gave the Governor power of issuing marriage licences, but these were issued indiscriminately, without question, on payment of a fee. The Bishop had obtained the repeal of the Ordinance, but Lord Grey, the Colonial Secretary, had hesitated to confirm the repeal. In 1851 the Bishop wrote:

In the present state of the marriage question at St Helena, I think of instructing the Clergy, before marrying parties who bring the Governor's licence, to put the usual questions which are required to be put in England, and act accordingly. You will remember that the Queen's Advocate in St Helena stated that it was DOUBTFUL whether the Governor could refuse licenses to ANY that applied. I know that no inquiries were made, and the Queen's Advocate states that under the existing arrangements Jews were married by the Clergy, and great facilities were afforded to parties who touched at the island (which is VERY rarely for more than twenty four hours). I cannot consent to allow the Clergy to be made instruments of effecting all sorts of marriages. There is one case of bigamy which has already come before me. I shall instruct Mr Kempthorne in this whole matter to adopt a conciliatory line, and if he has any doubt to refer to me before acting. I am grieved to say that during the past year the spirit of the Cape has been spreading in that little island. Ours are almost the only papers they see, and they feel a greater interest in what passes in this Colony than anywhere else. K. tells me that a radical party is agitating the parish against vesting the church now being built,in the See. I understand they are about to memorialize Lord Grey on the subject. They are headed by a Jew. Where else they would vest it I know not. The Patent, you know, constitutes the See a body corporate, etc., for the express purpose of affording a good and secure tenure for Church property.[74]

Thus it was that on the Bishop's second visit in 1852, he was unable to consecrate the new Country Church because of this dispute. He left Cape Town on 3 January in HMS *Vulcan* and arrived at St Helena on the 15th. Although he found large congregations and numerous communicants, he also found that a 'violent democratic spirit had grown up.' He left St Helena for England on 2 February in the *Persia*.

His third visit was a happier one and he said that it seemed quite a holiday. Accompanied by his wife Sophy, he arrived on 27 October 1857 aboard the *Granger*. Governor Drummond Hay gave them his rooms at the Castle in Jamestown for a fortnight, and they spent the next two months at 'Terrace Knoll', a country house where 'the rest did Sophy good'.[75] The previous objections had been overcome and the Bishop consecrated the new Country Church on 9 December, and appointed Kempthorne Archdeacon. He left aboard the *Celt* in January 1858 for England, where he was to have talks, amongst other matters, on the establishment of a separate Bishopric of St Helena.

Kempthorne remained until 1859. When he left he was presented with a Testimonial, signed by about 190 inhabitants:

Venerable Sir, We, the undersigned Members of the Church in St Helena, contemplating the Ecclesiastical changes effected in the Community desire to take the present opportunity of recording our grateful recognition of the

Christian benevolence, Paternal kindness and Urbanity of Manners which have ever characterized your intercourse with us. A Ministry among us, extending over some Twenty years, so faithfully and assiduously discharged – your judicious counsels – your liberal support of every object, religious, social or intellectual – our Churches enlarged and multiplied – our Clergy increased – our Poor instructed – for these, and for many other benefits, we want language to express the fulness of our gratitude. In then affectionately bidding you Farewell, we would fervently hope for you all manner of prosperity, that your domestic reunion should ensure the fullest measure of earthly happiness, and that your career of usefulness may be prolonged in the services of Him who rewards eternally.

Bishop Claughton, first Bishop of St Helena, wrote: 'Kempthorne will leave many behind him who will always regard him as their faithful pastor and Guide.'[76]

Richard Kempthorne succeeded Claughton as Rector of Elton, Huntingdonshire and died in 1888 at the age of 84.

2

The Bishops of St Helena

The First Bishops (1859-99)

The Diocese of Cape Town initially consisted of South Africa, roughly south of a line from the mouth of the Orange River to Durban, together with St Helena. Bishop Robert Gray soon found the need to divide his unwieldy Diocese. In 1853 the Dioceses of Grahamstown and Natal were founded and in 1859 the Diocese of St Helena.

His proposal to make St Helena a separate See had been discussed with some leading laymen during his visit in 1857. In a printed letter dated 19 November 1857, he proposed that the See should comprise St Helena, Ascension and perhaps Tristan da Cunha together with the pastoral oversight of the English congregations on the Eastern coast of South America. A Bishopric Endowment Fund of £5,000 would be needed, of which he asked St Helena to provide £2,000. The Colonial Bishoprics Fund contributed £1,000 and SPG offered £200 annually for three years.

A public meeting welcomed the suggestion but, pleading poverty and the present needs of the Church, could only offer £1,000. This was to be raised by a loan, and it was proposed to ask the Governor to institute a Property Tax to pay the interest.

The Letters Patent of Queen Victoria under the Great Seal, dated 6 June 1859, constituted the Island of St Helena: 'hitherto ... comprised in the ... Diocese of Cape Town, and also the Island of Ascension and the Island of Tristan D'Acunha (which two last mentioned Islands have not hitherto been, and are not at present comprised in any See or Diocese) to be a distinct and separate Bishop's See and Diocese ... "called the Bishoprick of St Helena", subject to the See of Cape Town.' Piers Calveley Claughton was appointed the first Bishop and the Church of St Paul was to be the Cathedral, although the Letters Patent gave the Bishop authority to make any present or future Church in Jamestown the Cathedral. 'And we do ordain and declare that the said town of Jamestown in the Island of St Helena shall henceforth be a City to be called the "City of James Town".'[1]

No mention is made of the English congregations on the east coast of South America, presumably because the Queen had no jurisdiction over those parts. But that they were to form part of the pastoral oversight of the Bishop is clear from a letter of 1866 to Bishop Welby, the second Bishop, in which Bishop Gray stated that he understood it had been agreed by the Government that the Bishop should receive the Colonial Chaplain's stipend of £500 and be at liberty to visit 'Ascension, Tristan, the South American Churches and any part of the Province as freely as any other Diocesan Bp. without any loss or diminution of income, or without asking the leave of the Govt.' (The Government had proposed to withhold the stipend for any period that the Bishop was absent from St Helena, visiting the rest of the Diocese.) In a postscript, Sophy Gray confirmed that money had been raised in Montevideo towards the endowment of the See of St Helena.[2] A list of the Diocesan clergy in 1860 included Charles Bull as Vicar of the Falkland Islands. However, in 1869 the Diocese of the Falklands, which included Argentina and Eastern South America, was formed.

Perhaps Bishop Welby had been wondering, as many have since, why St James' had not been chosen as the Cathedral, for in the same letter Bishop Gray wrote:

As to the Cathedral. It was because it was the generally expressed wish of the Inhabitants that the Country Ch. should be made so, that it was named. My view would have been to have made St James'; but I yielded to a general wish.

Maybe the proximity of Plantation House, the Governor's residence, was a consideration.

BISHOP CLAUGHTON

Piers Calveley Claughton was consecrated the first Bishop of St Helena in Westminster Abbey on Whit Tuesday 14 June 1859. His mother wrote, 'I don't think the title of Bishop will make you any dearer to me than you were before,' and sent her blessing. He and his wife left England on 3 October, arriving on St Helena on the 30th. J.C. Melliss, the Colonial Surveyor, placed Oakbank, a very fine country house, noted for its luxuriant grounds, at the Bishop's disposal and it became his residence. Claughton described it as 'so English in its character as to make us feel ourselves at home',[3] and he wrote: 'I have every reason to be satisfied with the spirit in which I have hitherto been met by all classes, not excepting our Dissenting brethren.'[4] He also suggested that young priests would benefit from a few years in St Helena or the colonies, not as missionaries but as parish priests.[5] A year later he wrote to SPG that he intended to purchase Oakbank for the See, using £1,000 of the Endowment Fund and what was invested at the Cape.

Part of the Diocese was not going to be easy to administer. In February 1860 Claughton wrote to the Chaplain of Bahia in South America that he would be glad of any information at any time. The Chaplain replied that:

your letter contained the first official information I have received of your appointment so that even now I am ignorant of the precise relation in which, as Chaplain to the British residents here, under licence from the Bishop of London, I stand to your Lordship or the extent of your authority.

But he went on to say that he would be glad of advice.[6]

The Bishop wrote to the Society for the Propagation of the Gospel (SPG) in 1860 that he was 'endeavouring to reach the low and dissolute class of people in Jamestown itself, Christians in name only, especially the poor fallen creatures that derive their very subsistence from sin. I am trying to establish a House of Refuge for them, and have promise of assistance from most of the residents of the island.'[7]

The welfare of the negroes on the island was also one of Claughton's major concerns from the first. Thus in January 1860, he wrote to the SPG:

In St John's [parish], I have a great many negroes landed some years ago for which nothing was done (as we are trying to do) towards teaching them Christianity when they were first brought to the Island, the consequences is that they have most of them continued heathen and learnt the vices of Christians instead of their virtues.[8]

The Liberated African Depot had been established in Rupert's Valley twenty years earlier, in 1841, to receive the slave ships captured by the Royal Navy, and to look after the unfortunate Africans who had been captured by the slavers. They were released, fed, clothed and nursed. Most of them were taken, as free men and women, to the West Indies, where there were employment opportunities, when they were well enough, usually after a stay of about three months. Some remained on St Helena. Between 1,000 and 3,000 Africans were released at Rupert's Valley every year between 1841 and 1863. The Depot was finally closed in 1866. Many of them were dead when they arrived, many died in hospital. Many thousands were buried in Rupert's Valley, some in mass graves. When Bishop Gray visited in 1849, there were 600 in the Depot, of whom 300 were in hospital, and there had been 21 deaths that week.

The transient status of the Africans and the language problem created difficulties for evangelism. Henry Frey, a German missionary schoolmaster, whom Bishop Gray made Deacon during his visit, had

done what he could to teach them, but Lord Grey, the Foreign
Secretary declined to provide a stipend for a teacher, because of the
short stay of the Africans. The Baptist Minister, Mr Bertram showed
great concern for their plight and wrote movingly of them.

Very soon after his arrival, Bishop Claughton, assisted by the
brothers George and Edward Bennett, SPG missionaries who had
arrived in 1858, began systematically to prepare the released Africans
for Baptism. Three times a week, they assembled with an interpreter,
Jacob Faithful, in the one spot in that barren valley where there was
some shade. 'Much patience and repetition was necessary, and the
want of memory was a great difficulty.' In January 1860, before a
number were to leave for the West Indies,

I proposed to them that if they really believed our words they should be
baptized, telling them plainly it was for them to choose individually, and that it
should not be done to please us, but from conviction; I gave them some days to
consider, and then I asked for their answer; it was a glad and universal consent.

[On 28 January] on the proposed site of a church which we hope to build ...
I found three large tubs of water placed, neatly covered with branches, and
round these we assembled. The negroes walked in line to the spot, managed by
my two assistant clergy, the Revs G. and E. Bennett. We each had a person to
attend on us to take down the name, and after reading the opening prayers of
the Baptismal Service, we administered the solemn rite to two hundred and
thirty of these so lately heathens, using the form for private baptism as more
suitable to the place and circumstances of their case, baptized thus before they
could master the language sufficiently to understand the exhortation or the full
service ... The ceremony lasted two hours.

Thus the Africans were sent to new homes in the West Indies 'either
entirely converted and made Christians, or at least brought some steps
on the way'.[9] The Bishop would commend them to their new Dioceses,
giving exact information as to the amount of teaching they have
received. A reply from the Bishop of Kingston, Jamaica, in May 1860,
thanks him for doing so, but continues:

Glad indeed should I be to be able to inform you of any satisfactory provision
for their future welfare. But in a short time they will be dispersed in all
directions; and meanwhile they can receive only a moderate share of ministerial
attention in this city of 35,000 souls. I shall endeavour to trace them to the
estates to which they will be removed; and then make a special representation
of their care to the clergymen of their respective districts.[10]

The same year Prince Alfred visited the island and the Bishop
presented an address from the liberated Africans at their request,
accompanied by some of their number.[11] But the proposal to build a

Chapel in Rupert's Valley had to wait over 130 years for its fulfilment! In 1861 516 adults were baptized by Edward Bennett, Vicar of St Paul's, who had the especial charge of the Depot.

Claughton visited South Africa in December 1860 for the Consecration of Archdeacon Mackenzie for the Mission to Central Africa, the first missionary Bishop to be consecrated overseas. He arrived on Christmas Day and found Bishop Colenso of Natal there. Colenso was a controversial figure because of his alleged modernist views, and was eventually to be deposed by Bishop Gray. Claughton wrote in January 1861 to the Bishop of London concerning Colenso:

He is deeply imbued with the views of Maurice and, I fear, Jowett; in short, is at issue with the Church on some most important points. Now I am giving my own private opinion of my dear Brother Bishop to you, and I admire and love him in the great features of his character, but what I feel is the question is 'Will it be the Gospel of salvation by Jesus Christ that he will be proclaiming to the heathen.' I talked with him much and could not find that the Atonement or Redemption of the Blood of Jesus Christ had any place, certainly not the first place, in his system. [12]

Later that year, after publishing his controversial Commentary on Romans (which Bishop Gray condemned as 'bristling from beginning to end with heresies'), Colenso wrote to Claughton:

I hope you will not take such a very decided view of my book on the Romans ... as to be unwilling to eat with me. I have there treated of questions which, as you say, must come before us in our intercourse with natives, and though I do not expect R. Capetown and H. Grahamstown to agree with me, I do not expect you to agree fully, yet I must confess to some surprise at finding that the Metropolitan speaks of the guilt of having opinions, which are no other than have been preached for years past in the metropolis, under the very wing of the Bishop of London and Archbishop of Canterbury, by such men as Maurice, Kingsley, Davies and Vaughan. [13]

He goes on to discuss Essays and Reviews, a recent work by seven liberal scholars which had caused a furore in England and concludes on a pastoral note:

I have not lost sight of Mr Frey. But SPG has cut us so short that it is utterly impossible for us to introduce another clergyman until they can increase their allowance.

Evidently Claughton had been trying to find a post for Mr Frey whom Bishop Gray had made Deacon. He had previously tried Grahamstown but the reason he received from the Bishop that no place could be found was rather different;

as regards Mr Frey ... I am very sorry that I am not at present able to offer anything suitable for him ... the problems of German pronunciation with English congregations ... we are just now rather overstretched with German clergymen.[14]

In February 1861 Claughton wrote to the Bishop of London:

I am trying the experiment of open-air preaching in my metropolis. Alas I fear that in size only it differs from yours in the extent of its depravity ... I was much amused, and much gratified, on the last occasion, by the Baptist preacher posting himself at my side ... I am certainly looking forward to my first visit to S. American congregations – I hope I may go before July.[15]

It is good to see at least a little easing of the animosity between the Established Church and the Baptists!

In his Primary Charge, delivered in the Cathedral on 12 July 1861, Claughton looked back on his chief work on the island as its division into three parishes. When he arrived:

I observed that the clergy had no settled partition of labour, and anyone might be required to visit the most distant parts of the island. On the Sunday much time was lost, and needless bodily fatigue incurred, by the complicated system of rotation in their duties.[16]

By the Government Ordinance of 8 April (No.2 of 1861) the island was divided into separate parishes, Jamestown, St Paul's and Longwood, although the District of Longwood would not actually become a parish until its church was built. To quote the Bishop again, 'It is, in a word, the Parochial system, which for the first time has been established in the Island.'

Accordingly on 13 April 1861 the Bishop instituted George Bennett to the Rectory and Parish Church of Jamestown; Edward Bennett his brother to the Vicarage and Parish Church of St Paul; and Henry James Bodily to the Curacy of the District of Longwood. On 29 April, on Ascension, he licensed Arthur George Berry, a Royal Naval Chaplain, to the Chaplaincy of the Island of Ascension.

On 17 October 1861 his infant son, Piers Edward died aged three months, and was buried just outside the east end of the Cathedral. There is a memorial window in the north wall of the Chancel.

On 3 March 1862 Claughton left to become Bishop of Colombo. In 1870 he became Archdeacon of London and in 1875 Chaplain-General to the Forces. He died on 11 August 1884 and was buried at Elton. His portrait, painted by J. Edgar Williams RA and exhibited in the National Gallery in 1881, was given by his son Alan O. Claughton in 1950. It now hangs in Bishopsholme.

BISHOP WELBY

Claughton was succeeded by Thomas Earle Welby. Born on 11 July 1810 at Clifton, Gloucestershire, and educated at Rugby, at the age of 16 he became an Ensign in the 26th Regiment of Foot. He was ordained in Toronto in 1844, and in 1847 became Rector of Newton-near-Folkingham, his family home in Lincolnshire. Bishop Gray persuaded him to come to South Africa and he arrived at Cape Town in February 1849 with his wife and eight young children, to be given the parish of George. He became very popular with both Robert and Sophy Gray. Bishop Gray wrote in December 1850, 'You will be glad to hear that Welby is appointed Archdeacon. He is a first-rate man, and much admired by all who know him. When I left home on this Visitation I gave Sophy a letter to the Archbishop, recommending him for my successor if I never returned.'

In 1862 he was appointed Bishop of St Helena, the last South African Bishop to receive Letters Patent from the Crown. He was consecrated in Lambeth Palace on 29 May 1862 and sailed in the schooner *Wizard* with his wife, children and servants (18 in all), arriving on St Helena on Sunday 26 October. He preached that evening at St John's.

St James', like the rest of Jamestown, had been devastated by white ants, brought ashore in the timbers of a slave ship in the 1840s. The church was closed for worship because of its dangerous condition and needed extensive repairs. Welby had hardly arrived on the island before he was petitioned by the parishioners of Jamestown to decide whether St James'was their Parish Church and whether they had an obligation to maintain it. His decision was confirmed by the Government Ordinance No.3 of 1863 which declared the Church of St James to be the Parish Church of Jamestown. The Church on St Helena was still part of the Establishment!

In a report to SPG, written from Oakbank in January 1864, Welby described the state of the Diocese as he found it:

The condition of Jamestown is so very sad, the profligacy of the poorer classes in it is greater and more shameless than I have ever seen in any other place – the indifference of the more wealthy to a state of things to which they have long been accustomed – the ignorance, poverty, and indolence of a large native coloured population of E Indian, African, Malay, Chinese and all European races blended together, presenting such difficulties to be overcome that I do not hesitate to ask for the continuance of that aid which the Society have hitherto afforded ... the dwellings of the poorest classes are miserable sheds for which they pay heavy rents, and inhabit them as long as the white ants spare the roofs sufficiently for safety.[17]

It must be remembered that the Bishop was making a plea for continued support. He was having great difficulty in paying his clergy adequately. He hoped to pay an unmarried curate £160 a year, 'the smallest income on which even a single man can in Jamestown support himself'.

Welby's five unmarried daughters lost little time in finding husbands, and their names appear in the Marriage Register: in 1863 Penelope, aged 21; 1864 Wilhelmina, aged 17; 1867 Caroline, 19; 1873 Katherine, 24; 1884 Edith Frances, 31!

Bishop Gray paid a brief fourth visit to the Diocese in June 1867 on his way to the first Lambeth Conference, just long enough to allow of an interview with Welby. He and Sophy were sailing in the *Briton*. 'The ship is comfortable, but we have an intolerable number of screaming children, who bellow from morning to night.' He probably discussed with Welby a matter on which he had written to the Bishop of London on 8 May:

A draft of an Ordinance on ecclesiastical discipline has lately been published at St Helena by which the right of final appeal to Her Majesty is done away with or ignored. The only appeal mentioned or allowed by the draft of an Ordinance from any decision of the Bishop of St Helena is an appeal to the Bishop of Capetown. I do not know whether such a draft of an Ordinance can take away from any subject the right of final appeal to Her Majesty, but it seems meant as an attempt in that direction.[18]

For some reason Bishop Welby was not happy with Claughton's division of the island into parishes. 'The division of the Island of St Helena into separate parishes and districts has been found to be inconvenient,' declared Government Ordinance No.3 of 1871. The Ordinances of 1861 and 1863 were repealed and from the following Easter Monday there was to be one Parish of St Helena, with the Church of St James as the Parish Church. There were to be three Churchwardens and the Colonial Chaplain was to be ex-officio Minister and to Chair the Vestry Meeting.

The Colonial Chaplain was, in fact, the Bishop. However in 1873 Downing Street declared that as the revenue for the island for that year fell short of the Estimates by £2,000, it would no longer be possible to pay the Bishop the Colonial Chaplain's stipend of £500, and suggested that he should explore the possibility of residing in Cape Town and making periodic visits to St Helena. (This was indeed to be seriously considered in 1898, when Welby wished to resign.) As an alternative, the Colonial Secretary suggested to the Archbishop of Canterbury in August that since the Bishopric of Gibraltar was to fall vacant:

it occurs to me that the Bishop of St Helena, whose office it will I fear be necessary to abolish or rather to withdraw from him the payment from colonial funds in consequence of the bankrupt state of the island, would be a good man to succeed Bp. Harris.[19]

An earlier Colonial Secretary had suggested a link between St Helena and Sierra Leone, 'since on any further vacancy in either, a union of those sees might be advantageous – so that the Bishop during the bad season at S. Leone might have the advantage of change to the healthier air of St Helena without leaving his Diocese.'[20] This proposal came to nothing.

Welby commented that it would separate St Helena from the Province of South Africa, and there would be difficulties of communication, letters from Sierra Leone to Ascension having to go via the Cape. A better scheme would be to annex Namaqualand, Clanwilliam and the northern part of Malmesbury to St Helena, which 'would be an immense relief to the Metropolitan'.[21]

Fortunately by May 1874, it was agreed that the Bishop might continue to be paid as Colonial Chaplain but at the reduced sum of £400 per annum and so neither proposal was taken further. (The Bishop also received about £440 from Bishopric investments, which had to suffice for all his expenses, including travelling.) In 1884 the Government withdrew the remaining £400.

In 1874 Welby had two deacons ready to be ordained priest, but only one priest, Whitehead, to assist. Fortunately, the visit of two Naval Chaplains, J. H. Lang of HMS *Active* and T. E. Treffry of HMS *Encounter* enabled the Bishop to ordain Hands and Goodwin as priests on 30 April. The unexpected problems of a small Diocese![22]

'I have lost ... the very dear personal friend of more than 23 years,' wrote Welby in 1873, when Robert Gray died. As acting Metropolitan, Welby was to be involved in two delicate negotiations in relation to the appointment of the new Bishop. On the one hand the Province of South Africa was anxious to establish its autonomy *vis-à-vis* Canterbury. Welby therefore wrote to the Archbishop:

We deem that he shall receive consecration at your hands, but in reference to the fourth Resolution of the Synod of Bishops of this Province, ask that you will accept from the Metropolitan of South Africa the oath as binding only to such due reverence and obedience to the Archiepiscopal See of Canterbury as may be consistent with the Constitution and Canons of the Church of this Province. If in this way the oath is understood to be required, it will, I think, remove the objections at present made to it.[23]

On the other hand there was a body of Churchmen in South Africa,

represented by the C of E Defence Association, suspicious of the
Church of the Province and anxious to insist that the Church was part
of the Church of England. Their chairman wrote to Welby asking that
the new Bishop should be 'untrammelled by any pledge to what has
been called the Church of the Province of South Africa, so that he may
come among us as consecrated and understood a Bishop of the Church
of England'.[24] Welby wrote an eirenical reply but was firm on one
point:

> one request with which I am unable to comply 'untrammelled by pledges to
> CPSA' ... by this term which has unhappily been so long an offence to you and
> other Churchmen in South Africa, I understand only the branch of the Church
> of England which has taken root in South Africa .. I would gladly do anything
> in my power consistent with my own convictions of what is right to unite the
> members of the same Church, who are now divided from one another, and to
> promote peace and charitable forbearance ...[25]

However, to Canterbury Welby wrote stressing the importance for the
new Bishop to have qualities of 'firmness, gentleness and moderation
and wisdom ... without these qualifications ability, experience and zeal
will not avail to heal the present divisions in the Diocese.'

From matters of high ecclesiastical import, Welby had to turn to the
question of the white ant! Its wave of destruction had reached Oakbank
and in 1878 Welby moved to Red Hill, which he bought personally.
(This was later to be known as Bishopsholme, and its foundations can
still be seen next to the Old Trade School, now the Vehicle Testing
Centre, above the present Bishopsholme. Oakbank was to remain the
property of the Diocese until it was sold to Mr Homagee in 1899 for
£750 during the interregnum, when it was uninhabitable owing to the
destruction of nearly all the woodwork. The money was then used to
buy Red Hill for the Diocese from Bishop Welby's executors.) But
accommodation problems were not all-pervading and Welby attended
the second Lambeth Conference of 1878.

Contemporary documents give a picture of the Church services
during Welby's episcopacy. Minutes of a clergy conference held at
Oakbank in 1877 show that services were held for the remote parts of
the Island at High Peak School House, Rock Mount or neighbourhood
(Luffkins or Peakgut), Sandy Bay School House, Shipway's or Rock
Rose, Longwood (Deason's) and Half Tree Hollow. *A Few Notes on St
Helena and a Descriptive Guide* by Benjamin Grant, the leading local
journalist and printer, published in 1883, gives a summary of the
services at the main churches:

	SUNDAYS	WEEKDAYS
Cathedral	11 a.m. and 4 p.m.	Fridays 4 p.m.
St James	11 a.m. and 7 p.m.	Wednesdays 7 p.m.
St Matthew	11 a.m. and 4 p.m.	
St John	11 a.m. (Third Sunday) and 7 p.m.	
RC Mission	11 a.m. and 7 p.m.	
Baptist – Town	11 a.m. and 7 p.m.	Wednesdays 7.30 p.m.
Knollcombe	11 a.m.	
Sandy Bay	3 p.m.	

Grant also mentions a military chapel among the Garrison barracks at the top of Ladder Hill. Coming down the hill from High Knoll, a pathway to the right led to the Observatory (later demolished), the Officers' Quarters, the Royal Engineers stores and workshops, 'and theatre, lately converted into a temporary Garrison Chapel'. When it closed, furniture from this military Chapel of All Saints was given to the island churches by Captain William Harry Turton RE, later to write the hymn 'O Thou who camest from above' and a religious best-seller *The Truth of Christianity*, which sold 40,000 copies from 1895 to 1919 and was translated into Japanese, Chinese, Italian and Arabic. In 1889, 'A large teak wood press with glass cupboard and drawers now used in the vestry and a quantity of Church fittings formerly used at the Ladder Hill Chapel' were taken to St James', and in 1890 the benches were taken to St John's Church, which the Military then attended.

By 1885 Bishop Welby had evidently found that there was something to be said after all for his predecessor's decision to divide the island into several parishes. Consequently a Government Ordinance of April 1885 gave authority for the division of 'the Parish of St Helena into four or more separate Districts, for Ecclesiastical purposes only, of which the Cathedral Church of St Paul, and the Churches of St James, St Matthew and St John shall be ... the District Churches.' Each District was to have its own Vestry and elect two Churchwardens.

The first Diocesan Synod was held in September 1885 in the Cathedral. In his charge the Bishop, while referring to 'the present and future difficulties which greatly hinder and enfeeble the work of the Church in this small and impoverished Diocese', was at pains to remind the Synod of its concern with spiritual as well as temporal matters.

There was one important constitutional issue to settle. The Provincial Synod of 1870 had resolved:

Inasmuch, further, as St Helena, being a Crown Colony has most of its Ecclesiastical matters ordered by law, and is therefore differently situated from other Dioceses of this Province, for these reasons the Acts of this Provincial Synod shall not be considered as having force in the Diocese of St Helena, except so far as they can be, and shall be hereafter, received through the voluntary action of the Bishop, Clergy and Laity of the said Diocese.

Accordingly the Diocesan Synod resolved that:

This Synod hereby accepts the Canons of the Church of the Province of South Africa, generally, so far as they are not in any way opposed to English Ecclesiastical Law, or the Canons of the Church of England, nor contrary to any local Laws, or Ordinances which may be in force in this Island.

(The Synod of 1916 was to delete this Resolution and pass in its stead an amended version without the reservations.)

The Bishop's charge gives some interesting figures on clergy stipends. Between 1863 and 1884 the Diocese lost £940 a year in grants previously given by the Government, resulting in a drop in stipends. Thus while in 1863 the Vicar of St Paul's received £250 a year and parsonage, by 1885 this had fallen to £150 and parsonage.

By January 1886, Welby was feeling his age. 'Inspection and supervision of three Government schools and five charity schools, in different parts of the island, and preaching on Sundays and sometimes other days, and holding yearly Confirmations, make up all the work I am now equal to.'[26]

On the 25th anniversary of his Consecration as Bishop, in May 1887, he received a tribute from his people, signed by 642 individuals, of whom 79 had put their mark.

A 4-page penny pamphlet, *The St Helena Church News*, was published monthly in 1888. Sadly it ended after two years, due to lack of funds.[27]

At the Fourth Diocesan Synod in 1891, the Bishop was 81 years old. In his charge he reminisced about his arrival at the Cape in 1849, and how when he went to George, in the whole Archdeaconry, which stretched from Swellendam to Plettenberg Bay, and up to Beaufort West and the Orange River, there was not a single church building, not even in George itself, and he was the only Anglican clergyman. He had attended every Provincial Synod, from the first one in 1870.

His advanced years did not prevent the Bishop from visiting Tristan in February 1892 in HMS *Raleigh*. Unfortunately the rough weather prevented him from landing during their 24 hour stay, but he was able to hold a Confirmation on board for the islanders and some sailors.

On All Saints Day 1895, the Bishop instituted four Canonries which were to constitute the Cathedral Chapter. He was in his 86th year and in his report to SPG he wrote: 'with us it is the day of small things, but they will not be disregarded by our Lord.'[28] Mrs Welby died in October 1897 and by order of the Government all shops and offices were closed on the day of her funeral.

The Seventh Diocesan Synod of 1897 was to be Welby's last. His age had prevented him from attending the Lambeth Conference that year, and in 1898 he announced that he proposed to resign and asked the Councils of each District to consider the future of the Diocese. The Councils of St James', St Matthew's and St John's all agreed that much as they would wish for a resident Bishop, they could not see how they could raise the stipend and decided that they must accept a periodic visit by a Bishop from the Cape. However the Metropolitan persuaded Welby to remain.

On 6 January 1899, at about 5 pm as he drove home from Jamestown in his carriage, there was an accident in which Welby was killed. The sad event was described by James Homagee, Treasurer of the Board of Finance:

On going up the Ladder Hill road his mare shied at something and swerved round and started down the road, the servant could not overtake the animal, the poor Bishop held on to the reins for about 200 yards, the horse going from side to side, at last the Bishop was thrown out, receiving terrible cuts over his forehead and was killed instantly – the horse continued to run and smashed the carriage to bits. The servant had been driving and when the mare shied, the Bishop told him to go to her head, but owing to the narrowness of the road, the man got jammed and could not stop the mare.[29]

When I wrote an account of Welby's death in a booklet for schools about local church history, pupils wanted to know exactly where the accident had occurred. Emma Gough, who was in her nineties, regularly came to Evensong in her wheelchair, having recently had both legs amputated. I asked her, 'Emma, do you remember where Welby's coach overturned?' 'Of course I do,' she said; 'My uncle was the coachman!' An example of the importance of writing local history while it still lives in people's memories.

Welby's body was removed to his son's house in Jamestown and was buried the following afternoon, in accordance with the regulation that burials had to take place within 40 hours of death. Welby was 88, and had been Bishop of St Helena for 36 years, the longest episcopate of any Bishop in the Province. He is buried in St Paul's Churchyard, on the site of the Old Country Church, next to his wife. The inscription on his grave runs:

Thomas Earle Welby D.D.; second son of Sir William Earle Welby, Bart. of Denton Hall Grantham Lincolnshire.

Born 11th of July 1810, Died 6th January 1899.
Bishop of St Helena from 1862-99 and Member of Council.
Thy light is come and the glory of the Lord is risen.

Twentieth Century Bishops (1899-1979)

BISHOP HOLMES

On St James' Day 1899, the Very Reverend John Garraway Holmes MA, Dean of Grahamstown, was consecrated Bishop of St Helena by the Archbishop of Cape Town. His wife and daughter accompanied him to St Helena where he was enthroned in the Cathedral on 13 August by the Reverend J. W. Williams, who had been Vicar-General during the vacancy of the See. Holmes' first impression was that the state of morality in the island was very bad and that 'our few well-to-do people have no idea whatever of proportionate almsgiving.'

Communications with the island, which had become increasingly isolated with the advent of steamships and the opening of the Suez Canal in 1869, were, in one respect, greatly improved in 1899 by the arrival of the Eastern Telegraph Company's submarine cables from the Cape and from Ascension. This provided up to date news of the war in South Africa, which was just as well since in April 1900, Boer prisoners of war, including General Cronje, began to arrive, reaching 6,000 by 1902. They brought a Dutch Reformed Pastor with them. There was a consequent rise in food prices (eggs cost 3d each) and problems with the guards – 'the streets are noisy day and night with drunken soldiers'. In June 1900 an influenza epidemic cost 59 lives among the island population, in that month alone.

Bishop Holmes' letters in Canon Porter's Diocesan Magazine are marked by a concern for growth in spirituality and intercessory prayer. He visited England in May 1901 to recruit a priest for St Paul's, returning in March 1902 unsuccessful, but bringing a horse to enable him to get around the island. In May 1902 the SPG sent £1,000 via the Province for the Bishopric Endowment Fund.

The Bishop's wife died on 14 July 1904, and the Bishop, in ill health himself, left for England with his daughter ten days later. He died at Worthing, Sussex, on 26th September.

BISHOP HOLBECH

William Arthur Holbech was consecrated as the next Bishop of St Helena on 24 June 1905 in Cape Town Cathedral, arrived in St Helena on 31 July, and was enthroned on 6 August. Born on 14 December 1850, the third son of the Reverend Charles William Holbech of Farnborough, Warwickshire, he was educated at Eton, Brasenose

College, Oxford and at Wells Theological College. He was priested in 1876 and became Chaplain to the Bishop of Bloemfontein, Archdeacon of Kimberley (1895-1901) and Dean of Bloemfontein (1902-05).

The Diocesan Archives contain a book of private prayers and 'Sacra Memoranda' including a book of notes on lectures at Wells Theological College in 1874, Rules of life and intercessions which he compiled from 1880 onwards, and five books of notes for lectures which he gave between 1877 and 1891.

His report to SPG in 1906 spoke well of his clergy, Canon Porter and Harry Gibbons and also of the elderly Canon Hands who, although no longer active, 'did what he could with kindness and perseverance'.

The problems raised by the ownership by the Diocese of properties no longer required for Church use was tackled by the Bishop. Although the price of property on the island was not very high compared with rents, the cost of repairs was increasing. It was also undesirable for the Bishop to be a landlord. Thus the tenant of the 'Star and Garter' in Jamestown had turned it into a public house against the Bishop's wishes. He therefore asked the Provincial Trustees for permission to sell some of the properties. Estcourt, in Jamestown, was sold to the Foresters Friendly Society in 1905 for £150, and Rock Rose to Messrs Solomons in 1907 for £450.

In 1907, Bishop Holbech inaugurated a lace-making association to encourage the industry, which had been founded a few years earlier by the schoolteacher and historian, Mrs E. L. Jackson.

The Bishop attended the Lambeth Conference of 1908.

In April 1909, Holbech appointed Lawrence Walcott, a coloured priest, to be Vicar of Jamestown. Walcott's father was a West Indian barrister and his mother English. Educated in England, Walcott was well received by the parishioners, but a few on the island were affronted by the Bishop's action. While the Bishop was at a Synod in South Africa, Canon Hands invited Walcott to exchange pulpits and on 19 September Walcott took the service at St Matthew's. The same day both Churchwardens of St Matthew's resigned and sent a petition with 35 signatures to the Bishop, protesting against this 'retrograde step' and asking for an assurance that no coloured priest would be appointed to a country parish. The Bishop replied that in view of the fact that the majority of the inhabitants were coloured, it seemed reasonable to appoint a coloured priest. At this 'unsatisfactory reply', two members of the Executive Council resigned from St Paul's, one writing that he would not 'support in any way any Church in the Diocese'. However in Jamestown parishioners countered with a strong remonstrance signed by 515 people, supporting Walcott and asking the Bishop to 'frustrate any wicked design against our much respected Vicar'.

Finance poses a problem for every Bishop of St Helena, serving such a small impoverished community. In 1911 the Bishop asked for one pound a year from each parish towards the Diocesan contribution of £5 to the Provincial Common Fund, and also negotiated fire insurance for all the Diocesan churches and vicarages. In 1912 he wrote to the clergy on the problem of the unpaid portion of their stipends. If the parishes could not or did not raise their share of the stipend, the Vicar would have to go short. The Bishop could only suggest that arrears be cancelled and the parishes begin afresh each year. At this time the clergy were expected to pay their own fares from England. When Canon Hands retired, after 42 years at St Matthew's, with only one three-month break in South Africa during the whole of that time, he wrote to his friends in England that he would dearly love to go and see them, but he could not afford the fare. The Bishop's stipend was only £250 a year. He was to address these financial problems in each of his four Diocesan Synods.

At the Synod of 1906, Holbech announced the forthcoming building of a school at Blue Hill. The Hussey Charity would pay for the building costs, but the running of it would be in the hands of the Bishop.

In his charge to the Synod of 1909, the Bishop stressed the need for plain giving by all parishioners for the support of their clergy. At present, the stipend of £200 a year was only half met by the parishes, the remaining half coming from the SPG grant to the Diocese of £325 a year. The 1909 Synod passed regulations on the calling and constitution of the Diocesan Synod.

The Synod of 1913 considered and accepted the new Provincial Clergy Pensions Scheme, but expressed doubt about the ability of each parish to raise the annual premium of £9. The Districts of St James and St John in lower and upper Jamestown were to be united.

At the Synod of 1916, the Bishop was concerned with the impact of the War on the island and with support for the National Mission of Repentance and Hope in England. It would seem that Walcott was still not accepted by some in St Matthew's parish, for the Bishop spoke sternly of his sorrow that those responsible for the Church had refused to allow 'a marriage party to enjoy the ministrations of a priest whom they love and respect' because of his difference of race. The Synod rescinded the Resolution of 1885, concerning the acceptance of the Provincial Canons by the Diocese, and passed a new Resolution which unreservedly declared the Diocese to be a part of the Province of South

Africa. Discussion took place on the advisability of the clergy being paid from a Diocesan Fund, administered by the Board of Finance. When St Matthew's fell vacant in April 1921, by the resignation of Sydney Ruscoe after less than a year, due to ill health, the Bishop decided that to save money on clergy stipends, the two parishes of St Paul and St Matthew would in future share a priest. Canon Porter left in July 1921 and from then until Frederick Ashworth came in November, the Bishop himself looked after the two parishes. The journey on foot from Bishopsholme to St Matthew's took him an hour. Ashworth's brother George, who was in ill health, became an assistant priest in the Diocese. It would be fourteen years before the two parishes would again have their own Vicars.

Canon Porter had edited and printed the Diocesan Magazine for 22 years. When he left in 1921, the Bishop bought his printing press, moved it to Jamestown, and Canon Walcott became its editor and printer for the next 30 years.

In 1923, at the age of 72, Bishop Holbech visited Tristan, travelling in HMS *Dublin* from Cape Town. He spent two days in Holy Week on the island, confirming 63 of the population of 127. On his return, he took charge of the two country parishes himself for six months from March to September 1923.

Throughout his episcopate the Bishop kept duplicate copies of letters, using an 'Anchor Copying Letter Book', and also carefully compiled Episcopal Registers. He left in the Diocesan Archives a leather-bound manuscript book containing 51 Confirmation addresses.

In June 1929, the Bishop went to the Cape for medical treatment. The following January the doctor sent him to England, but he died on 7 March and was buried at Farnborough.

Some of his clergy had not always found Holbech easy to please, but Canon Walcott wrote:

I can look back on 21 years of unbroken friendship, unclouded and unmarred by any kind of disagreement whatsoever ... Very few realized how completely generous he was ... A good and devout man was our Bishop, kindly and charitable, a lover of Christ and His Church, catholic, evangelical and orthodox, with a strong, and rightly strong regard for the dignity of the episcopate.

BISHOP WATTS

Charles Christopher Watts, the Fifth Bishop of St Helena, was educated at Corpus Christi College, Cambridge, and Cuddesdon and became Archdeacon of Swaziland (1918-27) and Warden of Zonnebloem College, Cape Town (1930-31).

He was still a young man, and this encouraged the authorities in England to consider a radical change in Diocesan structure. The Archbishop of Canterbury had asked the Bishop of Salisbury to consider the question of the Chaplaincy of the Cape Verde Islands, and in January 1931 the Bishop suggested the creation of an 'Atlantic Diocese'. The Diocese of St Helena should include St Helena, Tristan, Ascension, Cape Verde and the Canaries, including Las Palmas and Tenerife, as well as Madeira. They 'are linked by Union Castle and Royal Mail steamers and would give the Bishop of St Helena a real task.' He should live at Cape Town.[30] Nothing came of the suggestion and Watts was consecrated Bishop of St Helena in Cape Town Cathedral on 11 June 1931, and enthroned on 12 July. He visited Tristan in January 1932.

When Frank Oxley, Vicar of St Paul's and St Matthew's, left in 1932, Bishop Watts decided not to appoint a successor, but to take charge of the two parishes himself. The money saved in stipends would be used for the repair of the churches and schools. Walcott, the only priest on the island, was to help by looking after the Blue Hill area, and the Bishop also appointed a number of laymen as Readers. (To enable the Bishop to attend the Episcopal Synod in November 1932, Gilbert Turner came at his own expense from Cape Town to look after the parishes in the Bishop's absence.)

In his report to the Missionary Council of the Church Assembly in England for 1932 Watts wrote:

Work is terribly scarce, and there are restrictions on immigration of coloured people to the Cape. The economic position is very bad and grows steadily worse. All Church buildings are much out of repair, caused by white ant and dry rot. The Bishop's salary is under £250, and he has to provide his own travelling expenses to the Cape, and also to provide transport on the island itself. His position should be looked into by the Church Assembly Missionary Council. His work is practically that of a parish priest, except for an occasional exercise of his Episcopal functions. That being the case, his salary should be raised to that of the Parish Priest, and he should receive a travelling allowance.[31]

The Thirteenth Diocesan Synod was held on 1 May 1933, the first Synod since 1916. Canon Walcott was the sole representative of the House of Clergy. The need for lay people to assist in conducting services in country districts and in visiting was stressed. In September 1933 the receipt of a gift of £100 from England enabled Bishop Watts to be the first Bishop of St Helena to buy a car. Petrol on the island then cost 2s 3d a gallon.

Yet another scheme to solve the Diocese's financial problems was mooted in 1934 when Watts was invited to become Bishop of Damara-land, while continuing as Bishop of St Helena for a year to see whether it was feasible to link the two Dioceses. He left for his new Diocese in May 1934, and in the same month Archdeacon B.H.Warner arrived with his wife from England to be Vicar-General and also Vicar of the two country parishes for 14 months. The people of St Helena did not like the idea of a non-resident Bishop and the scheme was seen to be impractical. Bishop Watts returned in February 1935 for two weeks, during which he ordained Fenwick Hall to the priesthood, and finally left on 3 March 1935. In 1936, he wrote a small book entitled *In Mid Atlantic*, based on talks about the Diocese which he was accustomed to give to liner passengers.

BISHOP AYLEN

William Aylen, a Keble College graduate, was another Cuddesdon ordinand. He was consecrated Bishop of Zululand in 1930 and translated to St Helena on 8 May 1935. He arrived on 9 June, with his wife and small son and was enthroned on 28 July.

He looked after the parish of St Paul, and also that of St Matthew when Fenwick Hall left in September 1937. However he had been able to visit Tristan in March, travelling via the Cape.

St Helena's depressed economy had made it important for islanders to be free to emigrate to Britain and, more usually, to the Cape, – though, as Bishop Watts had noted, this was not encouraged. In 1936 the South African Government introduced a new policy requiring immigrants to have at least £100. During his visit to the Cape, Bishop Aylen secured a relaxation of this requirement for St Helenians, provided their employers could give a guarantee of at least £25, and in November 1936 he wrote an article stressing the poverty of the island entitled 'My lonely Island Diocese' for the South African journal *Outspan*.

Even before Aylen's arrival, Archdeacon Warner, in his reports to SPG has emphasised the devotion of St Helenians, their poverty and yet their generosity:

The Church means everything to these people, and it is most encouraging to see how they cheerfully undertake really severe walks every Sunday to attend their Church service; quite elderly people covering arduous journeys as a matter of course ... In Lent a sum of £3 was handed in as Lent savings in the Cathedral parish alone, made up chiefly of farthings and halfpennies. The relief of extreme poverty is a work of considerable strain on the Church. Quite a large sum is distributed to these half fed people from Church funds each year, and if it was not for this help it is difficult to see how these very poor people could continue to exist.[32] Much of Aylen's episcopate was spent in raising money to put the Diocesan finances on a sound footing. SPG had warned him that they might not be able to continue their annual grant of £277. However they did offer £500 to the Province, for whatever purpose the Bishops wished. The Synod decided that the whole amount should be made the nucleus of a Diocesan Endowment Fund for St Helena. In return SPG asked that Bishop Aylen should make himself available to them in England from May 1938 to assist in raising the money. The Archbishop agreed to send Gilbert Turner, then Vicar of Muizenberg, to St Helena to be Vicar-General and Archdeacon, and to look after the country parishes. Turner had been Vicar of St Paul's and St Matthew's from 1922 to 1924.

Aylen left for England in March 1938. His letters tell of an exhausting schedule, over 120 sermons and addresses in four months, from the south coast of England to Yorkshire and Lancashire, and in Wales and Ireland. Although he was a little pessimistic, 'with Income Tax at 5*s* 6*d* in the pound', he raised £1,000. In a letter to the *Sunday Times* dated 16 August 1938 he wrote: 'Cannot all friends of St Helena band themselves together into an Association and see that she obtains the simple requisites to sustain for her a peaceful happy life?' Perhaps his schedule was too exhausting, for at the end of the year, he resigned the See, without returning to St Helena. When Bishop Aylen died in England on 15 August 1972 at the age of 90, Bishop Capper commented: 'Those were days of great poverty on the island and he and Mrs Aylen are still remembered for their kindness and charity.'

After Aylen's resignation, the Archbishop of Cape Town, the Most Reverend John R. Darbyshire, came to see conditions for himself, arriving on 16 March 1939 in the *Dunluce Castle*. He preached at the annual meeting of the Church Provident Society for Women, confirmed in St Paul's and St James' parishes, and on the Sunday preached in all three parish churches. He stayed at Plantation House and no doubt discussed the question of Aylen's successor with Governor Pilling, for soon after the Archbishop left on 24 March, the Vestry meeting was able to congratulate Gilbert Turner, already in their midst, on his appointment as their next Bishop.

BISHOP TURNER

Gilbert Price Lloyd Turner, then 50 years old, had had a wide and varied experience. Trained at St Augustine's College, Canterbury in

1909, he gained his Licentiate of Theology at Durham University in 1912. He was SPG Missionary in Labuan and Sarawak (1915-16) and Chaplain to the Forces in Salonika and Constantinople (1918-20), after which he joined the Church of the Province of South Africa. He was Consecrated Bishop of St Helena in Cape Town Cathedral on 29 October 1939, and returned to St Helena on 19 November. He was enthroned on 26 November in St James' Church – not in the Cathedral, as white ants had made the roof unsafe.

The Second World War had just begun and St Helena found herself isolated in the middle of the South Atlantic, with problems of supplies reaching the island. However, there were some compensations – the flax industry prospered, and the garrison provided work and brought money.

During the whole 21 years of his episcopate Turner acted as Vicar of St Paul's parish. Much of his energy in the first six years was directed to the restoration of the Cathedral roof and raising money to pay for it. The account of the restoration will be found in Chapter 4. At first he lived in the old Bishopsholme (formerly Red Hill), but this too was rapidly falling to pieces due to white ant, and in 1947 he moved into what is now St Paul's Vicarage.

A serious epidemic of poliomyelitis struck the island at the end of 1945. The Government acted swiftly to minimize the risk of infection and on the Saturday before Advent Sunday ordered all church services to be cancelled. This was later modified by an order prohibiting church services and public meetings held in any buildings, except for church services with fewer than twenty people and where all were over seventeen years old. Walcott reacted somewhat strongly in the January issue of his magazine, but published a letter the following month from Fenwick Hall, Vicar of St Matthew's, who objected to his article as 'unfair and uncharitable criticism against the civil authorities who are doing their utmost and their best under difficult circumstances to control the spread of a terrible disease.' There may have been overreaction on both sides, but the Bishop, who was in the Cape at the time, took strong exception to Walcott's attitude when he returned.

The wartime Garrison finally left in 1946, having occupied the barracks on Ladder Hill since 1939, and the Church was again almost entirely composed of islanders.

Two sects arrived in 1949, the Seventh Day Adventists, in the person of Mr Camphor and his family, and the Jehovah's Witnesses, who established themselves particularly in the Levelwood district, where they still have a significant influence.

The College of Arms granted arms to the Bishop of St Helena by a Warrant dated 24 November 1949, carrying the seals of Garter, Clarenceux, Norroy and Ulster Kings of Arms. These arms had been designed 90 years earlier by Bishop Claughton on the formation of the Diocese, but had never been properly granted. They are almost identical with a mediaeval seal of Dunwich which was a Bishopric and a Borough on the Suffolk coast in Saxon times. Claughton's correspondence shows that he adopted it as being eminently suitable for an island Diocese. The only substantial difference is in the direction of the wind – blowing from ahead of the Dunwich ship and from astern of the St Helena ship.

In 1952 Tristan passed from the Diocese of St Helena to the Diocese of Cape Town.

The Union Castle liners resumed the 'Cape run' after the War, calling regularly at St Helena and making it possible for Bishop Turner to attend the Lambeth Conferences of 1948 and 1958. The Provincial Archivist, the Reverend C.T. Wood, visited in July 1950 to calendar the Diocesan Archives. The Archbishop of Cape Town, the Most Reverend Geoffrey Clayton, visited between 2 and 8 June 1951 when he preached in the churches of St Paul and St James. Bishop Turner was in the Cape from June to December 1955 attending Episcopal and Provincial Synods, but also convalescing from an illness.

The shortage of land in Jamestown's narrow, overcrowded valley, turned attention to the neglected old cemeteries of Jamestown. Responding to a Petition of the Government Secretary, in 1951 Bishop Turner signed a Deed of Deconsecration of the Cemeteries 'known in these days as Middle Cemetery and China Lane Cemetery, formerly as Central Cemetery and Upper Cemetery ... which have for many years been in a condition of much neglect and misuse.' In July 1953, the Bishop also signed a Deed of Deconsecration of 'the ancient neglected ... Lower Cemetery'. Headstones from these cemeteries were placed in the enclosed area north-west of the Porch of St James' Church. The land was used for schools and playgrounds.

Bishop Turner made a chapel, which he named 'Arabia', at Bishopsholme (the present St Paul's Vicarage). The altar had come from St James' Church in 1906. The reredos was made by Herbert Nicholls in 1956 from a simplified design of Sir Gilbert Scott, but incorporating a central Calvary made by Richard Scott Constantine in 1941 and side panels of St Augustine of Canterbury and Bishop Robert Gray, made by him in 1949 for a previous reredos.

The Centenary of the Founding of the Diocese was celebrated on

Sunday 7 June 1959 with a visit by the Archbishop of Cape Town, the Most Reverend Joost de Blank, accompanied by Archdeacon C. T. Wood. At the Centenary Eucharist in the Cathedral, the Archbishop read a letter from SPG, presented the Churchwardens with an illuminated address (now in the Cathedral), and the Cathedral with a lectern edition of the 'Coronation Bible' inscribed:

This Bible is presented to mark the centenary of the consecration of Piers Claughton as the first Bishop of St Helena on June 14th 1859 ... Among those who contributed were the parishioners of Elton where Dr Claughton was Rector, the Diocese of Colombo to which he was translated in 1862 and many friends from the mother Diocese of Cape Town.

In the same month Her Majesty the Queen paid tribute to Bishop Turner's ministry by appointing him an Officer of the Order of the British Empire.

At the May 1960 Vestry meeting, Bishop Turner announced that he would be retiring on Saturday, 1 October 1960. At Evensong that day 174 people gathered in the Cathedral to receive his last Blessing as Bishop of the Diocese. He continued as Vicar-General until the end of the year, when he retired to South Africa. He died on 3 November 1968 at the age of 80.

Before Turner came to St Helena in 1922 as a priest, Holbech had heard of his high churchmanship, and had commented: 'If he is ultra-Catholic, that is beyond our mark, we stop at Catholic; but I like what you say of him.' In *Isle of St Helena* Oswell Blakeston gives an account of a tour round the island with Bishop Turner in 1957. He claims that Turner discussed whether a hanging pyx was more 'spike' than a tabernacle! The copy in Bishopsholme library has Turner's notes in the margin: 'Did I really say that?'. Bishop Turner also made very full and delightful comments week by week in the St Paul's Service Registers. They reveal a lovely personality, with a great pastoral concern. It is sometimes said that he is remembered more as a parish priest than as a Bishop, perhaps understandably in view of the fact that he looked after St Paul's parish for the whole of his episcopate. Today in many country cottages, with the picture of the Queen, one can also find a photograph of Bishop Turner. At a Requiem Mass in the Cathedral on 14 November 1968 Bishop Capper said, 'Thus an old Saint takes the people of St Helena with him into Heaven, and there you have your friend.' Bishop Turner left a substantial sum as an endowment with the Provincial Trustees, the interest to be paid to the Bishop for the time being of the Diocese of St Helena. If the Diocese of

Jamestown from Ladder Hill

St Helena ceased to be part of the Province, then the interest was to go to the Sick and Aged Clergy Fund of the Diocese of Cape Town.

BISHOP BEARDMORE

Harold Beardmore succeeded Bishop Turner in 1960. Born in 1898, he entered the Royal Navy from HM Training Ship *Conway*, and was a midshipman in the attacks on Zeebrugge and Ostend in 1918, as a member of a crew of three in a coastal motor boat laying flares. After the War he joined the Clan line and sailed round the world as fourth mate in a cargo boat. He trained for the ministry at Knutsford Ordination Test School, King's College London (AKC 1923) and Wycliffe Hall, Oxford.

He was Chaplain of the South African Railway Mission in 1925 and a Chaplain in the Royal Navy (1927-47). The Reverend Gordon Taylor in his book *The Sea Chaplains* gives some account of his work. In the East Indies station he had 'led the forwards in the Fleet Rugger XV with much vigour both physical and vocal.' Admiral Sir William Davis, who was to become the first Chairman and later first President of the St Helena Diocesan Association, was his Commander in HMS *Hood* (1939-41), and recalled on one occasion 'seeing a real old-timer at the defaulter's table, for, I think, his usual offence of trying to give the

Master-at-Arms a black eye on return from shore leave late at night. I said to the Master-at- Arms: "Is this to be a Captain's Report or a talk by the Chaplain?" The accused burst out: "Not another talk by the Chaplain please Sir!" [33]

Beardmore was appointed an Officer of the Order of the British Empire (Military) in 1941. In 1944 he published *The Waters of Uncertainty*, a book of advice for Naval Chaplains. After six years as Archdeacon of Basutoland (1952-8) he was consecrated Bishop of St Helena in Cape Town Cathedral on 27 November 1960. He arrived with his wife Nona and two Basotho ponies and was enthroned on 29 January 1961. This was not Harold Beardmore's first contact with the Diocese. He was Chaplain in HMS *Dorsetshire* when she visited St Helena in October 1933 and he preached in the churches of St James and St Paul. He was also Chaplain in HMS *Carlisle* when she took Bishop Aylen to Tristan in February 1937.

The present Bishopsholme was bought by Beardmore in April 1961 from Homfray Welby Solomon, grandson of Bishop Welby, with the help of an SPG Budget of Opportunities grant of £2,000. It was formerly known as Prince's Lodge, after its original owner, the early 19th century merchant, Richard Prince. In its grounds are the foundations of the old Bishopsholme into which Bishop Welby had moved in 1878. By a curious coincidence, the blue and white Flemish tiles in the fireplace, with Biblical scenes and texts, are identical with those in Bishopscourt, the Archbishop's residence in Cape Town. Beardmore made a chapel upstairs, using the altar and reredos from 'Arabia'.

Beardmore set up a small Trade School, above Bishopsholme, where boys were taught metal work, plumbing and car maintenance, at a time when there was no other such provision on the island. It was to continue until 1979. Beardmore also revived the Church Lads Brigade in St Paul's parish.

Serious financial problems dogged Beardmore's episcopate. Stipend levels were £320 p.a. for a single priest, £420 if married and £500 if he had children. (In considering these figures one must remember the difference in cost and standard of living in those days. The author recalls that as a curate with a wife and three children in the early 1950s in England his monthly stipend was £30 and a house.) The Bishop formed a Senate of Clergy and lay people in the hope that they would work for larger stipends through increased parochial contributions. It was a time when SPG had had to reduce their grant to £135 p.a.

By 1962 there were clergy in all three island parishes, and with the advent of John Crawford as the first Vicar of Ascension (as distinct from Naval Chaplains), the Diocese had for the first time a full complement of clergy.

Beardmore produced a monthly printed Diocesan Magazine of which only the February 1963 issue has survived. As well as giving the services in the Country Churches for that month, there is an interesting editorial which illustrates the Bishop's forthright nature:

What sort of people do they think we are? The question can be asked today of the Colonial Office by any thoughtful person living in this isolated Colony.

Tristan da Cunha has captured the imagination of the general public because they had to be evacuated but we do not pray for a volcanic eruption in order that we may become News and therefore remembered.

Fortunately we are not a troublesome people, we are law-abiding loyal citizens of a British Colony. Because of this it seems, that in spite of the fact that His Excellency the Governor has sent numerous urgent telegrams to London regarding the serious position we are in, having only one over-worked Doctor – responsible people in London have not yet given him any firm hope of the second Doctor's arrival. This is really serious and if there is a question asked in the House of Commons, as to why a Governor of a lonely outpost populated by people who are living souls and worthy of attention cannot get any satisfaction, there would be an outcry among the people of England ...

It is therefore our earnest hope that the Governor will find it possible to go to England and perhaps make History in that he might well be the first Governor who has had the courage to tell those in authority the truth about this 'Island of abandoned schemes'...

I would willingly go myself but (a) I am not a Governor and (b) like the Government – I have no money.

Readers may well feel that, at least until the 1980s and substituting the Falklands for Tristan, things had not changed very much in twenty odd years.

The Bishop set up the St Helena Diocesan Association in England, around a nucleus of several retired Naval officers who were his friends. The Association has continued to this day, and provides a valuable support, being largely responsible for helping with the ever increasing fares for clergy and their families. Today many parishes and individuals support the Diocesan Association with prayer and money.

Bishop Beardmore resigned in March 1967 and returned to England in poor health. He died on 3 November 1968 at the age of 70 at Bray, Berkshire.

BISHOP CAPPER

He was succeeded by Edmund Michael Hubert Capper, who came with over 30 years' experience of overseas service, mainly in Africa.

Born on 12 March 1908 he trained at St Augustine's College, Canterbury in 1928, went to the University of Durham in 1932 and was ordained Priest in 1933. Edmund Capper served with the Universities Mission to Central Africa (UMCA) in 1936-62, being Archdeacon of Lindi, Masasi (1948-54), Archdeacon of Dar-es-Salaam, Zanzibar (1954-7) and Provost of the Collegiate Church, Dar-es-Salaam (1958-62). He was appointed an Officer of the Order of the British Empire in 1961. After being Chaplain at Palma de Mallorca for five years, he was consecrated Bishop of St Helena in St George's Cathedral, Cape Town, on 13 August 1967 and enthroned in St Paul's Cathedral on 3 September 1967.

A complete reorganization of the Diocesan finances was one of Bishop Capper's important achievements. The Bishop was no longer to be personally responsible for the finances, which were placed in the hands of the laity, in the form of a revived Diocesan Finance Committee. Bishop Capper appointed a leading business man and landowner, Mr Donald Thorpe, as honorary Diocesan Treasurer and instituted a system of parochial quotas.

He was also able to raise capital for a Clergy Stipends Endowment Fund. He had ministered pastorally to Mrs Helen Gilles, the widow of a former Director of Medical Services in Northern Nigeria, and somewhat of a recluse. When she died she left her house, 'Harlyn' and its contents, including a small grand piano, to the Diocese as a thank-offering. Part of the proceeds were used to form the Helen Gilles Clergy Endowment Fund, which today, considerably augmented, provides over a third of the money needed for clergy stipends. As a result of his work, clergy stipends were raised to £600 for a single priest, £720 for a married one.

Thus in his report to the Diocesan Association in 1972, the Bishop was able to say:

It is 4 years since I came to you with a grim report of serious financial difficulties in our little Diocese. Now I rejoice to tell you of our thanksgiving as the clouds have lifted through efforts on the part of our own people in the Diocese, and with your help, and the help of USPG and the Church of the Province.

He also reported that he had been able to raise £6,000 (£1,500 from USPG) to increase the capital of the Bishopric Endowment Fund. In the four year period the Diocese had given away £1,000. In 1971 Mr John Beadon, a retired Bank Manager, became Honorary Diocesan Treasurer, a post he was to fill for 10 years.

Bishop Capper invested part of Mrs Gilles' legacy with the Provincial Trustees to provide a small income to help with the upkeep of St Paul's Churchyard. In return St Paul's parish undertook to keep her grave in good repair, and to place flowers on it on her Year's Mind, 28 June.

As a new Bishop, he attended the 1968 Lambeth Conference. In giving his impressions, he spoke enthusiastically of the leadership of Archbishop Michael Ramsay, but, except for the worship, he was somewhat disillusioned with the Conference.

Bishop Capper was presented to Her Majesty the Queen at Buckingham Palace during a visit in 1970.

The regular schedules of the Union Castle ships enabled Bishop Capper to keep a close relationship with the Province and with the St Helenian community in Cape Town, resulting in further financial help for the Diocese. It also made visits by Provincial Officers possible. Bishop Stanley Pickard, the Provincial Executive Officer, visited St Helena in September 1970, and John da Costa, Rector of St Mark's, Cape Town, visited for two days in August 1972, shortly before becoming Provincial Director of Mission. The Archbishop of Cape Town, Robert Selby Taylor, visited St Helena in November 1972 and preached in all three parishes.

That month, Bishop Capper blessed a new Volkswagen Beetle given by USPG for the Bishop's use. Twelve years later, it was still transporting the present writer. Throughout his episcopate, the Bishop edited a Diocesan Gazette of which only a few issues have been discovered.

Bishop Capper resigned in March 1973 on reaching retiring age. He became Chaplain at Malaga in southern Spain and now lives at Blackheath, London. He is an Assistant Bishop in the Dioceses of Europe and Southwark.

BISHOP GIGGALL

George Kenneth Giggall was the tenth Bishop from 1973 to 1979. After gaining his BA at the University of Manchester in 1937, he trained at St Chad's College, Durham, and was ordained Priest in 1940. He was a Chaplain in the Royal Navy (1945-69), being appointed an Officer of the Order of the British Empire (Military) in 1960. He was an Honorary Chaplain to Her Majesty the Queen (1967-9) and Dean of Gibraltar (1969-73). When his appointment as Bishop was announced, as befits a senior ex-Chaplain of the Royal Navy and in accordance with the hospitality of the Senior Service, he received the splendid assurance from the Chief of Staff to the Commander-in-Chief Fleet:

'The Fleet is at your disposal for getting yourself and your belongings to St Helena.' Accordingly he sailed on RFA *Tidereach* accompanied by HMS *Apollo* and HMS *Rhyl*. At St Helena his 'belongings' were offloaded onto the lawn of Plantation House, the Governor's residence, by 12 sorties of HMS *Rhyl*'s helicopter, one for each of the 12 Apostles, as the island observed.

He was consecrated Bishop of St Helena in the Church of St Saviour, East London, South Africa on 4 May 1973 and presented with his pastoral staff made by shipwrights in the dockyard in Gibraltar. His pectoral cross was a gift from the congregation of Gibraltar Cathedral. He sailed for St Helena on the Union Castle Mailboat *Southampton Castle* for his enthronement on 20 May 1973 in St Paul's Cathedral.

A link was formed between the second youngest Diocese of the Province, Port Elizabeth, and the fourth oldest, St Helena, in 1975 at the instigation of Fr John da Costa, then Director of Mission, CPSA. It was to be a link of mutual support by prayer, and the Port Elizabeth Diocesan Council also generously agreed to help with clergy stipends, to pay clergy pensions premiums, and the first 400 Rand of expenses incurred in South Africa. All this has been of inestimable help to St Helena.

Since 1966 the Province had an Augmentation of Stipends scheme whereby the wealthier Dioceses contributed to a central fund to help the poorer Dioceses pay a minimum stipend. However by 1976 it became obvious that the gap in stipends between the richer and poorer Dioceses was widening, and the following year a Parity of Stipends scheme was inaugurated, whereby the minimum stipend of a poorer Diocese was to be increased at a faster rate each year than in the richer Dioceses, until there was equality of stipends throughout the Province. To avoid 'pauperization' of the poorer Dioceses they were to pay a proportion (at first one third) of the increase each year. When it seemed likely that St Helena would not be able to benefit from this scheme, since Bishop Giggall felt he could not commit the Diocese to finding this increasing amount of money each year, the link Diocese of Port Elizabeth generously offered to pay St Helena's contributions. In fact they have each year since then paid an annual contribution of 2,000 Rand which has been added to the capital of the St Helenian Clergy Endowment Fund, the increased interest enabling St Helena to pay her share. In addition Bishop Giggall adopted the policy of adding any surplus money to the capital. Thus during his episcopate he was able to raise the capital of the Endowment Fund from about £1,000 to £19,000 and to more than double clergy stipends from £720 to £1,500 a year.

Since St Helena is in the Sterling area, he aimed to build up funds in the United Kingdom to avoid the rise and fall in the value of the Rand. The importance of the shipping link for all aspects of life on St Helena cannot be exaggerated. Yet ironically travel to and from St Helena actually became more difficult as the century progressed. The island has no airstrip and is therefore totally dependent on shipping. For many years two Union Castle ships each called monthly enabling comparatively short visits to be made to Ascension and to South Africa. (This service was interrupted in 1973 when the *Good Hope Castle* caught fire between Ascension and St Helena and had to be abandoned. Passengers and crew in lifeboats were picked up by a passing ship and the *Good Hope Castle* was eventually salvaged.) In November 1977 both Union Castle ships were withdrawn. Furthermore, since the Royal Navy had withdrawn from Simonstown, visits by British warships were very rare. However the Bishop was able to attend the Provincial Synod at Johannesburg by a return passage on HMS *Tiger*. On this occasion he himself arrived by helicopter on Plantation House lawn. After a year of occasional chartered ships, by which means the Bishop was able to attend the Lambeth Conference, a scheduled service was resumed in October 1978 with the RMS *St Helena*, a vessel of some 3,000 tons, carrying cargo and 70 passengers. But a single ship, shuttling between England and Cape Town, calling at Ascension and St Helena on the way, and taking two months for the round trip, causes many problems. To visit Ascension means staying nearly six weeks, waiting for the ship to sail to England and return. To attend a Synod means staying two months in South Africa.

One remarkable eccentric who was on the island in the Bishop's time was Mrs Louisa Hawker, known affectionally to all, islanders and expatriates alike, as Auntie Lou. A lady of some social standing and beauty, she claimed to have become disillusioned with society, and travelled extensively around the world in her Ford V8 motor caravan, known as the 'Suzy Wong'. She eventually arrived at St Helena where she parked her van under the cliffs in Upper Jamestown and constructed a remarkable garden on the barren rock. She lived in the van, and welcomed visitors to her garden where they might find the contrast of a beautiful flower growing out of a broken teapot, and an exquisite chiffon scarf worn over a somewhat grubby apron, set off with a valuable necklace. She seldom left her domain, save for an annual visit to Plantation House for her birthday party. She died on 10 September 1981 but sadly her great wish to be buried at sea in the 'Suzy Wong' could not be realized as it was considered too dangerous an undertaking, and she was buried in St Paul's Churchyard.

Bishop Giggall resigned on 30 September 1979 and left St Helena a month later. He first became Chaplain of San Remo, Italy and then retired to Lytham, Lancashire, where he is Assistant Bishop in the Diocese of Blackburn.

A Personal Interlude (1979-85)

'It must have been difficult writing about yourself' said a daughter-in-law, after reading a first draft, in which I had tried to be objective about my own episcopate. Well, yes, it was difficult and I was not really happy about the result. So I decided to throw objectivity to the winds, just for one section.

I had been a Royal Air Force Chaplain for 20 years, retired in 1974 to become Chaplain and Head of Religious Education at St Margaret's School, Bushey, a girl's boarding school run by the Clergy Orphan Corporation. When my wife Eunice and I were asked if we would go to St Helena, we had to look it up on the map! We knew nothing of St Helena or South Africa.

Becoming a bishop means, amongst other more important things, acquiring a whole new outfit. Family, school, previous parish and USPG rallied round generously. So did the Royal Air Force. In January 1937, aged 16, I had joined the RAF as an Apprentice and was trained at the Electrical and Wireless School, RAF Cranwell. We should have passed out in December 1939, instead we were sent to our operational stations at four hours' notice on the evening of 1 September, not even knowing our assessments. But in 1979, the workshops of my old School offered to make my pastoral staff. So that September, on their parade ground, I was presented with a beautifully made staff, in a case adorned with my old Apprentice badges. The Station Commander had done his home-work in the Air Ministry Archives and on parade read out my marks and final position, just 40 years later to the month!

We met the St Helena Diocesan Association, who told us that they would pay for the shipment of our baggage, as was their custom. I knew they had little money left in their funds, and I was concerned when the shippers added another £200 to their original estimate. Somehow this came to the ears of the Dean of Hereford, Norman Rathbone, and he and Mrs Rathbone kindly arranged a coffee morning in the Cathedral and gave us a cheque for £200.

We had to fly to South Africa for my Consecration. Our flight was arranged by the Salvation Army, who are expert at arranging the cheapest flights for missionaries. At Johannesburg we met the Provincial Officers and were taken to Soweto by the Director of Mission. We had no idea it was so vast, with an estimated population of two million. At an early morning celebration in the Cathedral, Bishop Desmond Tutu, then General Secretary of the South African Council of Churches, rose from his knees and pressed a cheque into my hand 'to help with expenses'.

We flew to Cape Town where Archbishop Bill Burnett and his wife Sheila gave us a warm welcome at Bishopscourt, and we enjoyed their hospitality and their garden, reputed to be the finest episcopal garden in the Anglican Communion. We shared with Donald Nestor, to be consecrated Suffragan Bishop of Lesotho, and his parents, the vital spiritual life of Bishopscourt.

The Consecration was in Cape Town Cathedral on the evening of 14 October. Bruce Evans, Bishop of Port Elizabeth, and Liam Manning, Bishop of George sponsored me, and the Dean kindly arranged for Eunice to receive Communion with me.

We then had ten days to wait for the sailing of the RMS *St Helena*. By a lucky chance, Arthur Collins, Archdeacon of Cape Town and a contemporary at King's College, London, and St Boniface College, Warminster, was going on leave and lent us his rectory in return for looking after his parish. The Archbishop gave me Bishop Turner's pectoral cross, made in the form of a Canterbury Cross, to take back to the Diocese.

We found the RMS *St Helena* to be a happy ship, with a British and St Helenian crew. After a voyage of five days, we arrived at Jamestown in the early hours of 30 October, and were greeted by Bishop Kenneth Giggall who was to leave next day northbound, and the other two clergy, Archdeacon Richard Lindsay and Fr John Harvey. We enjoyed the hospitality of Governor Geoffrey Guy and Mrs Guy at Plantation House for two days, before moving to Bishopsholme. Bishop Giggall once described its style as 'decayed elegance' and no doubt it had seen better days, but we liked it. The rooms, though few, were spacious, and the grounds, though partly overgrown, were extensive, with a terraced garden in front, once the pride of Mrs Beardmore. To the north – we are in the southern hemisphere – is a pleasant view over a sea devoid of ships, save for a few fishing boats and, twice every two months, the RMS *St Helena*.

My enthronement as eleventh Bishop was on Sunday morning, 4 November, in the Cathedral, broadcast over the island radio. There are no Servicemen on St Helena, and visiting dignitaries, having inspected the police, go on to inspect the Scouts, Guides and Church Lads Brigade. Wishing to add dignity to the occasion, the Archdeacon had arranged for a fanfare to be blown by the Scout Buglers, as he placed me in the Bishop's throne. As I sat down the call rang out. In my Service days we used to put words to the different calls, and the words which came back into my mind at that solemn moment were 'Oh, he won't get to Heaven when he dies, when he dies'. I think no one else in the Cathedral realised the appropriateness of the call, and I believe my face did not betray it!

There was an interregnum at St Paul's parish when I arrived, so I was able to look after the parish for the next three months. This was most useful in getting to know the people, and during my six years as Bishop I always welcomed the opportunity of taking over a parish during the absence of clergy, quite apart from the help this measure gave to the Clergy Stipends Fund! St Paul's parish, with its five churches, covers the western half of the island. Every Tuesday morning was devoted to taking the Blessed Sacrament to the housebound in different areas of the parish.

I used to enjoy those mornings, taking the car as far as we could go, and then tramping over the hills to remote cottages. Churchwarden Reggie Constantine always came with me, at first to show me where to go, and then to keep me company. 'It's wonderful how far you can get, if you just keep going steadily' he used to say as we climbed some particularly steep hill. The older St Helenians were used to walking a great deal, over very hilly terrain. Two dear old ladies, Iris and Harriet, used regularly to walk several miles, rain or shine, to the 8a.m. Communion in the Cathedral every Sunday. Sadly Reggie died in the 'flu epidemic of 1980, while I was on Ascension. He was a wonderful Christian gentleman. There are many classical surnames on the island – Constantine, Augustus, Plato, Leo, Scipio, Hercules – a relic of the old slave days. Sometimes Eunice would accompany me on these Tuesday mornings and she was always especially welcomed. Usually at the last cottage, coffee and sandwiches would be produced, or I would be sent home with a gift of fruit or vegetables.

If someone was seriously ill or dying, at home or in hospital, the priest was always sent for, and anointing was expected, while the family gathered round. Such a ministry was a great privilege. When a death occurred, there was, before the church service, a little ceremony, often in the mortuary chapel, when family and friends, including children, came to say goodbye at the open coffin, and there would be a hymn and prayers. I thought this was a good and healthy custom, although some of the clergy found it difficult to accept. After the service in church, the congregation would gather round the open grave and

A typical St Helenian dwelling

after the committal the children would drop flowers on the coffin. Then we would sing a hymn and remain in silence while the grave was filled in and mounded very efficiently by two grave diggers, and floral tributes arranged.

Weddings were great occasions, although comparatively few guests came to the church. At the reception the bride and groom would sit in two chairs in the middle of one side of the room, and guests would come to offer their felicitations. I found it somewhat reminiscent of receptions at Malay weddings, and it is possible that it has come down from the early days of the East India Company. It was the task of the priest to read the telegrams and propose a toast. The clergy were always invited to join the family and many friends who remained behind after the 'official' guests had left, for the splendid meal which followed. There was no chance of going away for a honeymoon, and the celebrations would continue until the small hours. Often Eunice and I have felt sorry for a young bride, desperately tired, but bravely persevering.

As well as taking assemblies once a week in the four Government schools in the parish, I was asked to help with some Religious Education in the Country School. At first I was a little surprised when Mrs Lilian Greentree, whose class it was, elected to remain in the classroom with me. I soon realized how wise she was. There were absolutely no discipline problems, but it could be very difficult for a newcomer to understand what the children were saying, and at first I often had to ask for help. I found the sessions very enjoyable, and the children most responsive. And always Mrs Greentree would end the afternoon sessions with prayer.

Our first Christmas was very joyful, if busy, with services in all five churches of the parish. Jamestown on Christmas Eve had an almost Dickensian air, with the shops open and everyone doing their last minute shopping, almost up to the time for Midnight Mass. We discovered one happy link with the past. All Saints Convent, Oxford who had supplied St Margaret's School, Bushey with wafers for Holy Communion also supplied St Helena as part of their missionary work. Sister Alice SAS, who ran the bakery, had an honoured place on our Diocesan prayer list.

At the beginning of the year, the RC priest, Peter Paul Feeny, the Baptist Minister, Norman Longstaff, and Howard Sercombe, the Salvation Army Captain, all preached in the Cathedral. It prepared the way for the formation of a Minister's Fraternal (see Chapter 5).

Fr Clay Knowles and his family arrived in February to take over the Cathedral parish. There is a delicate situation on St Helena in that the Bishop is also the Dean, and therefore would normally have responsibility for the Cathedral and its services. However, in this case, the Cathedral is also the principal church of the parish. It was evident that it was prudent to keep a very low profile as Dean, and although I asked to be consulted before any substantial changes were made, I generally allowed the parish priest a free hand. People often comment on how splendid it is to have such a small Diocese where the Bishop can know all his clergy and people. This is indeed true, but one must also remember that on such a small island, news travels fast, and it is almost impossible not to know exactly what is happening in the three parishes. It is therefore important that the clergy should not feel that the Bishop is breathing down their necks!

One great work of Fr Knowles, was to prepare three mentally retarded people for Confirmation, and it was a wonderful experience to give them Holy Communion. Linda came each week with her mother to St Andrew's, and her joy in receiving was evident. Cyril, an older man, was gifted as a violinist, and used to come with us each month to the Mental Hospital, to accompany the hymns for the Eucharist. They were both confirmed in Bishopsholme Chapel, but Deanna lived in a remote cottage and was confirmed in her home. On the monthly home Communion rounds we always celebrated the Holy Communion in her cottage, which was more meaningful for her than taking the Reserved Sacrament. She soon learnt how to prepare the vessels.

Lent has always been strictly observed on St Helena. No one would think of asking to be married in Lent, and dances were not held. The custom began to be questioned in some quarters. Eunice and I thought the best way of making the point was to hold a Pancake Party each Shrove Tuesday at Bishopsholme, which proved very popular, and involved us in making some 200 pancakes each year! But customs were changing, and in the end I had to ask that at least there should be no parties in Holy Week.

Easter Monday was traditionally the day when all the parish Sunday Schools gathered on Francis Plain for an annual treat and picnic – always a substantial meal, as are all St Helenian picnics.

The Société Napoléon chartered the RMS *St Helena* for a three day visit in 1980. Some 70 French members came, led by Prince and Princess Napoleon and accompanied by descendants of Napoleon's entourage, such as Baron Gourgaud and Count Walenski. We found it a fascinating visit.

Our first visit to Ascension, to collate Fr Richard Davison as Vicar, was in July 1980. On our return six weeks later, Fr John Harvey went to South Africa on furlough, so I was able to look after St Matthew's parish for three months. That gave the opportunity of getting to know another batch of House Communicants. I always remember one elderly lady, who lived in very simple surroundings, who could recite not only the whole service with me, but the seasonal collects as well. A little beyond her was Deadwood Plain, where one could often catch sight of a wirebird, the island's only indigenous landbird, running along on its slender legs.

When we arrived on the island, we were told that the endemic St Helena Ebony (*Trochetiopsis melanoxylon*) had been extinct for over a hundred years. Imagine our excitement when two small bushes were discovered on a remote cliff face by Mr Quentin Cronk of Cambridge University and the World Wildlife Fund and Mr George Benjamin, a St Helenian with an extensive knowledge of and love for the island flora. It was successfully propagated and numbers of cuttings and seedlings planted around the island.

In October 1980 came the news of the Algerian earthquake. I issued an appeal, thinking we might raise about £300 or so. In the event, the islanders raised £1,800, mostly in small amounts. I estimated that a very large proportion of the islanders had contributed, and I was touched by the way poor people would stop me on the road and give a contribution.

Although the island is small, the terrain does isolate the clergy to some extent from one another. We held a monthly Chapter meeting and from time to time a quiet day for the clergy. Although each priest has a full time job, there is a certain lack of pressure which helps a life of prayer, but the lack of normal facilities for retreats and the limited choice of a spiritual director are problems. Local leave also presents difficulties, which I endeavoured to mitigate by taking over each parish for a week or so, usually after the Festivals.

For some reason, the island does not get thunderstorms. 1 June 1981 saw the first for 40 years, albeit out to sea. Since the last thunderstorm had coincided with an outbreak of poliomyelitis, there was some apprehension as to what this one might presage but in the event no new disasters befell the island.

We sailed for Cape Town in October 1981 for meetings of the Episcopal Synod and Provincial Standing Committee. During the routine stay of two months in South Africa, while waiting for the return ship, we hired a car and drove along the 'Garden Route' and on to Johannesburg, whence Eunice flew to England to see the family. (She was to find herself stuck there, when the RMS *St Helena* was requisitioned for the Falklands crisis, and eventually returned to St Helena in June 1982 in the replacement 500-ton *Aragonite*, a voyage of three weeks.) After the Synod, and a retreat at the Convent of the Sisters of St John the Divine at Durban, I acted as curate to Tim Bravington of St Martin's, Durban. It was an especially rewarding experience, ministering to the mainly Indian population in Phoenix township. After a visit to our link Diocese of Port Elizabeth, I left Cape Town on 23 December, and celebrated Midnight Mass on board. Sadly, on Christmas morning, one of our St Helenian passengers, a sick man hoping to return to the island, died only an hour after receiving his Christmas Communion, and was buried at sea.

I paid another visit to Ascension in March 1982. While I was there the invasion of the Falklands occurred, and I was still waiting to return to St Helena, when the British Task Force came through.

The Fourteenth Diocesan Synod, the first since 1933, was held in St Paul's Cathedral on 30 January 1983. Unfortunately, but almost inevitably, it was not possible for any representatives from St Mary's, Ascension to attend. In my charge I reviewed the life of the Diocese over the last 50 years. (The portion dealing with the present and future can be found in Appendix A.) The Synod resolved to work towards financial independence, called for a Campaign for Stewardship and commended tithing. It challenged the Church to consider seriously the call to priesthood and lay ministry, including work among youth. It revived the Diocesan Board of Finance, with elected members, in place of the Diocesan Finance Committee and set up a Diocesan Council. A message was sent to the Prime Minister concerning the right of entry of St Helenians to the United Kingdom. The Archbishop of Cape Town was requested to invite the Diocesan Council to express their views when the election of a Bishop of St Helena was pending. The Governor was asked to repeal the Parish Ordinance (Chapter 79) which conflicted with the present Canons 26 and 28 concerning Vestry meetings and Churchwardens. The proceedings were published locally.

Eunice and I travelled to England in May 1983 on RMS *Centaur*, the successor to the *Aragonite* as a temporary replacement for the RMS *St Helena*. The next five months were taken up with visits to 16 supporting parishes, a month's course on the 'Bible and the Land' at St George's College, Jerusalem, interviewing prospective clergy and marrying our youngest son Nigel to Sally-Anne. The Diocesan Association had kindly bought us a 'banger' which took us all over England from Weston-super-Mare to Durham, before expiring in August at its MOT test.

On our return to St Helena, Fr John Harvey retired to South Africa. Once more I could act as parish priest of St Matthew's for three months. We visited Ascension in June 1984 for the institution of George Bradshaw as Vicar, when I paid a brief visit to the Falklands at the request of the Archbishop of Canterbury.

With regard to Diocesan finance, I continued my predecessor's policy of giving priority to increasing the Clergy Endowment Fund. With continued help from the Diocese of Port Elizabeth and the Provincial Parity of Stipends Fund and by increasing substantially annually the parochial contributions, clergy stipends were raised from £1,500 to £2,675, plus a children's allowance, and the capital of the Clergy Endowment Fund from £19,000 to £34,000. The clergy were now able to live, if simply, at least without financial worries. However, clergy stipends had now outstripped the Bishop's stipend, and partly to redress the discrepancy, about £4,000 was, over a period, added to the capital of the Bishopric Endowment Fund.

The dramatic fall in the Rand/Pound Sterling exchange rate in 1984 caused financial problems for the Diocese. All money received from South Africa, such as interest from Endowments invested with the Provincial Trustees, and grants from the Diocese of Port Elizabeth and the Parity of Stipends Fund were all reduced by 27 per cent. Happily, at the meeting of the Provincial Standing Committee in November, which I attended, both the Diocese of Port Elizabeth and the Parity of Stipends Committee offered to increase their contributions in 1985 to make up for the low exchange rate.

The sad but inevitable decision in 1980 to remove the spire of St James' – described in Chapter 4 – together with other restoration work cost nearly £16,000. This was raised by an appeal by the Governor, Bishop and Vicar, and thanks are due to Mr Geoffrey Guy, the Governor at the time for personally supervising the appeal.

An appeal by the Bishop, Vicar and Churchwardens in 1984 for the restoration of St Paul's Cathedral raised about £10,000, including 500 Rand from the St Helenian community in Cape Town during the Bishop's visit in December 1984. Although the bulk of the money in both these appeals came from charitable trusts in England, substantial sums were raised by parishes and individuals, both in the Diocese and overseas.

In 1981 Mr John Norris was appointed Honorary Diocesan Treasurer, to be succeeded in 1983 by Mrs Ivy Ellick.

I was able to attend only two Episcopal Synods, the second being in November 1984 at Modderpoort. The Synod elected Paulino Manhique as Bishop of Niassa, and Desmond Tutu as Bishop of Johannesburg. Afterwards Philip Mokuku, Bishop of Lesotho, invited Eunice and me to spend three weeks in his Diocese. It was a wonderful experience. He and his Suffragan, Donald Nestor – we had been consecrated together – took us to Confirmations in remote villages in their mountainous Diocese. The villagers and especially the Mothers' Union in their colourful uniforms would escort us with singing and dancing, and what with the feasting afterwards, a village Confirmation could last six hours! We spent some time with the Sisters of the Community of the Holy Name and were privileged to attend the Profession of a coloured Sister into the contemplative Society of the Precious Blood. Fr David Wells ssm took us on a memorable drive into the central mountains to the Anglican Mission Hospital at Mantsonyane.

Back in Cape Town we learnt that the ship would be delayed. We were staying at Bishopscourt and the Archbishop and Eirene Russell took the news wonderfully, even though their family was arriving for Christmas! The RMS St Helena had had a fire in her engine room on her northbound run, and the passengers had had to spend several hours in the lifeboats, dangling from the davits while the fire was brought under control. The ship wallowed helplessly in the Atlantic for two days until a tug arrived to tow her to Dakar. Fortunately the only casualty was an engineer with badly burned hands, rescued from the engine room by a colleague. After repairs, the ship returned to Cape Town and we left on 23 December, so once more we were able to celebrate the Nativity on board. Before we left, St Aidan's, Lansdowne, arranged a splendid rally of Saints – St Helenians – living in the parish.

The Governor invited me, as Bishop, to serve on the Education Committee. It was good to be involved at a time when, after 16 years of negotiations, we could finally plan the new central Prince Andrew High School, and also when Basil George, the first St Helenian Chief Education Officer, could lead the planning. During my time the schools could offer only two 'A' level subjects, so to provide a third I taught five trainee teachers 'A' level Religious Education. They had to study at the same time as doing their teacher training, and it says much for their intelligence and application that, with few reference books, they obtained one A Grade, two B Grades and two C Grades in an examination where E Grade is a pass. They were better results than I had usually obtained with full-time pupils!

Early in 1985 I completed a history of the Diocese which had, perforce, to rely on the sources available on the island. Professor Musiker, Librarian of the University of the Witwatersrand, where the Provincial Archives are kept, kindly gave a grant of 500 Rand from the Canon Wood Fund, Mrs Pat Musk typed it as a labour of love, the Reverend Michael Crook made available his word processor and the Governor kindly allowed it to be printed by the Government printer, that stalwart churchman Arthur Bizaare.

In September 1984, I announced to the Diocesan Council that I had offered my resignation to the Archbishop of Cape Town, to take effect from the end of 1985. The reason for the unusually long notice was to give time for the Diocesan Council to express their views to the Archbishop. This they did, thus implementing for the first time a Resolution first passed by the second Diocesan Synod in 1887 and renewed by the Synod of 1983. Under the Provincial Canon Law, in any Diocese where there are fewer than ten priests, the Bishop is elected by the Bishops of the Province.

At its meeting in February 1985, the Episcopal Synod elected James Nathaniel Johnson to be the first St Helenian Bishop. The day before his appointment was made public, I went to Hutt's Gate to tell Mrs Johnson that her son was to be the next Bishop. It was a very proud moment for her.

In my last week on St Helena I did something I had wanted to do for some time, and produced Henri Gheon's *Christmas in the Market Place* with a mixed St Helenian and expatriate cast, with myself playing Old

Melchior. We played it in Jamestown in the open air on the Court House steps, and also in the Cathedral and at Blue Hill. We left St Helena on 21 December 1985 and spent ten days on Ascension taking the Christmas services before flying to England.

A St Helenian Bishop (1985-1991)

James Nathaniel Johnson was born on St Helena in 1932 and went to primary school at Hutt's Gate and to the Secondary School at Red Gate. In 1955 he and his wife Joyce, whom he had married two years earlier, went to England as domestic servants – virtually the only way to obtain entry into the UK, then as now. Sadly, if the British Government's proposal, announced in July 1991, to phase out by 1995 the special quota of work permits for unskilled and semi-skilled workers from dependent territories is implemented, St Helenians will no longer have this opportunity of entry into Britain. James joined the Church Army and then trained for the priesthood at Wells Theological College, while Joyce continued her work as a shop assistant to support both them amd their son Brian. James was made Deacon in 1964 and became Curate at St Lawrence Weston, Bristol. In 1966 they returned to St Helena where Fr James spent two tours in the Cathedral parish. He thus follows Frederick Baker and William Samuel as an island born priest. He returned to the UK in 1971, was USPG Area Secretary for Exeter and Truro Dioceses (1972-4), then Rector of Coombe Martin and later Rector of Thorpe Bay. Bishop Giggall appointed him an Honorary Canon in 1975.

The importance of having indigenous clergy, where possible, is nowadays taken for granted. People often comment how splendid it must be to have a Diocese small enough for the Bishop to know all his people. Of course they are right, but they sometimes forget that there are disadvantages – especially if, for example, one is related, however remotely, to many of the islanders, who may remember you as a schoolboy. All the previous Bishops had come to the Diocese with hardly any previous knowledge of it. Bishop James had known it, both as a young man and as a priest. But it was not to be the same island that he had known. There had been changes in the last 14 years. Most people enjoyed a higher standard of living, although there were still pockets of poverty. There was a rise in 'consumerism', many people had enough money to buy a video recorder (there was no television) and video nasties had infiltrated the island, as well as drugs. Education and welfare provision had markedly improved. Perhaps not quite so many people went to church, Lent was not so strictly kept and sport on Sundays had considerably increased. Things had indeed changed.

The Johnsons flew to Johannesburg in October 1985, where they met some of the Provincial Officers. Bishop Leslie Stradling conducted the retreat at the Roman Catholic Centre at Schoenstatt. Their daughter Ruth joined them for James' Consecration as twelfth Bishop of St Helena in St George's Cathedral, Cape Town, on All Saints' Day. Bishop Bruce Evans of Port Elizabeth preached. The Bishop attended the Episcopal Synod, and then spent some time in the link Diocese of Port Elizabeth. The Bishop and his wife arrived in St Helena on 19 December, and there was an official welcome in the Cathedral on the morning of Sunday 22 December, at which the Bishop delivered his charge to the Diocese.

The Most Reverend Philip Russell, Archbishop of Cape Town, accompanied by his wife Eirene, arrived on 23 January 1986, having flown to Tenerife and come south on the RMS *St Helena*. (Unfortunately the length of stay at Ascension had not allowed the Archbishop to land.) The Enthronement was on 26 January. The Archbishop preached and later wrote to his family:

Sunday was the great day, and great day it was. The little Cathedral was full, Scouts and Guides marched and blew bugles (two later did the fanfare in the Service); the Governor was there in full regalia; singing was good ...

(I am sure the Church Lads Brigade was there as well.) The service was relayed to people outside and later broadcast. The next day the Archbishop took a Quiet Morning for the clergy. In the afternoon the Bishop took him and Eirene to Sandy Bay. The Archbishop wrote:

The roads in St Helena are almost all single track, with occasional passing bays. The speed at which they travel, the narrow escapes (a car will suddenly appear from nowhere in the mist; both cars swerve madly, and then the drivers stop, completely blocking the road to have a chat) took years off my life.

On the following three days the Archbishop spent a day with each of the parishes, and of course there were dinners and receptions at Plantation House, Bishopsholme, and parish socials. They left on 1 February for Cape Town via Tristan. The Archbishop wrote to the island:

I want to record my gratitude to all who made the stay ... the truly memorable event it was ... do continue to keep alive that warmth of human relationships which gives St Helenians that special characteristic known far beyond the shores of the island.

The Archbishop's visit, the first since Archbishop Selby Taylor's in 1972, did much to make the people aware of the reality of the

92 ST HELENA

relationship of the Diocese to the Church of the Province of Southern Africa.

Another visitor that year was Miss Gwen Abbott, sadly now deceased, a Reader in Gloucester Diocese. On her previous visit in 1985 to advise on the education of deaf children, she had preached in virtually all the Anglican churches.

Michael Crook was ordained Priest in the Cathedral on 7 September 1986, the same day that Desmond Tutu was enthroned Archbishop of Cape Town. Michael Crook had been a Consultant Surgeon in the Far East for many years and retired to St Helena. He studied for the non-stipendiary ministry, first under Bishop Leslie Stradling in Cape Town and then under the present writer on St Helena, and was made Deacon on 1 September 1985. It was the first time that there had been an ordination of a Deacon on the island since Harry Gibbons in 1901, and of a Priest since Maurice Geen in 1963.

Fr Peter Cowen moved to St Matthew's parish in October 1986 and the Bishop looked after the Cathedral parish for three months. Fr Cowen represented the Diocese at the 1987 Partners-in-Mission Conference at Modderpoort.

Bishop Johnson's first visit to Ascension (since 1971) was in May 1986. He paid a brief visit on the shuttle of the RMS *St Helena* in May 1987, and called for ten days in April 1988 on his way to the Lambeth Conference and to visit supporting parishes in the UK. He returned via South Africa to attend the Episcopal Synod there. Fr Price was appointed Vicar-General. In July a whole-day Diocesan Conference for clergy and laity was held at St Mark's, to pray for the Bishops at Lambeth and to discuss the four Lambeth themes in the context of the Diocese.

An exchange between Fr Cottingham of Ascension and Fr Houghton of St James' took place for two months at the end of 1988. This was valuable, both personally for the two priests, and to cement the two parts of the Diocese.

Realization of the priceless heritage in Diocesan and parochial records had grown during the 1980s. Although they had been preserved from the ravages of the white ants which in years past had attacked other valuable records on the island, the writer decided in 1983 to send the Diocesan records to the Central Record Library of the Province at the University of the Witwatersrand in Johannesburg. They were microfilmed and a copy of the fiches and a reader were given to the Diocese. It was felt that it was too risky to allow the Baptism, Marriage and Burial Registers to leave the island and so the Provincial Archivist,

Mrs Anne Kotze, visited St Helena from February to April 1989, armed with a microfiche camera, to make a copy of the Registers. During that time not only did Mrs Kotze work very hard in difficult conditions in the Government Archives in the basement of the Castle, since the door which was closed to keep out the light also kept out the air, but she played a full part in the life of the Church, and was there for Holy Week and Easter. She later wrote of her experiences in a little book, *St Helena Journal*, which captures the flavour of the island splendidly. She has kindly allowed me to quote from her concluding entry:

What shall I take away from this Island of St Helena which a poet once called an emerald set in a ring of bronze?

I shall think of an island of contrasts – lush green hills and barren soilless mountains, of brilliant sun on silken sea and soft grey rain misting the inland countryside.

I shall remember the deep, simple religious faith of the Saints which is integrated into their everyday lives.

I have appreciated the unlocked Churches, houses, hotel room with no fear of robbery or vandalism.

It has been a special pleasure to have no anxiety about personal safety and to walk anywhere alone at night.

I like the islanders' good-humoured acceptance of shortages. I will not forget their generosity in business, shopkeepers having told me many times where I could buy the same thing cheaper in another emporium.

I have loved the St Helenians' home-made activities and their readiness to take part with enjoyment and unselfconsciousness.

I shall recall an archivist's paradise with historical material to hand at every turn.

I shall remember a rich experience and good friends.[34]

The Bishop left in May to attend the Episcopal and Provincial Synods in Durban. Mrs Joyce Johnson was the first ever Lay Representative of the Diocese at the Provincial Synod.

The Society for the Propagation of the Gospel, (now USPG) has assisted the Diocese of St Helena since 1704 when, only three years after the SPG was formed, it gave £5 worth of small tracts to the East India Company Chaplain, Charles Masham. The first SPG missionary was William Bousfield, in 1847, since when the Society has given the isolated Diocese of St Helena great assistance by making itself responsible for the recruitment of clergy. It must be said that in recent years it has become increasingly difficult to find clergy from this country willing to serve overseas, and whilst there are still some volunteers, the

Diocese has been fortunate in being able to recruit clergy from Africa as well. The Society pays clergy fares at the end of a tour (the Diocese, or the Diocesan Association, pays the outward fare) and for furloughs. The Society also pays a furlough allowance, Clergy Pension and National Health contributions where appropriate, and other incidental expenses. However, it was not until 1989 that an official of the Society had ever visited the Diocese. Mr Mark Parker, USPG Short Term Experience Programmes Officer, flew to Ascension in May, spent a week with Fr Ron Cottingham and then caught the ship for St Helena. He visited all three parishes before leaving on 9 June.

His report is a very competent account of the situation of the islands and the Diocese. He echoed the thoughts of Mrs Kotze when he wrote: 'I was impressed many times during my short stay at the simple yet devout faith of ordinary St Helenians on both islands'. He considered that 'this faithful lay presence is the greatest asset of the Diocese' and he stressed the need for training lay ministers. Mr Parker was concerned for unity at both Diocesan and Provincial levels. He commended the recent exchange between priests of the two islands, and suggested a Diocesan Conference every two years. At Provincial level the valuable link with Port Elizabeth might be strengthened by exchange of clergy, and more clergy might be recruited from the Province, although he appreciated that the islands were deeply British. He concluded:

Finally I must say how encouraged I was by the people of the Diocese. It was a shame that I could not make my visit at a time when the Bishop was in the Diocese but he clearly has much in the islands of which to be rightly proud. The Church may be losing influence and numbers but the clear faith and love of the Christians was very evident. I thank God that He is doing so much among them.[35]

In February 1990, the Bishop left for the Episcopal Synod in Johannesburg. On this voyage, once a year, the RMS St Helena goes to the Cape via Tristan. Thus the Bishop, at the request of the Archbishop of Cape Town, was able to confirm ten candidates on Tristan. He returned via England, where his daughter, Ruth, was seriously ill, but fortunately she made a good recovery.

The Bishop had appointed as Vicar-General, Bishop Leslie Stradling, who visited St Helena from February to April 1990. Bishop Stradling was particularly struck to have arrived on the anniversary – a hundred years to the day – of the arrival of the Zulu prince Dinizulu who was brought to St Helena as a prisoner (see Chapter 4).

No one had realized this, and it took me some time to convince anyone that this was an important anniversary. As Chief Buthelezi's predecessor he is more interesting than Napoleon to South Africans.

I had come as a sort of spiritual consultant since PIM (Partners in Mission) had identified the Island Church as being in need of teaching about prayer. I conducted 3 Quiet Days ... and preached 31 sermons ... I was sorry to see only small congregations except ... on Mothering Sunday and at an ecumenical service at the end.

In the absence of the Bishop, I took the chair at the annual meeting of the Women's Provident Society. Before it, the St Helena band marched 100 behatted and beribboned ladies to the Church for a service and then marched them up again, with the clergy, the Governor's wife and other VIPs at the end of the procession. They agreed without trouble to increase their subscriptions without getting any more benefits. 'But', I was told, 'there will be plenty of grumbling afterwards.'

I visited the prison which had only 4 male and 3 female prisoners and it reminded me of a well run boarding house. One young man asked me if he could have a Bible – I hope not only to impress me – and before I could answer, a warder had gone off at the double and fetched one.

Whether there is much drug abuse I am not sure. On arrival, every one of my cases was searched from top to bottom – an indignity I have suffered nowhere else in the world – and I presume this is what they were looking for. Videos – widely described as blue, though not having seen one I cannot say how blue – are very common. Illegitimacy is rapidly on the increase and few seem to think it a disgrace. Litter has become a way of life. And inevitably in so circumscribed a community, gossip is unusually rife.

I shall remain permanently grateful for much wonderful hospitality ... for the green hills and volcanic rocks and for the courageous faith of the minority who hold fast their Christian faith and practice.[36]

During his episcopate Bishop James was especially concerned with the repair and upkeep of church buildings, including the vicarages and Bishopsholme. In 1989 he invited Mr G. H. Edwards PhD to survey all the churches, vicarages and church halls. Dr Edwards produced a comprehensive illustrated report, with his recommendations, amounting to some 74 A4 pages. It will be an invaluable reference for the Church for years to come. Dr Edwards is now ordained. A great deal of work was done, which cost a considerable amount of money. While much came from the island parishes themselves, a large proportion was raised by the Bishop himself, not only from grants from the Diocesan Association and supporting parishes and from the Association of St Helenians in the UK, but also from individuals.

Bishop Johnson celebrated the Silver Jubilee of his Ordination to the Priesthood on 19 December 1990. In April of that year, the Bishop had announced his resignation, to take effect from February 1991. At its meeting in September 1990, the Synod of Bishops elected the Right Reverend John Harry Gerald Ruston OGS MA to be the thirteenth Bishop of St Helena. John Ruston was born in England on 1 October 1929, and after graduating from the University of Cambridge was trained at Ely Theological College, and ordained Priest in 1955. He was a Tutor at Cuddesdon Theological College (1957-61) and went to South Africa in 1962. He became Archdeacon of Bloemfontein in 1976 and was consecrated Suffragan of Pretoria in 1983. The Oratory of the Good Shepherd (OGS) is a dispersed society for celibate priests living under a rule of life.

Bishop John should have arrived in his new Diocese in February 1991. However, a new RMS *St Helena*, which had just been built, after certain tribulations, broke down with engine trouble on her maiden voyage and had to limp back to the UK for repairs. Her temporary replacement, the *Lowland Lancer*, also broke down on her way to Ascension, and had to await repair. (She had previously visited Ascension in 1982 as the RFA *Sir Lancelot* when she was part of the Task Force.) The *Lowland Lancer* eventually travelled to Cape Town via Tristan, on one engine, and brought the Bishop from Cape Town to St Helena, (and Bishop James from St Helena to Ascension) in April 1991, two months late. It was a salutary introduction to the communication problems of Bishop John's new Diocese!

Bishop John was accompanied by Robert Selby-Taylor, one-time Archbishop of Cape Town, who, on behalf of Archbishop Desmond Tutu, enthroned the new Bishop in St Paul's Cathedral on Sunday 14 April, when Bishop John gave his charge to the Diocese.

Bishop John paid his first visit to Ascension from 24 July to 28 August 1991, when he took charge of the parish until the arrival of Fr Nicholas Turner and his wife, the Reverend Ann Turner, on 20 August. Meanwhile, Fr John Ryder, the Senior priest, and Fr Ronald Cottingham, were responsible for the three parishes on St Helena.

3
Early Church Buildings

When in 1861 the Diocese was divided into parishes, two existing churches formed the natural focus for two of the parishes – the Town Church of St James and the Country Church of St Paul. The District of Longwood was to become the third parish once the Church of St Matthew had been built.

It was not only the Anglicans who were involved in the building of Churches in the mid 19th century: about the time of the construction of St John's in Jamestown and the new Country Church, the Baptists bought property for a Mission House in 1846, and the Roman Catholic Church of the Sacred Heart was built in 1852.

However, both the Town Church and the Country Church already possessed venerable pedigrees, which can be traced back into the 17th century.

The Churches of Jamestown (1671-1874)

The first Anglican church in Jamestown must have been built soon after the arrival of the East India Company's first Chaplain, William Noakes, in 1671. There is no record of its construction, but it was probably not a substantial building, since by 1678 it already needed repair, having 'suffered damage by the extreme heat of the weather'. That year half an acre of land around the church was enclosed for a churchyard, 'the said enclosure shall be by a bank cast up out of a ditch that shall be five foot in breadth and five foot in depth upon the Topp whereof shall be set Lemon Trees round the whole enclosure and a Gate shall be made with a bridge to go over the ditch for a comely and convenient entrance and passage to and from the said Church and Churchyard'.[1] By 1691 'The Chappel in Town in bad repair and the roof in danger of falling'.[2] Little seems to have been done, and when the Churchwardens in 1711 petitioned that 'whereas our Churchyard at the Fort is very small and hardly room to dig a grave for rocks and graves already digged also our yard wall is very bad and irregular we pray that we may inlarge our yard backwards by cutting the water in a new course near the hill ...', the Governor and Council replied: 'that its commendable in them to promote the putting that piece of rubbish

called the Churchyard in order; its for the credit of the Island and we advise you to repair the Church or it will tumble down in a little time.'[3]
   In 1732 the Churchwardens reported that 'the Chapple at the Fort ... is so much out of repair that it is shameful a place set apart for the celebration of divine service and in open view of all strangers especially of foreign nations'.

ST JAMES' CHURCH

Eventually, 40 years later, in 1772, preparations were made for building a new church, the present St James', during the time of the Chaplain, William Bearcroft. The accounts for October 1772 for workmen and materials for the new church show:[4]

29 days Carpenters work		£2	3s	6d
120 days Masons		9	0	9
31 days Overseer	@ 1/6d	2	16	10
18 days Overseer	@ 2/-	1	16	0
12 days Smiths			18	0
25 days Stone sawyers		1	17	6
154 days Labourers		£77	5	3
Lead		£3	19s	4d
Nails			16	7
Timber		161	10	2
Elm boards			12	3
Oak planks		9	16	8

and, finally:

10 gallons Arrack for workmen	1	12	11

On 4 April 1774, the Church was reported to be 'complete, all but the Balustrades for the Communion ... likewise the Revetments'. Final expenses included:

Pulpit and Desk hangings	£1	10s	0d
Communion Table cloth		10	0
8 cushions for 2 pews	1	5	0
3 cushions for altar		9	0
4 stool covers, etc.	1	17	6
Carpenters, Painters etc.	5	14	0
Books: 18 Bibles etc.	27	6	0

Three houses (the present 1, 2 and 3 Main Street) were then built on the site of the old church for the use of the Company servants.[5] Captain James Cook admired the new church when he visited the island,

St James' Church, Jamestown. 'Scene taken from the Castle Terrace' from View No.3 of
Views of St Helena *(London 1815) by G.H. Bellasis, from a sketch made in 1804*

St James' Church, Jamestown. From a colour plate by Vincent Brooks from A Few
Thoughts for the Stranger and Resident in St Helena. *London 1868. Artist*
unknown

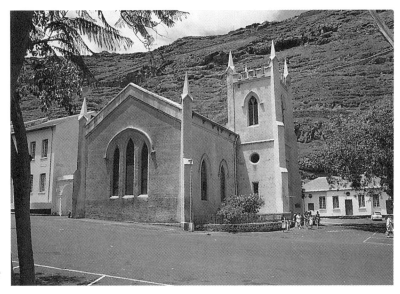

St James' Church today

returning homeward from his second voyage, in May 1775. It is the oldest existing Anglican church south of the Equator.

The church originally had a tower at the west end, but no spire, and no north porch. This can be clearly seen in a picture of 1815 by George Hutchins Bellasis, *Scene taken from the Castle Terrace*,[6] and in other contemporary pictures. Within 60 years fears were expressed for the safety of the tower. A report in 1833 stated that the south or weather side had cracked or settled and investigation of the masonry under the rendering showed it to be of an 'inferior description', using dirt mortar. A contributory factor was the leverage on the walls exerted by the principal timbers of the internal galleries. In 1835 G.W.Melliss reported a bulge in the south face, opposite to the clock, and considered the steeple (tower) to be dangerous. Accordingly it was dismantled and in 1843 a new tower and porch were built by the north door, as it is today, but with a spire surmounting the tower. The new Colonial Government gave a grant of £1,000 to help meet a total cost of £1,300.

The condition of the fabric was to be a constant source of anxiety in the years to come. The records repeatedly refer to repairs to the roof and concern for the safety of the tower and spire – indeed the spire was eventually demolished. (But these are matters bound up with the chronicle of parish events which forms the subject matter of the next chapter, and are related there as they occur.)

The site of the church was conveyed by the Governor, Sir Patrick Ross, to the Bishop of Cape Town on 29 March 1849, during the Bishop's first visit and was consecrated as the Church of St James on 4 April 1849. The Deed of Consecration gives the dimensions: '... in length from East to West ninety feet and in width from North to South forty two feet including the tower fifty three feet'.

Details of the provenance of some of the items and furnishings within St James' Church at this time may be of interest. The font is a white marble basin, standing on a cylindrical pillar of black marble set upon a square plinth, also of black marble, inscribed 'J. Malcott. London.' Malcott was a marble mason in Newgate Street, who died in 1766.

The turret clock was made by Aynesworth Thwaites of Clerkenwell in 1786 and placed in the tower of St James' Church in 1787, having been provided by the Governors of the East India Company. It was taken down in 1834 and in 1841 was placed in the Court House. In 1845 it was replaced in the new tower of the church.

The stone reredos with its three panels was presented by Saul Solomon in 1845. In 1937 Canon Walcott removed the curtain which, for some reason, had covered it for over 30 years. The teak altar rail enclosing the sanctuary was made in 1848 in memory of Mr Thomas Ford Thompson, a former schoolmaster and parish clerk.

St James' was the first church to be reached by the inexorable march of white ants across the island. By 1862 it had to be closed for public worship, services being held in the Court House and in St John's. The damage was such that in December 1864 the Vestry set up a Committee to decide whether to repair the church or to rebuild. They reported in February 1865 that it was not necessary to rebuild but they listed the following recommendations:

taking down the base of the steeple, which now occupies a considerable amount of room at the West end of the Church.

taking down the present Vestry walls, adding the space thereby acquired to the body of the Church.

remove the gallery entirely.

a new floor of asphalt to be laid in the space occupied by the seats, the stone paving being continued in the aisles.

a space of 22 feet by the width of the Church is proposed to be set apart as a Chancel, the floor of this portion to be paved with ornamental encaustic tiles. Within this space of 22 feet it is proposed to erect the organ, pulpit etc. The proposed seats are open benches of teak, as also the pulpit and chancel fittings. It will be necessary to have a new east window.

the roof to be so framed as to admit of a ceiling if found necessary hereafter. The roof to be plain iron framed and covered with slates on iron laths, but it is proposed to get designs from England. Considerable elevation will be given to the roof over the present one; and ventilation will be provided under the eaves by openings in the ends of the Church.

The sum required was estimated as £1,550, made up as follows:[7]

Paving and asphalting the Church floor	£100
Paving the ...	75
Sittings of teak	200
Pulpit and Chancel fittings	100
New East window and stone work to same	80
New stonework to remaining windows	120
New doors etc.	20
Taking down organ	5
Plastering the interior	60
Do exterior	50
Principals for roof with £60 more if ornamental	180
Rafters, purlins and laths	100
Iron ridge	10
Eaves, gutters, spouts etc.	20
Slates, nails and putty	55
Taking down present roof and erecting new one	130
Making a new Vestry	95
	£1410
Add 1/10 for contingencies	141
	£1551

By mid-1866 worship had been resumed in St James' Church, and the Government had promised £200 a year for five years to help pay for the repairs. Since the walls of the old vestry under the tower had been removed, the present vestries were built on to the west wall of the church in 1869.

The Vestry of 1874 found that they had a balance in hand and used it to buy the stained glass window of the Good Shepherd in the centre light of the east window. The two outside lights depicting St James and St John were decorated later in memory of William Newton Corker, Churchwarden (1923-50).

The Colours of the St Helena Regiment were laid up in St James' Church in 1887. They were still there in 1903, when they were mentioned by Mrs E. L. Jackson, but they have since disappeared.

ST JOHN'S CHURCH

In June 1849 Sir Patrick Ross granted to the Diocese a plot of land at the top of Jamestown for a new church. The need for another church only a mile from St James' is probably related to the squalor and immorality on which Henry Whitehead commented in 1867 (see Chapter 4) as characterizing this part of Jamestown, and indicates the degree of social concern felt by the Church in 1849. Sir Patrick died suddenly in August 1850 and it was largely due to the efforts of his widow, Lady Ross, that money was raised to build St John's Church. She is commemorated by a plaque in the church. Even so, it took time to raise a sufficient sum, and although the cornerstone was laid by Lady Drummond Hay in 1857, the church was not completed for another four years. Bishop Claughton reported in December 1859 that the roof had just arrived from England. He consecrated the Church on 25 January 1862.[8] The New School Room near the Church was built in 1870.

The Country Church (1671-1860)

If the East India Company's first church was built in Jamestown in about 1674, it could have been only a few years later that the Country Church, near the present Cathedral, was constructed. In 1678 we read of a Churchwarden for the Country Church[9] and in 1684 an order about registration of lands was 'to be affixed and set upon the Church doors in the Country'. However by October 1691, 'The Church in the Country in bad repair – the windward part much decayed it being all done with Boards'.[10] So in April 1699, 'whereas the Church in the Countrey is much decayed being made all of Timber it was thought convenient that it be rebuilt with stones and for that end the day's work be for the gathering of stones towards the rebuilding of a new Church'.[11] Evidently, the rebuilding had to wait over 30 years, for in 1732 a Vestry meeting was held 'concerning ruinous condition both of the Chapple in the Country and the Chapple at the Fort the former of which has laid level with the ground for two or three years'.[12]

The site of the new stone church was the flat area of ground south west of the present Cathedral, approached by a stepped path flanked by old cypresses. A pen drawing, hanging in Plantation House, inscribed on the back 'on loan from Mrs Marais of Klein Nektar, Hout Bay, Cape Province' shows the Old Country Church with the same avenue of cypresses. The small church has a square tower without a spire at the west end, as also in a lithograph by Lieutenant Stack made in the mid 1840s. However, earlier pictures show the old Country

Church with a spire, as in a picture by Burchell of 1808[13] and some East India Company plate which shows Plantation House with, on the hill above it, the Old Country Church. Lieutenant Read's map of 1816, which correctly depicts St James' Church with a west tower, shows a spire on the old Country Church.

It is not clear when the spire was removed. An entry in the records of 22 July 1835, 'Church steeple in danger of falling and ordered to be taken down', could refer to either the Country Church or St James, although 'steeple' normally meant 'tower'. Thus Melliss could write of a new steeple and spire erected for St James, evidently using steeple to refer to the tower. A framed plan in Plantation House shows the precise location of the Old Church.

A Government order of 1822 lays down the seating plan in the Old Country Church:

Pew   1.   Governor and his family
         7.   Members of Council and their families
         2.   Senior Company's servants
8 & 13.   Senior Company's servants
         9.   Chaplain's family
3 & 14.   Inhabitants of 1st class
        15.   Inhabitants of 2nd class
        13.   Churchwardens and such as are eligible to serve that office
5 &   6.   Plantation House servants
        11.   Respectable Bk. women and Cn.
Gallery   School children and teachers
Beneath   Men of colour & Soldiers in uniform

By 1848 it had been decided to replace the Country Church. In a letter to *The Builder* in 1853, Mr Joseph Lockwood, the Public Works Officer who was to build the new church, wrote:

It was in a very dilapidated condition, the walls hanging over in every direction, at all kinds of angles, kept up by strong props and struts, and threatening at every gust of wind to topple headlong down.

The cracks and flaws in the interior had been so often pointed and repaired, that it was seamed in every direction with these unseemly joints. At last, a part of the wall tumbled bodily into the governor's pew and alarmed all the congregation.[14]

A report of the Church Building Committee[15] presented to the Vestry on 21 August 1848 gives some interesting information:

The new Church being required to hold 450 persons, we are of the opinion, looking at the size of the present one, holding 320 (nearly), and the nature of its

The Old Country Church. From a photograph by Sister Lilian Hepworth of a pen and ink drawing in Plantation House (courtesy Governor of St Helena)

building materials, that they would not supply more than one third of such as would be required in the new Edifice.

By choosing a new site, it is probable that the works of another Church may be carried on to within Six Months of their completion, without interrupting Divine Service in the present one; this important advantage, joined with the income arising from the Pew Rents (about £50), which would otherwise be lost for Two Years, obliges us to relinquish the idea of building on the present spot.

The Governor was asked if he would give a plot of ground, comprising 'the bank in front of the Church Gate, and also the Cottage and Field occupied by Walton' in exchange for some ground at the back of the old church.

Some authorities have stated that the new Country Church (the present Cathedral) was designed by Sophy Gray, the Bishop's wife, who had designed many churches in South Africa. This was not the case. Her plan was not accepted by the Building Committee, as the following extract shows:

Two Drawings of Churches were received from the Lord Bishop of the Diocese, a short time previous to our Third Meeting, with a kind intimation in reference to one of them, that if it proved acceptable, the working plans could be immediately prepared in His Lordship's own Family. Both these Churches appearing to be of larger dimensions than requisite, as well as too expensive, we feel much indebted for His Lordship's consideration in forwarding at the same time a letter of introduction to BENJAMIN FERRY, Esq. Architect, of London, requesting him to favour us with a plan and estimate, more accommodated to our circumstances.

Benjamin Ferrey was a well known architect, who had designed the Church of St Stephen, Rochester Row, Westminster, endowed by Angela Burdett-Coutts, also a benefactress of the Diocese of Cape Town. Mr Ferrey was Churchwarden of St Giles-in-the-Fields, London (1844-5).

The Committee's letter to Benjamin Ferrey dated July 1848 is worth quoting in full for the light which it throws on the problems of commissioning such a building at a distance and with a limited budget:

To B. Ferry, Esq. Architect.

SIR, Having received from the Rev. R. KEMPTHORNE an introduction to you, which the Lord Bishop of Cape Town has been kind enough to transmit, with the view of assisting the erection of a new Church in this Island, we are induced to solicit your aid in furnishing us with a Design, and a working plan of a Church capable of containing Four Hundred and Fifty persons, (perhaps some raised recess or Gallery could be appropriated for the School Children, estimated at 80 out of the 450) together with a Chancel, Tower, Vestry, and Registry Office.

Our own views are very decidedly in favor of the early English style, but we are of course prepared to leave this matter in a great measure to your option; the first application to the Bishop of the Diocese on this subject mentioned Norman Architecture, under the impression that it would be the least expensive, this latter point being under any circumstances essential in our deliberations, inasmuch as the poverty of the Parish renders even the Estimate prepared for them some time since (£3200) a terrific document to the majority of the Rate payers; this leads us to apprehend that such ornamental part of our Structure as may not be absolutely necessary to be fixed or provided for in the first instance, must be delayed until a future period.

You will now allow us to lay before you some hints which we hope may be of use in framing your Plan.

The nature of the Buildings here is generally what we understand to be known as uncovered Rubble Walls, about two feet in thickness; the Stone available for the purpose is a kind of Lava, either cellular or compact, and of a very hard nature; there is also a red kind of Sand stone, so much softer than the Lava, that it is rarely made use of for the exterior of Buildings: the Mortar is of an inferior quality obtained from the earth in the vicinity of the Building; the Walls are afterwards pointed or plastered with Lime. We have subjoined a list of the Local prices of some Building Materials, in the hope that you will favor us with your recommendation as to the best means of obtaining from England such as may be required for the new Church; our own decided opinion being, that this would be the best plan to be adopted with regard to all the Materials except the Stone, and perhaps the Lime, unless you conclude from its price and the local expense of conveyance, that it would be better to import it.

The timbers of the roof, and the framework and sashes of the Windows should also be prepared in England, and we would propose Slate for the covering of the Roof, as we find this material best suited to the Climate; Zinc has been lately introduced for Ridging etc., but we are unable to decide at present on its merits in preference to Lead. Such Columns, Pilasters, Circular Work, Mouldings, etc., as are necessary to afford sufficient decorations to carry out your views we should be compelled to obtain from England; we have read of Iron having been substituted for Stone in some of these respects. We venture to include in our wishes some stained Glass for the Windows, and Encaustic Tiles for the Floor of the Chancel.

We should of course be anxious to obtain the address of any person who would undertake to supply from England the materials you recommend, and we are further desirous of obtaining the assistance of a practical Builder, one who might possess such a knowledge of the various parts of the structure as to be useful throughout the work: the terms we proposed to recommend to the Parish, to secure the services of such a person would be somewhat as follows:

To pay his passage from England to St Helena, estimated to cost £40. To pay him at the rate of £12 10s per month whilst his engagement lasts. To pay his passage back to England if he wished to return within a certain time after his engagement with the Parish closes, estimated at £30, there being at the same time every reason to believe, that he would meet with such numerous demands on his professional skill, as to hold out the fairest prospects of a comfortable competence, in case he should settle in the Colony.

We have forwarded a Plan of the Ground on which our new Church is to be erected, to show the intended line of approach, both from the eastward and from the westward, and also a section to indicate the inclination of the ground.

Although we are most happy to avail ourselves of this introduction of the Bishop of the Diocese, in opening a correspondence with you upon a subject so important and interesting to this Island, we shall of course be prepared to meet any expense which may be necessary to the accomplishment of our object as well as to testify our sense of your kindness in the event of your giving any of your valuable time and attention to the erection of a Church in perhaps the most beautiful spot of our distant Island.[16]

On October 30th 1849, Richard Kempthorne wrote from Oaklands to Bishop Gray that he had received Mr Ferrey's drawings and liked them:

The West end ... runs up into rather a high Bell turret, containing three bells. This rather disappoints me, as I had set my heart upon a LARGE bell. It will however, if correctly carried out, be doubtless the prettiest building in the Island. The foundation is now being dug out.[17]

The foundation stone, which can be seen in the north wall, was laid by the Governor, Sir Patrick Ross, on Wednesday 6 February 1850.

The *St Helena Gazette* for 23 March records the removal of the wall tablets from the Old Church; and the issue of 30 March has a notice by the Churchwardens – 'Tenders invited for loan of money (£1,000 or any part) stating interest, for building of Country Church – repaid over 20 years.'

The project was reported in the *London Standard* on 12 January 1850:[18]

A novelty in exportation has just been completed by Messrs. Winsland & Holland, the eminent builders of Duke Street, Bloomsbury. This consists of an entire Church, capable of accommodating 300 persons, which is intended to be erected on the rock of St Helena, for the accomodation of the English residents on that island.

The edifice is in the early English style of Architecture, from the design of Mr Benjamin Ferry.

It is composed of stone, all of which has been hewn into form on Messrs Holland's premises. This portion of the material is already on its way to St Helena in the bark *Glentanner*. The roof and other woodwork of the building, the ironwork, paving slates etc. are all completed and will be shipped on board the *Juliana* in a few days. The dimensions are as follows: the body of the church is 75' long by 30' wide, the chancel 25' by 18', the vestry 10' by 10' and a muniment room of the same size. The design includes a belfry and a porch. The pulpit is of carved stone, and the seats of stained pine.

Doubtless the ships' crews were glad of the ballast, on their empty outward journey through the Bay of Biscay. The hewn stone referred to was that for the doors, windows etc, the main part of the walls were of local stone, some taken from the Old Country Church.

In the letter to *The Builder* referred to above, Lockwood gives a full account of the problems involved in transporting the materials up to the site of the Church, some 1900 feet above sea level, and some details of its construction:

It was a work of some months to get all the stone and timber up to the churchyard ... The stone work was carried up by trucks and drags. Embargos were laid on every empty vehicle going towards the church, even if only to carry up a single stone, which was submitted to with very good grace by the inhabitants, who, for their own convenience, were anxious to get the church finished. All the long timbers and curved trusses for the roof had to be carried up by manual labour. A considerable quantity was taken up by the voluntary labour of the inhabitants. The governor lent us a considerable number of poor Africans, who had been but recently liberated from a captured slaver ... a purlin was a fair load for a dozen, and at least twenty were occupied at one of the trusses. When they reached their destination ... they were rewarded with each a pipe and bit of tobacco, and refreshed with wine and water in the sober proportion of one bottle of wine to a pail of water.

The stones for the foundations were not quarried, but gathered from the

St Paul's Cathedral. From a colour plate by Vincent Brooks 1868

neighbouring hills, where they laid about in confused heaps among the stunted bushes of bringall and prickly pear. We selected the largest and flattest slabs that could be found ... they were used in the rough, just as they were found, the flattest side being laid downwards ... The trenches for the foundations were 4 feet wide. As soon as they were carried down to the proper depth, the first course or footings was laid down, and well rammed in a bedding of properly tempered mud, prepared like mortar. All the irregularities were then levelled up by means of thin slabs, and stone chips driven into every open space by mallets, till the first course had assumed the shape of a compact bed of stonework. A thin layer of mud was then spread over the whole, and a second course laid down ... No lime mortar was employed in the foundations. The mud here spoken of is a kind of coarse puzzolana – mostly consisting of decomposed feldspar and other materials – it is commonly employed as mortar in St Helena for mud roofs and all kinds of common masonry. All the stones used in the foundations were of a hard dense lava ... A considerable quantity of iron hooping was used in these basement walls; it consisted of the longest hoops we could obtain from old tubs, barrels and waterbutts ... From the plinth upwards, lime was employed to the whole of the wall, except in the middle of the west front, which carried the turret; here a portion of the middle was filled in with the puzzolana, to economise lime, which was at that time difficult to be obtained in the island. The best of the lime was quarried in the island; some came from England; but the greater part was shell-lime from the Cape of Good Hope, which is of very fair quality. Much of the sand was from the coasts of

Africa, brought to the island in captured slave vessels; the rest was beach sand, always used unwashed, especially whem mixed with the island lime.

There was some difficulty in obtaining qualified masons, as only one in the island – a soldier – had ever seen a similar work ... The clerk of works was no less a personage than the adjutant of militia, who kept the men in good order ... though he knew nothing either of the qualities of materials or of construction ... The hard lava plinths were dressed by a gang of five French masons from Bourbon – accidentally left in the island – who proved quite a Godsend, for two or three weeks.

The Bath stone windows, quoins and door arches contrast very well with the deep grey of the lava ashlar wall, and it looks on the whole like a veritable Kentish church, with its rough ragstone walls.[19]

In a sermon preached by Richard Kempthorne on Wednesday 3 September 1851 at the opening of the new Church, he said:

A strong interest was always felt in our old Country Church. Apart from all questions of expense, many earnestly wished that it might be spared: and when demolition had been decided on, in order that the chief materials might be reserved here for their original sacred purpose, though their place was changed, our last Sunday in that Church passed off heavily.

A fragment of stone, built into the clergy vestry below the window, bears the name of Charles Hutchinson, Governor (1746-64). In his sermon Kempthorne mentioned 'a decent Font, of a size allowing the dipping of the child in Baptism, where the parents desire the rule of the Church to be carried out'. The smaller font from the old church was later given to St Matthew's Church, where it now is.

Not all were to approve of the architecture. Robert Sterndale, Governor (1897-1902), was later to say that the church was 'utterly devoid of architectural beauty, outside or in'. Some contemporary copies of *The Ecclesiologist* are of interest. The issue for April 1850 stated:

This church by Mr Ferrey is interesting from its having been manufactured so to say in England, and sent out to S Helena to be erected there. This arrangement of course necessitated great simplicity in the design. Still we think that Mr Ferrey might have thrown far more life and variety into the design than he has done. We are the more sorry that this design should have been so hastily put together, when we consider the isolated locality for which it was destined. We in England can see many churches – so that the inferiority, it may be, of our own parish church is not a matter of such moment as it would be to the islanders of S Helena, to whom this building will be for ever their one type of Christian Architecture and Ritualism.

In 'Thoughts on Tropical Architecture' in the February 1851 issue, a Mr Scott is even more scathing:

St Paul's Cathedral today

By way of illustrating what we mean in the way of incongruity in scenery, we would ask such of our readers as have seen bananas and plantains grow, or who know what the colour and shape and size of the basaltic cliffs of the Atlantic islands, all extinguished volcanoes, are, how they think a smart white smug 'Early English' church, all natty and nice, with its trim neat windows and a cocky little spire would look like under such associations? Because this is exactly the principle of what Mr Ferrey has done in sending out a ready made stone church either for Ascension or S Helena (we forget which).

The last word was with Lady Ross, the former Miss Eliza Bennett of Chubb's Spring and widow of Sir Patrick, who wrote in the following issue:

The truth is that the scenery amidst which the church is placed is, with its hills, fields and hedgerows, exactly of an English character; so similar, that it might well be taken for a rural scene in one or other of the English counties.

On the whole we agree with Lady Ross.

Bishop Gray was unable to consecrate the church during his second visit in 1852, because of a dispute about the church being vested in the See, and it was not consecrated until 9 December 1857, during his third visit. It was dedicated to St Paul.

The mural tablets from the old church were fixed in the new church, and also the old Colours of the St Helena Militia, which had been laid up when new Colours were presented in 1847. Sir Patrick Ross had then directed that the old Colours should be placed over the memorial tablet of Sir William Doveton, who had been their Commanding Officer for many years. They are still today over his memorial in the present church.

The stained glass for the east window was given by Sir Patrick Ross, at a cost of 50 guineas.

St Paul's Church became the Cathedral in 1859.

It may be useful to gather together here the different episodes in the story of the vicissitudes of the church belfry and bells. It will be recalled that to Kempthorne's disappointment, the original design for the belfry had three small openings for bells. In 1867 it was decided to hang two bells in the belfry, expert opinion having advised that it might be done without risk. (The third bell was to be given to St Matthew's Parish in 1887.) A photograph taken after June 1867 (the date on a grave in the foreground) shows the Cathedral belfry pierced by three openings, with two small bells hanging in the two lower openings.

A larger bell, said to have come from Half Tree Hollow cemetery, was installed in 1886, and it was presumably at this time that the two lower openings were made into one. This was to cause problems, for the belfry was not designed for a large bell. The first warning was given the following year by Sapper Robert Newhouse, who wrote:

If any casualty ever occurs with the Bell in Turret at St Paul's, I should advise the bell to be stationary and a double clapper fixed upon Cill of Turret, then there will no strain upon Bolt only Vertical.[20]

Repairs were carried out in May 1905, as the bearings and clapper had worn, and again in 1938. In 1943, while the church was closed for roof repairs, the bell was removed for safety. It was replaced in March 1945, but was out of order the following year. One night in 1948 the church bell settled down upon the floor of the bell turret, hurling part of its heavy iron bolts and nuts to the vicinity of the Governor's Gate into the Churchyard , and it was taken down and hung in a belfry near the North Porch.[21]

The bell was replaced in the belfry in 1967 but had to be taken down in 1978 and again hung near the North Porch, where it is today. At the Fourteenth Synod in January 1983, in reply to a question, the Bishop replied: 'The Civil Engineer advises that it would be dangerous to replace the bell in the Cathedral belfry, and accordingly the Bishop would not be willing to issue a Faculty'.[22]

Kempthorne would again have been disappointed!

St Matthew's Church, Hutt's Gate. From a colour plate by Vincent Brooks 1868

The Church of St Matthew (1680-1862)

The Church in Town and the old Country Church were first built in the 1670s, but the people around Hutt's Gate and Longwood had to wait nearly 200 years. It was not for want of trying. The inhabitants of the Eastern Division of the Island had petitioned in 1680 to build a place of worship and a school, 'being at soe great a distance from the church', but with no result. A proposal in 1832 to devote £300 of Parish Funds to build a chapel at Hutt's Gate was negatived in Vestry by 12 votes to 7. However, in 1849 Bishop Gray preached in the billiard room in New Longwood House, which had been built for Napoleon, though not used by him, and licensed it for Divine worship.

The cornerstone of St Matthew's Church was laid in December 1861 by Lady Drummond Hay, wife of the Governor. There are very few houses near, and the site was probably chosen because it was at the intersection of three roads, to Jamestown, Longwood and Levelwood. The Benevolent Society had already built a school near by. The Church was built of corrugated iron lined with wood, and measured 59 feet by 26 feet. It was a prefabricated building made in England, and Canon Hands was to recall later how he had seen it temporarily erected at the maker's works before it was sent out. The only parts now remaining are the attractive metal roof trusses, which were incorporated in the present church. The ground for the church and burial ground was conveyed by the Governor to the Bishop in February 1862. The Diocesan Archives have a plan and artist's impression of both the interior and the exterior. The church had a small rectangular sanctuary, about 8 feet deep, with a porch or vestry on each side, an entrance porch at the west end, and a small belfry, built within the walls of the church at the south-west corner. At that time the road from Plantation to Longwood ran close to the church porch – the present bend in the road above the church is of a later date – as can be seen in a ground plan of church and churchyard attached to the Petition to the Bishop to consecrate the new church. The font from the Old Country Church, dated 1825 and inscribed with the names of the Churchwardens, was placed in St Matthew's Church.

Bishop Claughton consecrated the Church on St Matthias' Day 1862. The Rectory, which stood beside the site of the present Vicarage, had been briefly the residence of General Henri Bertrand, who was on Napoleon's staff. General Bertrand later moved to Longwood.

4
Parish Life

St James' Parish (1861-1991)

The Parish of St James was formed in April 1861, when Bishop
Claughton divided the island into three parishes. George Bennett, who
with his brother Edward had been on the island since 1858, was
appointed the first Rector. The parish is the smallest of the three in
area, comprising the city of Jamestown and its immediate surrounds.
Part of today's parish, Rupert's Valley, just north-east of Jamestown,
was then the site of the Liberated African Depot which was the
responsibility of the Diocese as a whole. Jamestown is confined in a
narrow valley, over a mile long, rising steadily from the sea. For most of
its length it is only one street wide, vulnerable to rock falls from the
steep bare sides of the valley, broadening out a little as it nears the sea.
Here is the seat of Government, the Castle, the Court House, the
Prison, the Public Library and St James' Church. The top of Jamestown was a problem area, as Henry Whitehead, who, after four years as
Curate, was given responsibility for St John's in 1867, reported:

St John's ... comprises the worst part of Jamestown, many of the inhabitants
being sunk in the lowest depths of vice and immorality, and from their bodily
and mental condition, peculiarly open to the various temptations of a garrison
town, which is also frequented by vessels of war and troopships.[1]

Whitehead moved to St Paul's in 1871 and was succeeded at St John's
by Thomas Goodwin, who had come out as a schoolmaster for the
Benevolent Society in 1861 and who also worked as a catechist for the
liberated resident slaves. He was made Deacon on Trinity Sunday
1871. He left in 1874 for Natal, finding his stipend inadequate for a wife
and six children.

The division of the island into four Ecclesiastical Districts in 1885,
thus making St James' and St John's into separate districts, had
created a problem for the people of St John's district, which extended
down to the Botanical Gardens. They were very poor and unable to
find the stipend for their own priest. This apparently meant that they
were not entitled to any part of the SPG grant of £275 per annum. The
contention of the Churchwardens that part of the SPG grant was for

Jamestown and not just St James' did not alter the Bishop's position that it could be allocated to St John's only if they had a priest in sole charge.

J.C. Hands, the Vicar of St Matthew's, was priest-in-charge of St John's for one year and in April 1887 was replaced by Stephen John Ellis who had arrived to be Vicar of St James' in the previous year. However, by August the Bishop stated that: the services of the Reverend S.J. Ellis would now cease at St John's and the congregation were not required to contribute to his stipend, as the members of St James' Church had guaranteed the full amount required, at which Church Mr Ellis' services would for the future be absorbed.

The Bishop offered instead the Vicar of St Paul's for one Sunday morning a month at a cost to St John's of a guinea, and Ellis, who seems to have been popular with the people of St John's, offered an 8a.m. celebration on the first Sunday, free.

In the event, Ellis remained as priest-in-charge until 1889, when he was replaced by George Mushet, who became deacon-in-charge for two years at a stipend which seems to have steadily reduced. Hands helped by celebrating Holy Communion, mostly on a weekday.

One is inclined to sympathize with a Churchwarden of St Matthew's who in 1900 said that in his opinion, 'one good strong man could do both districts – SS James' and John's – very well.' The answer might lie partly in the fact that Canon Ellis' successor, Edwin Hughes, was evidently a sick man, and partly in a remark by the Bishop to St John's Church Council that he hoped that 'a better feeling may exist between the two districts'. I am indebted to Mr Lionel Yon and Mr Douglas Hudson for the comment that even in their childhood, any boy who strayed into the other district was likely to be roughly handled.

The records of St John's give details of church attendance during these years. Numbers at Morning and Evening Prayer, not held every Sunday, were almost always over 100 and could reach 300, but it is not stated how many of these were soldiers at a Parade Service. (From 1882 to 1901 St John's received a military grant of £4 p.a. and Canon Hands was Officiating Chaplain to the Troops.) The average number of Communicants was 15 to 20, at 16 to 20 celebrations a year.

Ellis had to leave St James in May 1891 after four years, because his wife's health required a return to England. He was followed by Edwin Hughes. When in 1895 Hughes had to resign because of ill health, Ellis was asked to return. He did so in October 1895 but, sadly, died of fever in Holy Week 1896 at the age of 39. He was buried on Good Friday evening, and 'no parish priest was ever carried to his grave with more genuine and affecting signs of the sorrow of his flock.'² He had founded the Church Lads Brigade in Jamestown in 1895, and although this lapsed two years later, it was revived in October 1899 by Canon Porter. Ellis was succeeded in 1896 by Edwin Heron Dodgson, the brother of Lewis Carroll. Edwin Dodgson had already served on Tristan for eight years, where he showed great devotion to his flock (see Part III). We know little of his ministry at St James. It seems that he did not get on well with the aged Bishop Welby. The Reverend W.A.C. Welby (his brother?) had written in 1897, 'I am afraid that poor Mr Dodgson is not the comfort to the Bishop that was anticipated.'³ Perhaps this coolness had a connection with Dodgson's championship of Canon Barraclough, a cleric whom Welby had to discipline for concealing his previous adultery and divorce (see below). Dodgson thought that Barraclough had been very badly treated and had told the Reverend F.W. Carré, the Bishop's son-in-law, 'You and I may not have fallen in the same way, but we may be as great sinners – if not worse – in God's sight.'⁴ However, there is a disturbing ending to the report to spg by James Homagee (Treasurer of the Board of Finance) of Bishop Welby's death on 6 January 1899. He complains that respect was shown by everyone, except by the Reverend E.H. Dodgson, who although he was in town on the evening of the death,

passed and repassed the house (where Welby's body lay) and never once enquired, but went to Church in the evening and requested the Organist to play Christmas Carols which she refused to do ... Mr Dodgson never attended the funeral. I am happy to say in contrast to his behaviour that the Baptist minister (Mr Aitken) made allusions from his pulpit on the evening of the accident to the sad event and again on Sunday. The Captain of the Salvation Army also referred to the loss the Church of England had sustained, and those who differ from us on points of religion could follow our dear Bishop's remains to the Grave – yet Mr Dodgson made himself conspicuous by his absence.⁵

At first sight such behaviour seems shocking, but in point of fact, Dodgson's behaviour may not have been so heinous as it seems. January 6th is the Feast of the Epiphany, there was evidently a service that evening – the organist was there – and Epiphany hymns might well be described as Christmas Carols. It is interesting that the Baptist Church also had a service on Epiphany evening. We cannot know why Dodgson did not attend the funeral. There is other evidence that Homagee, whose own life was not beyond reproach,⁶ did not approve of Dodgson. Edwin Dodgson left in June 1899.

By 1899 St James' Vicarage had fallen into 'such a dilapidated state as to have become scarcely inhabitable'. However, the sum of £55 was raised, of which £22 was spent on labour, and the rest on 64 sheets of iron, timber, cement, lime and wallpaper, and the vicarage was ready in time for the arrival of the next Vicar, Canon Alfred Porter,[7] from Grahamstown. He arrived in 1899 with Bishop Holmes, bringing his own printing press. The same year he began publishing *The St Helena Parish Magazine* which was to continue as the Diocesan Magazine until 1951 (under Canon Walcott after 1921) and is a very useful source for the history of the Church in that period. His training of local boys in printing was said by Government Secretary Geoffrey Kitching to have saved the art on the island.

In March 1901, Mr Harry Gibbons[8] arrived and was made Deacon the same month. He was priested on St Barnabas Day 1902 and became Curate of St John's. When Canon Porter was moved to the Cathedral parish in 1904 Gibbons succeeded him at St James', and also became Vicar of St John's. It was not until the Synod of 1913 that St James' and St John's were combined into one Parish.

In 1897 the roof of St James' was in a bad state of repair. Nothing was done, and by the end of 1902 it was 'leaking in all quarters'. It was proposed to replace the slates with corrugated iron but by the end of 1903 the sum of £300 had been raised, enabling new slates to be ordered from England. They were warranted to be of a durable nature having stood the test of over '25 years in England and over 300 years abroad ... Though not the most expensive slates in the catalogue, they are well recommended, and have been adopted by the best English architects.' In fact the saga of the slates had only just begun!

A Parish Room was acquired in 1904 for the use of parishioners and soldiers. The interior colour scheme of St James' was changed in 1905 from red and pink to two shades of green, said to harmonize with the new sanctuary hangings, and a new carpet placed in the sanctuary. The same year the vicarage roof was repaired at a cost of £100. In 1906 the altar, which had been the gift of Miss Isabella Solomon, was replaced by a longer one, more suitable to the proportions of the church. The old altar is now in Bishopsholme Chapel.

Harry Gibbons left in December 1907, to be succeeded, first by Frank Lane[9] for 15 months and then in 1909 by Lawrence Chase Walcott. Born in 1880 of West Indian descent, Walcott trained at St Augustine's College, Canterbury, and was ordained priest in 1906 in the Diocese of St John's, South Africa. He became greatly loved in his Parish, but there was an initial objection by a few people in other parishes to the appointment of a coloured priest (see Chapter 2). He was very interested in education, became Superintendent of Schools and was involved in Teacher Training. Within a few weeks of his arrival he had organized football for the Church Lads Brigade, and had made a club room in the Vicarage for the CLB and the choirboys. Magic Lantern shows for the Sunday School girls were to follow. In 1910 Cottage Services were begun at the Briars and at Rupert's Valley.

In 1911 the small piece of ground on the north-west side of the porch of St James' was enclosed and made into a garden, to match the piece on the north-east side enclosed by Canon Ellis in about 1895. The Sailors' Institute in Main Street was rented as a Parish Room and a Church Institute with recreation room and billiard table set up. A Guild of St Mary for girls was formed. St John's roof was painted for £6.

In 1914 Walcott was on leave in England and returned with a new organ, built by the Positive Organ Company, at a total cost of £205. It was erected by voluntary labour and dedicated by the Bishop on 21 October. The harmonium it replaced was moved to St John's Church.

The Vestry meeting of 1915 was poorly attended, but not as badly as it might have been, since several ladies took advantage of a recent alteration to the Provincial Canons which permitted them to sit in Vestry for the first time.

More holes appeared in the roof of St James', and in October Walcott wrote: 'the slates are insecure through resting on laths which were too old in the first place, too narrow, and too wide apart'. The result was that a gust of wind would shift or remove slates. New laths were put in throughout the whole roof, but by the following July,

the roof is still a source of anxiety ... the slates put on some ten or twelve years ago were of inferior quality, and have perished ... In other words we were done by some slick rogue in England. So rotten are these slates that some you can literally poke your finger through.

Further repairs were necessary to the roof of St James' in 1922, but by the end of the year the supply of slates was running out, and in 1925 the slates were replaced by sheets of iron.

In 1916 the financial position of the parish had improved, partly due to the wartime return of a Garrison. The Vicar's stipend was paid in full for the first time since 1909! Alas, the improvement did not last, the troops were once again withdrawn, and by 1920 the parish owed the Vicar, Gerard Day, £45.

Walcott left in 1917, after eight years. The Bishop spoke highly of his work, and his interest in youth. In addition to his own parish, he had assisted St Paul's by holding monthly services in Sandy Bay, and it was at his instance that the Chancel was built on to the Sandy Bay School. His successor, R.J.J.Garrod[10] stayed for only nine months and was followed by Gerard Day[11] for two years. Hearing of the Bishop's problems in finding a replacement, Walcott offered to return, which he did in May 1921, accompanied by his bride, Winifred Ida. By September, he had taken over the Diocesan Magazine on the departure of Canon Porter, instituted a daily Mass, was Scoutmaster of the Jamestown Troop which he had begun in 1915, and Mrs Walcott had started a Girl Guide Company. He once more took monthly services at Sandy Bay, walking from Jamestown.

Problems arose with the spire in 1925, the plaster coming away, exposing the soft red stone to the weather; and with St James' clock in 1933:

Now and again at rare intervals one of the massive weights which governs its movements crashes through the floor above into the porch below.

Heavy baulks of timber were placed across the floor above the porch, to lessen the damage on any future occasion and prevent the weight breaking through. Fortunately for the Church the clock was Government property.

At St John's, improvements were made to the appearance of the area in 1933 by the conversion of the enclosure on the north side into a flower garden by Mr and Mrs Isaac Williams and in 1936 by another garden made on the south side.

Canon Walcott dropped 'Diocesan' from the title of his monthly magazine in November 1933, to allow himself more freedom of comment on items of local news, but he included with it 'St Helena Diocesan Notes'.

To help St Paul's parish, Walcott began in 1934 visiting Blue Hill each month where he would take Evensong in the School, followed by Holy Communion the next morning. Similarly, once a month he would go to the St Mary's Guild working party and read to them while they sewed. The interior of St James was redecorated in 1934 by Mr C.H.Jameson and in 1939 the ant-eaten chairs in St John's Church were replaced by locally made pews.

Lord Baden-Powell visited St Helena in ss *Llandovery Castle* in May 1936 and afterwards wrote to tell Walcott:

... how agreeably surprised I was to find a group so large and so smartly turned out in uniform ... I carry away a very good impression of the Scouts of St

Helena – an event which I shall ever remember with pleasure ... I would like to congratulate you personally ...

Mrs Winifred Ida Walcott died in October 1941 and was buried in St Paul's Churchyard. As founder and organizer of the Girl Guides in St Helena, she was awarded the Medal of Merit by the Chief Guide, and also the Jubilee Medal of King George V. The Guides continue to flourish on the island and in 1985, on the 75th anniversary of the founding of the Girl Guide Movement in UK, Mrs Margaret Banks, Commissioner for Branch Associations (those Guide Associations which are in British Dependencies), visited St Helena. There have also been four visits by Girl Guide Association Trainers, Miss Barbara Ryrie in 1968, Miss Judith Emsley in 1979, Miss Joyce Murphy in 1987 and Miss Sheila Mathieson in 1989. Miss Murphy gave the address at the large 'Thinking Day' Parade Service for all the island Guides in St James' Church. By 1989 numbers had grown to 211 children (including newly formed Rainbow guides for 5- to 7-year olds) and 36 Rangers and Guiders.

CHURCH OF ST MARY THE BRIARS

The origins of the little Church of St Mary the Briars date from this time. For many years Mrs Edward Grant had made available a room in her house for a Sunday School at the Briars and Mrs Simon had run a class of 30 children. When the house was sold in 1946 other arrangements were necessary. Mr James George offered the ground for a Church Room and this was completed at the beginning of 1948 at a cost of £75. Used at first for the Sunday School, services began to be held there in Fr Flint's time and it was dedicated as the Church of St Mary by Bishop Capper on 8th September 1967 within a week of his enthronement. Bishop Capper consecrated the wooden altar in 1972 and the Church was registered for marriages in 1973.

Many improvements were made in Fr Houghton's time. A carved stone Head of Christ with Crown of Thorns, set above the altar, the work of Mr John Drummond, and also a new electronic organ, purchased by local subscription at the instigation of Mrs Hazel Stevens, were dedicated by the present writer in 1984. A ¾ cwt bell, presented by the Reverend Gordon Robinson of Somerset, England was installed in March 1985. The Church was extensively rebuilt in 1989. Thanks to an extra piece of land given by Mr Harold Williams, for many years Chapelwarden, it was extended at both ends, with a door at the west end, a sanctuary, a new pitched roof and a small vestry. Local craftsmanship was used, seen especially in the wooden

St Mary the Briars after extension (David Bentham)

altar rail and the cross on the roof. It was rededicated on 3 April 1989. In his sermon Bishop James commented on how fortunate they were on St Helena in that the churches could always be left unlocked without any anxiety.

By 1949 the rendering on St James' spire on the weather side had again crumbled, exposing the stonework. This was rendered in the early part of 1949 by Mr Harry Phillipson, single handed, and without any scaffolding, using a rope around the spire. He took five weeks and was paid £60. The Church also took out an Employers Indemnity Policy at a premium of £7 11s 3d.

In February 1950 a new 6 cwt bell, cast by John Taylor of Loughborough, was anointed and blessed by Bishop Turner, in memory of the Royal visit of 1947 and of a former Churchwarden. The bell cost £200 and is inscribed 'in memory of William A. Thorpe, 1842-1918. Honour the King 1947'. The old fixed bell was moved nearer to the clock which could continue to strike on it, thus leaving room for the new bell to swing.

Walcott resigned in 1950 but continued to live at Palm Villa and to publish the *St Helena Magazine*. He died in April 1951 aged 71 and is buried beside his wife in St Paul's Churchyard. The *St Helena Magazine* came to an end with his death. In 1986 on the 35th anniversary of his death there was a large attendance of Scouts and Guides at the Cathedral for a Requiem and laying of wreaths on their joint grave.

Douglas Humphrey Cumming was inducted as Vicar on 16 July 1950. He had been a missionary in Africa and came from a parish in Cape Town. He returned to South Africa in 1952.

On 7 October 1950 Bishop Turner issued a Faculty to the Vicar and Churchwardens of St James' to remove and replace the north to south wall Communion rails, and the wooden floor in the sanctuary. The work involved the extension of the sanctuary platform to the whole width of the church, as it is today, using as floorboards twelve of the old 15-foot teak pews, said to date from the restoration of 1866. Some parishioners felt that they had not been consulted, and Walcott was indignant both with his successor and with the Bishop for allowing the 'smashing up of the pews'. In his *St Helena Magazine* for December 1950 he printed an 'Old Man's Reverie' in which he mused on the scenes which had occurred in the Church as it was. After picturing rows of Confirmation candidates he wrote: 'Welby, Holmes, Holbech of saintly memory, Aylen, Watts, would never have allowed such a vision as that to lapse.' In the same issue he gives an account of the 1866 restoration, with pointed reference to the 'sittings of teak' and comments: 'It will be seen by the foregoing what a big say in these matters Parishioners had in those days, so different to what now seems to be the usual practice.'

Edgar James Mitchell[12] succeeded Cumming in 1952, having been Rector of a country parish in Wiltshire for 20 years. He found his island ministry a fulfilling experience:

The Vicar of Jamestown is also Chaplain of the Prison and I take a short service there every Sunday morning when there is a prisoner. I have also recently been appointed Court Missioner, which gives me an opportunity to speak on behalf of any accused person, and those on probation are placed in my care. I am also Chaplain to the Civil Hospital, and happily both the Sisters (European) are good Churchwomen. I take a shorthand class once a week ... The parish priest plays a large part in the life of the town. He is, happily, free to do the work of a priest. The work is onerous and means a good deal of loneliness. The people however are friendly and look to the Vicar as their helper and friend ... I have now been here for just over a year, and at the age of 61, I can say that this is the happiest bit of work since my ordination.[13]

He left in 1954 for South Africa and died in 1981.

In 1954 the corrugated iron roof of St James' was replaced by one of asbestos, and on 15 May 1954 Bishop Turner re-hallowed the Church, 'restoring the same for the worship of God after long neglect and decay.'

Keith Flint,[14] previously a Congregational Minister, was ordained in the Church of England in 1939. He became Vicar of Jamestown in 1954, where he served for nine years, leaving in 1963 to spend three years as Chaplain of Tristan da Cunha. He is still remembered in Jamestown with affection. His pastoral good sense can be seen in a report to SPG in 1955:

Seventh Day Adventists and Jehovah's Witnesses are as active as ever. It seems the best way of dealing with the heretical sects is to aim at the Church being so alive and her teaching so strong that the truth will triumph over error. That, rather than any head-on attack.

A Tabernacle, enclosed in African teak, on the altar of St James' Church was hallowed by Bishop Turner in 1955. By 1957 the wooden altar in St John's Church was infested with termites. The Vicar and Churchwardens, Robert Bizaare and Thomas Hopkins, asked the Bishop's permission to raise the marble slab on which the altar stood to see if it was suitable for use as the mensa of a new altar. It proved to be a tombstone, with the following inscription:

Lo, where this silent marble weeps
A friend, a wife, a mother sleeps.
A heart, within whose sacred cell,
the peaceful virtues lov'd to dwell.
Affection warm and faith sincere,
and soft humanity were there.
In agony, in death resigned,
she felt the wound she left behind.
Her infant image here below,
sits smiling on a father's woe:
whom, what awaits, while yet he strays
along the lonely vale of days!
A pang to secret sorrow dear
a sigh, an unavailing tear,
till time shall every grief remove,
with life, with mem'ry, and with love.

The new altar was built of red stone, gathered from the ruins at the back of the vicarage, with the centre filled with rubble, and the tombstone placed as a mensa, with the inscription downwards, and immediately beneath, the first chapter of St John's Gospel, between two pieces of glass. The two steps from nave to sanctuary were reconstructed as three steps. The altar was consecrated by Bishop Turner on 13 September 1957. A Reredos 'with a Crucifix of Christ Regnans thereon and Cherubim', together with a Tabernacle encased in iroko was blessed by the Bishop on 9 May 1958.

The Bishop dedicated new Choir Stalls, Priest's Desk and an altar frontal in 1958, 'gifts commemorating the Consecration of the Church by Bishop Claughton'. (In fact St John's Church was consecrated not in 1858 but in 1862.)

William Thomas Walter Samuel was St Helena's second island-born priest. He left St Helena in 1900 and was ordained Priest in 1930 in the Diocese of Cape Town. When he was parish priest of the Church of the Good Shepherd, Maitland, Cape Town (1941-59), he and his wife visited St Helena for three months in 1957. He was licensed to officiate in St James' parish from April to September 1959, during the absence on furlough of Fr Keith Flint.

Eric Kleb[15] from South Africa was Vicar in 1964-6 and was succeeded by Leonard Smith who was Vicar of St James and Archdeacon of St Helena until 1968, when he left for the Diocese of Gibraltar. In January 1968, ten days before his departure, the parish made strenuous efforts to persuade him to stay, even offering to increase his stipend by £100.

Richard Lindsay[16] was instituted as Vicar of Jamestown on 8 May 1968 and admitted as Archdeacon of St Helena and Canon of St Paul's. In September 1976 he married an islander, Cecily Ann Caroline Young.

Miss Helena Thorpe left a legacy of £5,000 (less Estate Duty) in 1969 to St James', the income to be used for the fabric and ornaments of St James' Church. At first invested in fixed interest shares, it was re-invested in 1984 in the Investment Fund of the Central Board of Finance of the Church of England, using USPG as Trustees, in order to provide for capital growth. Fr Cumming left a legacy of £75, and the Church Council purchased a pair of cruets and a tray in his memory. In October 1971 Bishop Capper dedicated anew the pulpit of St John's Church, which had been restored by Mr Arthur Bizaare senior and Mr Trevor Stevens.

Weekday House Communions were recommenced in Rupert's Valley in 1972 on two evenings a month. Noticeboards for the two Town Churches were made and given by staff and prisoners in the gaol. In December of that year the Bishop dedicated a nave altar in carved teak in memory of Mr Robert Francis Bizaare MBE, Churchwarden.

To mark their Jubilee year, in 1975 the Jamestown Troop of Scouts cleaned and renovated the interior of St James' Church. Metal tubular handrails to assist the infirm were installed at the altar steps by Messrs Solomons.

An electronic organ was bought for St John's Church in 1974 for £273 and dedicated in May by the Bishop.

The Centenary of the Church Provident Society for Women was marked by the installation of a wooden plaque depicting St Helena and the Cross on the South wall of St James' Church. This was dedicated by the Bishop at the Centenary service on 16 March 1978. The same year two wooden collection plates were made and given by Mr Arthur E. Bizaare.

The condition of the tower and spire of St James' Church had been giving cause for concern since 1968, and unsuccessful attempts had been made to find someone to undertake the work.

Scaffolding was erected around the spire in January 1980, and a complete inspection made. In March Mr Rodney Buckley and Mr Philip John of Solomons reported that the top 17 feet of the spire was a solid block of concrete weighing two tons. Below that the stonework had cracks extending right down the spire. The courses of local redstone had been bonded together with metal dowels, which had corroded and expanded, causing large cracks in the masonry. It was therefore decided that there was no alternative to the demolition of the spire, which was carried out by Messrs Solomons. The total weight of stone removed was approximately 37 tons, and the average weight of each stone was 80 pounds. The height from ground level to the base of the spire was 65 feet, and the height of the spire itself was 69 feet. The external diameter at the base was 13 feet. The dangerous operation was carried out without any accident to the workforce, consisting of Messrs Basil Yon, Gilbert Wade, Perry Stevens, Jeffrey Stevens, Danny Francis and Daniel Thomas, under the supervision of Mr Philip John assisted by Mr Michael Constantine and Mr Rodney Buckley. Prayers were said regularly in the church for their safety. Further restoration work included the roofing of the tower and the repair of its floors, the repair of its pinnacles, and the painting of the exterior of the church.

The total cost came to a little under £16,000. The Parish had £2,700 in its Maintenance Fund to which the Women's Guild was to add some £700. USPG provided a low-interest 'Festina' loan of £5,000. An Appeal was launched, personally supervised by the Governor, Mr Geoffrey Guy. Her Majesty the Queen graciously sent a donation, and a great number of individuals, churches, societies and firms, both on the island and overseas contributed, including many St Helenians living in England and South Africa. Substantial sums came from Charitable Trusts in England. Among the fund-raising events on the island will be remembered a Musical Extravaganza organized by Mrs Ivy Ellick, and a production by Mrs Edith Timm of *Murder in the Cathedral*, played in all three parish churches, with the Governor as Becket and the present writer as the Fourth Tempter.

Such was the success of the Appeal that the USPG loan, originally for a period of five years, was repaid by June 1981.

Richard Lindsay, with Cecily and their three children, left for England in December 1981 after over thirteen years service to the Diocese. He was made an Honorary Canon of St Paul's Cathedral, and became Vicar of Holmside, Durham. He died in February 1991.

David Neaum[17] was Chaplain of Tristan (1952-5) and Rector of a parish in Zimbabwe for sixteen years, before coming to St Helena with his wife Dorothy. He became Vicar of Jamestown on 6 January 1982 and Archdeacon the following month. He left in June 1984 and is now in retirement in Australia.

Michael Houghton[18] and his wife Diana had taught for three years in a Church School in Lesotho, before he was ordained. They arrived with their two children in 1984 and he was collated as Vicar of Jamestown on 5 June 1984.

In 1984 the Bishop gave permission for a short Victorian stave, carved with the Figure of St James, the gift of the parish of St James, Haydock, Lancashire to be kept in the Church and used in Procession. Permission was also given for an Icon of our Lord and the Blessed Virgin to be placed on the wall of St James' Church. It is a reproduction of an early 15th-century Russian icon, *The Mother of God Petroskaja*. The custom of the 'Blessing of the Seas' was revived at Peterstide 1986. Mr Isaac Douglas Hudson was made Sub-Deacon on 24 August.

The interior of St James' Church is a large plain rectangle. In October an application for a faculty to make a chapel for use on weekdays was not granted, but permission was given for the replastering and redecoration of the interior of St James'.

With the help of a visiting member of Alcoholics Anonymous, Fr Houghton set up a local branch in January 1987.

From April to July 1987 the Houghtons were on leave. A 77-year-old retired priest, Leslie Lovely, came from South Africa to look after the parish. When the Houghtons returned, Lovely moved to St Paul's Vicarage until October to help during the interregnum. Mr Arthur Bizaare Senior died in August 1987 at the age of 97. At one time Churchwarden of St James' he was for many years a very respected undertaker. In December Mrs Blanche Mercury died. She was a well-known character in Jamestown and one of the last lepers. Her early life was spent at the Leper Station above Jamestown. She was buried on Christmas Eve, just when the local radio station was broadcasting her recollections of Christmas in past years.

In October a new sanctuary carpet, a carved African Madonna and Child, an introit bell and pricket stand were placed in the Church of St James.

The Houghtons left in August 1989 after two tours of duty. They were succeeded in April 1990 by Louis Donald Ilett and his wife, but unfortunately the Iletts had to return to South Africa three months later for domestic reasons. In October, Ronald Cottingham, who had spent four years on Ascension, moved to St James, as priest-in-charge, becoming Vicar in July 1991.

In September 1990 work began on the reroofing, rewiring and redecorating of St John's at a cost of over £7,000. An anonymous donation of £1,000 was received via Mr Owen George, then Chairman of the St Helena Association (UK). A service of thanksgiving was held on 6 December. Plans were also afoot to rewire St James' as a memorial to Miss Helena Thorpe, benefactor of the parish.

THE CHURCH AT RUPERT'S VALLEY

Readers will recall that in 1860 Bishop Claughton proposed to build a chapel in Rupert's Valley, in which was the Liberated Slave Depot. Since 1910, services had been held in houses at Rupert's Valley, but the desire to have their Chapel was strong. When the spire of St James was demolished in 1980, the stone was taken to Rupert's Valley, to be used one day in building a Chapel. In 1984, during excavations in preparation for a new generating station at Rupert's Valley, a number of human bones were unearthed from an unmarked mass burial. That there were some mass burials from those unfortunates from the captured slave vessels who were either dead on arrival or died shortly afterwards was known, but not the location of all of them. A Commission appointed by the Governor in February 1985 agreed that the bones, which had already been put in boxes and placed in St Swithun's Chapel in the Cathedral, should eventually be re-interred at Rupert's Valley. It was planned that there should be a memorial garden, in conjunction with the proposed chapel. Mrs Diana Houghton, who was a qualified landscape architect, was asked to design and supervise the landscaping of the valley. A building fund was opened and, with the help of the Bishop, several thousand pounds were raised from parishes and individuals in Britain and the RMS *St Helena*. The Reverend Gordon Robinson found and presented the bell from the wartime HMS *St Helena*. The Government has given a plot of land, and building is expected to commence in the near future. An altar and other furnishings from St Stephen's College, Broadstairs, was given by the Sisters of the Community of St John the Baptist, Clewer, through the good offices of Fr Michael Houghton, when the Sisters closed the school. The work of the Liberated Slave Depot at Rupert's Valley from 1841 to 1866 is a piece of its history of which St Helena can be justly proud.

St Paul's Parish (1861-1991)
St Paul's parish was formed in 1861 with Edward Bennett as the first Vicar. It covers the western half of the island. There are no centres of population, save for the presently growing community in Half Tree Hollow. People live in isolated cottages, scattered over the parish. There are a few larger houses, built in the 18th and 19th centuries, many ravaged by white ants. And there is Plantation House, the home of the Governor, near the Cathedral, about 1,600 feet above sea level.

Edward Bennett was succeeded in 1863 by George Barrow Pennell. However, Bishop Welby had invited a Reverend Robert Gray to come as Vicar of St Paul's, and was evidently embarrassed by the appointment of George Pennell by the Colonial Secretary, apparently without consulting Welby. Hence the Bishop of Cape Town's remarks in a letter to Welby of March 1866:

First let me say that I am much grieved at your vexations, troubles, want of heart and unity among the clergy. I know not how young Pennell was appointed; but I never have, and never would allow any appointment to be made in my Diocese without my concurrence.[19]

Bishop Welby did his best by making Robert Gray a Canon in July 1863 and licensing him to officiate within the Diocese. Robert Gray's signature then appears as Secretary to the Bishop until June 1865. On Welby's recommendation, Gray was made Headmaster of the Government Head School in 1863, but he was dismissed by the Governor three years later for being notoriously negligent. It is not known whether he was a relative of Bishop Gray. At Bishopsholme there is a wooden staff, about 6 feet long, somewhat roughly made from three pieces of (possibly) cane, with a silver cap, which bears the initials R.G. and may have belonged to him, although its precise function is unclear. At Farm Lodge there is a similar staff, about 4 feet long, whose silver cap bears the name A. M. Hands, and presumably belonged to the wife of Canon Hands.

'Young' George Pennell married Emma Clare, the 22-year-old daughter of the Governor, Admiral Sir Charles Elliott, in 1864. Sadly she died a year later.

Henry Whitehead, Curate of St James' since 1863, and Military Chaplain since 1866, succeeded George Pennell at St Paul's in 1870. After furlough in England he volunteered to go to Tristan da Cunha in 1878 for 6 to 12 months, taking his 14-year-old son while his wife and four younger children remained on St Helena.[20] However the visit had to be abandoned as the ship which was to have taken him was wrecked[21] and the following year he became ill with a lung complaint. He died on 21 July 1884, aged 67 and is buried, with his wife, in St Paul's Churchyard. Welby wrote: 'He worked very hard and faithfully on this Island for 23 years.'[22]

The first island born priest was Frederick Henry Baker, who was born on 26 May 1850, the son of a merchant, Eden Baker, and his wife, Bertha Emma. He became Vicar of St Paul's in December 1884. Unfortunately in December 1893, at the age of 43, he had to resign because of 'the serious state of my throat, which has for a long time past prevented me from speaking without great difficulty.' In 1874 Baker had married Jane Mary Sophia Pritchard, with whom he lived for nearly 60 years until his death at Cradock in South Africa in 1933. Baker's mother died at Southerns on 11 November 1905, aged 86, having lived on St Helena for over 60 years. As Miss Hammond she used to play the organ in the old gallery in St James'. In spite of his throat affliction, Baker had been able to instruct Dinizulu and some of his entourage in the Christian faith.

Dinizulu, son of Cetshwayo, the Zulu chief, was brought as a prisoner to St Helena in February 1890. He stayed first at Rosemary Hall, then at Maldivia in Jamestown, and finally at Olive Cottage on Francis Plain. In 1891 the Bishop wrote, 'Dinizulu and two chiefs, his uncles, attend morning service at the Cathedral on Sundays with their Zulu interpreter, Paul, who is a Christian,'[23] and in the following year, 'Dinizulu now reads and writes in Zulu, and reads in English. One of his entourage is to be baptized.'[24] In 1893 the Bishop confirmed one of Dinizulu's entourage who had been prepared by F. H. Baker. In October 1894 Dinizulu wrote from Maldivia to the Bishop of Zululand:

I respectfully salute thee, servant of the Lord. I have read your letter which you wrote on August 1894, about my people who wish to be taught about Jesus Christ our Lord. I, Dinizulu, rejoice much to hear that you, the Bishop, are about to send a teacher, who is going to teach the people. I thank you very much.[25]

W. M. Carter, Bishop of Zululand, called on his way to the Cape in 1896, to the great joy of the Zulus.[26]

Three of Dinizulu's children were baptized at St John's, David and Solomon on 11 April 1894 and Victoria Helena on 10 December. The Bishop recorded that Dinizulu was himself desirous of Baptism, but there was the problem of polygamy.[27] In 1896 two more sons were baptized, this time at St Paul's: Arthur on 15 March and Samuel on 13 September. Dinizulu returned to Zululand at the end of 1897. At Bishopsholme there is (at present on loan to the St Helena Museum) a carved wooden object, a cup joined to what looks like a cigar rest, with the carved inscription: 'To Mrs Welby from Dinizulu'.

Mr Storer, the Churchwarden, wrote to the Bishop in 1887 for guidance about payment of fees for burials, as he felt 'unsettled in the matter' now that the Government had given permission to the Salvation Army to bury in the Cemetery adjoining St Paul's Churchyard. Mr Storer was Churchwarden from at least 1880 to 1894. At the Vestry meeting in 1891 he observed that 'the office was sometimes connected with difficulties'. Part of the cause may have been occasional forgetfulness by the ageing Bishop who, as Dean, kept a firm control on the Cathedral. In 1891 Bishop Welby, writing about a controversy over graves, admitted that 'as the permission was verbal ... I may not remember quite correctly what I said.' The Parish Council safeguarded themselves by asking the Churchwardens 'to get in writing from the Bishop the real wishes of his Lordship on the point, so that for the future there should be no mistake.'

Two years earlier Mr Storer had felt compelled to send the Bishop a letter oozing with anxiety:

My Lord, As the washing on the outside of the Church doors appears in your Lordship's opinion to be inconsistent, and in consequence of certain remarks having fallen from your Lordship with reference thereto and you having expressed a desire to have the said wash removed after an expense having been defrayed by and with the consent of my brother Churchwarden and feeling somewhat dubious in taking upon myself to carry out your Lordship's expressed wish without acquainting him, and feeling anxious to do everything to please your Lordship, I will, if not asking too much, feel thankful if your Lordship would kindly condescend to convey the above sentiments in writing, not from any personal motives but that I may be exonerated from blame for acting singly in the matter, also at the next Annual Easter meeting I may not be charged for spending monies out of the Offertory for illegal purposes.[28]

Edwin Arthur Barraclough became Vicar in July 1894, and was made a Canon in November 1895. At the 1895 Vestry he noted that the walls of the Cathedral, except for the Chancel, had not been cleaned for 35 years. By the following year this had been remedied, new lamps installed and the organ returned to its old position near the Chancel.

Sadly, the new Vicar was to bring some grief to the closing year of the Bishop's life. Welby claimed that Barraclough had represented himself as a single man, but it was later alleged that he had been married and had been accused of adultery in a divorce suit in 1893. This came to light when in October 1897 Barraclough left for England with a letter from Welby, giving him permission to exchange duties with the Bishop's son-in-law, the Reverend F. W. Carré of St Katherine's, Savernake, Marlborough. However the Bishop of Salisbury learnt of the divorce suit (which had been reported in *The Times* of 24 and 25 January 1893), and refused to allow Barraclough to officiate. The Bishop of Salisbury very charitably wrote:

It is fair to him to say that if there is any want of candour in the matter the blame must be equally shared by the Bishop of St Helena. I do not know that he was bound to confess his past life if his present Bishop did not think it necessary to allude to it.[29]

But this was the first that Welby had heard of it! A friend of the Bishop, Archdeacon P. P. Fogg, who was visiting, instructed Mr Homfray Welby Solomon, Churchwarden, (and the Bishop's grandson) to present Barraclough before the Diocesan Court, at which the Bishop deprived Barraclough of the office of Vicar of St Paul's. The Governor, as Acting Chief Justice, ruled the action of the Bishop to be illegal and ordered him to reinstate Barraclough. The Bishop refused to accept the Governor's ruling. After the Bishop's death, Archdeacon Fogg became Vicar-General, and reported to the Archbishop that:

On the second Sunday after the Bishop's death, Barraclough attempted to force his way into the Chancel of the Cathedral, but fortunately was prevented by the Churchwardens under my direction ... whereupon I cited Barraclough in my Court of Vicar-General ...[30]

Fogg was succeeded as Vicar-General by the Archbishop of Cape Town's Chaplain, the Reverend J.W.Williams. The Archbishop advised Williams that the appeal to the Privy Council which Welby had made should be withdrawn at the last possible moment, and to cite Barraclough under Provincial Regulations, on the charge of brawling ... There must be 2 clerical assessors, – only 2 clergy on the island besides Mr Barraclough, and the defendant has the right to 2 clerical assessors – I fear the case must necessarily break down, but the Church although unable to enforce its discipline by force of circumstances, will at least have exhausted every possible process available to her. Mr Barraclough will have, I fear, to be re-admitted to the Cathedral Church, but it must be under protest, and possibly after a formal excommunication, that the Church's conscience may be clear.[31]

At a Diocesan Court on 16 June 1899, Williams as Vicar-General upheld the Bishop, but by this time Barraclough had left the island.

The departure of Barraclough left St Paul's without a Vicar, and Bishop Holmes looked after the parish for his first four years. The Church Lads Brigade detachment in St Paul's parish was formed in March 1900, meeting at Half Tree Hollow School. In 1904 the Bishop moved Canon Porter from St James' to St Paul's.

Canon Porter left in July 1921 to return to England. He had served the Church on St Helena for 22 years, five years in Jamestown and 17 years at St Paul's, having come to St Helena in 1899 at the age of 43. He was a very well-liked and respected parish priest. He took a great interest in the education on the island, and was a keen cricketer. He had edited the Diocesan Magazine for 21 years. In a tribute, Dr Arnold, himself a well-loved medical doctor on the island, said:

There is much one would wish to say regarding the many virtues of Canon Porter, but it would be useless to say much in his praise for he would not believe it ... Canon Porter has always disliked publicity. He has not sought man's praise or man's reward. He has never asked others to do what he did not do himself, or which he was not prepared to do himself ... In men, as in things, you cannot excel the best. Canon Porter has proved himself to be of the best both as man and clergyman.[32]

With the departure of Canon Porter, the two country parishes of St Paul and St Matthew were to share one parish priest for the next 13 years. Frederick Ashworth[33] came for one year and lived with his invalid clergyman brother at Kingshurst.

Then in 1922 came Gilbert Turner (later to be Bishop) with his mother and sister; they lived at Enfield. He arrived to find the Cathedral floor in a dangerous state, due to the white ants, which had reached St Paul's by 1916. The Vestry floor had been cemented in that year, and the floor under the organ in 1920. Turner had the Chancel floor concreted in 1922, and the following year, schoolchildren and other volunteers brought stones to the church as they passed on their way to school or work, ready for the laying of a concrete floor throughout the nave. This was completed by the end of 1923 at a cost of £120.

Turner left in 1924 and was succeeded by Harold Lewty[34] (1924-6) and Frank Oxley[35] (1927-32). For the next 30 years, St Paul's was looked after by the Bishop (or Vicar-General).

By the time Gilbert Turner returned in 1938 as Vicar-General the ants had climbed from floor to roof, and in the summer of 1939, a few months before Turner was made Bishop, the Cathedral was closed by the Government due to its dangerous condition. It was not to be reopened until the new roof was constructed in 1945. There continued to be a celebration of Holy Communion in the Vestry on Wednesday mornings, and marriages took place there. Sunday services were held at Bishopsholme. An annexe – known as the Shelter – was built on to the outside doors of the dining room using cedar posts, with yew and eucalyptus poles as rafters and thatching for the roof and sides. This could seat 100 to 150, with the altar and choir stalls in the dining room.

During the war years £5,000 was collected and work began at the end of 1944. By November the old roof was off. Mr Harry Yarrow and Mr Herbert Nicholls contracted to do the work, under the supervision of Mr Hedges, the Government Architect, assisted by Mr Gammer of the Public Works Department. The eight large 1½-ton trusses were made by Mr F. Smith, foreman carpenter of PWD, and these were in place by February 1945. The result is a very fine roof indeed.

The last service in the Shelter was held on Ascension Day 1945, and the following Sunday there was a combined Thanksgiving for the Restoration and for Victory in Europe. The Litany was sung in procession from the East Gate of the Churchyard. Eight Hundred people were present. The Bishop celebrated the Eucharist and gave Communion to 98 persons.

On 4 August 1945, the Bishop consecrated the marble mensa, imported from the Cape. The teak altar, made in the 1850s by Charles Ormsby Western, was extended by Mr Richard Constantine to the width of the East window. Beneath the mensa were placed two pages of the Gospel according to St Luke, containing the account of the Institution of the Eucharist. The reconstruction of the altar was a memorial to Bishop Holmes. The Riddel posts were designed by Mr Hedges and made by Mr F.M. Smith. In June 1947 they were to be surmounted by angels, each one given by one of the Women's Guilds at Sandy Bay, Blue Hill, St Paul's District and High Point.

On Whit Sunday 1947 the new lych gate at the east entrance of the

Churchyard was dedicated. This was made by Mr Yarrow to a design of Mr Hedges and given by Mr Homfray Welby Solomon in memory of his grandfather, Bishop Welby. The old Victorian iron gate was moved to the west entrance. Electric light was installed in the chancel in 1947 and extended to the nave in 1949.

The stained glass window next to the pulpit was dedicated on 15 April 1951 in memory of William Bain-Gray, Governor during the war, who had given great support to the restoration of the roof. The window was unveiled by his successor, Sir George Andrew Joy, who spoke of the crushing burden borne by his predecessor during the War. The window had two lights, depicting St Peter and St Paul, together with some of the works helped by the Governor's encouragement. Under St Peter is shown the Cathedral with its restored roof, a man working in the field, and a woman gathering corn. Under St Paul, Governor Bain-Gray is shown receiving men, women and children, survivors from ss *City of Cairo*, sunk by torpedo during the war, who reached St Helena after about three weeks in open boats. The window was given by his wife, Ursula E. C. Bain-Gray.

CHURCH OF ST HELENA AND THE CROSS, BLUE HILL
On 8 August 1941 two acres of land known as Girling's Ground were conveyed by Solomon & Co to the Bishop for the sum of £20 and in 1951 the foundation stone of the new Church of St Helena and the Cross was laid by the Governor, Sir George Andrew Joy, the stone first having been blessed by the Bishop. The stone was a block of concrete with the letters in lead 'May 21st 1951' written within the arms of a cross. The new church was needed to serve the parishioners living in very scattered and isolated cottages in the south west of the island, some five miles from the Cathedral. The church was built by the Public Works Deptartment under the supervision and to the plans of Mr G. F. Gammer at a cost of £1,000 for the church and £60 for the pews. The church was dedicated by the Bishop on 3 November 1951 and the altar consecrated. In his address the Bishop paid particular tribute to the work of Mr John March and Mr Harry Yon. The Communion rails were reconstructed after being removed from the Cathedral. In December, the Governor, by a Proclamation under the Burial Grounds Ordinance 1895, declared that 'The Churchyard of the Church of St Helena and the Cross, or so much of it as the said Bishop shall from time to time consecrate for the purpose, shall be a private cemetery', and on 15 June 1952, it was consecrated by the Bishop.

On 13 September 1952, the building being now free from debt, the

St Helena and the Cross, Blue Hill (David Bentham)

Bishop consecrated the new church. He had previously typically asked the Archbishop about 'the ancient ceremonies used in the consecration of a church' to which the Archbishop replied that he doubted if anyone in the Province could answer Gilbert Turner's questions and referred him to the liturgiologist Canon Ratcliffe. There is no evidence that Turner did so refer, but in his Register of consecrations he gives details of the ceremony used, including the tracing of Alpha and Omega at the four corners 'on pavement by the Bishop with staff, in ashes previously scattered' and the anointing of the four consecration crosses. The simple iroko reredos was dedicated on 12 October 1952 and on 16 November the Bishop blessed and anointed a bell 'of which the date is 1856, and the name Mutlar, to be the bell to call the Faithful to Mass and Prayers in the Churchyard of St Helena and the Cross at Gurling's Gate. Formerly a ship's bell, for many years this bell served as house bell at Bishopsholme, to Bishop Holbech and subsequent Bishops.' The St Helena hymn, 'O God, Creator, at whose word our land arose from out the deep', was written by the Reverend D.H.Cumming, Vicar of Jamestown, for the Consecration of the Church of St Helena and the Cross, and the music composed by Mr Algernon Broadway. The church was licensed for marriages in November 1951.

St Helena is the patron saint of Colchester, although few would still maintain that she was the daughter of Old King Cole! Miss Clarice Chapman of Colchester designed a beautiful tapestry, taking the design from the portrait of St Helena depicted on the seal of the original Borough Charter of Colchester of 1189, and presented it to the Diocese in 1989. It now hangs in the Church of St Helena and the Cross.

The picture of St Helena on the front of the Cathedral pulpit is a copy of an Icon in the Chapel of St Helena in the Church of the Resurrection, Jerusalem. It was given by the Patriarch of the Greek Orthodox Churches in Palestine to Sir Spencer Davis at the time of his appointment as Governor of St Helena in 1932. It was used as the design for the 2s 6d stamp of the 1934 issue of St Helena stamps commemorating the centenary of Crown rule. According to the September 1955 issue of *The Wirebird*, the mahogany frame was made from fragments of a bookcase used by Napoleon at Longwood and destroyed by white ants. The picture was returned to the island by Sir Spencer Davis' nephew, Mr W. B. Davis, in August 1955.

The Centenary of the Consecration of the new Country Church by Bishop Robert Gray was kept on 15 December 1957, the third Sunday in Advent. Bishop Turner anointed two stones, one from the Cathedral Church of Christ, Canterbury, set in the sanctuary wall on the Gospel side, and one from the Cathedral Church of St George, Cape Town, on the Epistle side. Both are engraved with a cross and the years 1857-1957.

ST PAUL'S VICARAGE

The first St Paul's Vicarage had been Rock Cottage, near Sydenham. By 1921 this had fallen into disrepair, and the parish rented first Kingshurst and then Enfield as a vicarage. At this time the present St Paul's Vicarage, built in the time of Sir Hudson Lowe, was a school. When this also fell into disrepair the school moved down the hill to Luffkins. In 1926 Bishop Holbech proposed to the Governor that they exchange Rock Cottage for the old Country School. At first the Bishop wished to retain some of the flax land around Rock Cottage, but later, to pay for the repairs and conversion to a vicarage, he had to convey to the Government all the land around Rock Cottage, amounting to 10 acres. The vicarage was ready for use in 1928, but the Vicar Frank Oxley declined to move in, preferring to remain at Enfield. He complained that he had not been consulted about the conversion, that there was insufficient cupboard space and there was no water laid on. The vicarage was unoccupied until 1929, when Bishop Holbech put in a caretaker.

When Oxley left in 1932, the Bishop decided to look after St Paul's parish, and the vicarage was not needed. Thus when the Government needed Luffkins for the Medical Officer, the Bishop leased the vicarage to them, and it once more became the Country School, in February 1934.

In September 1947 the present Country School was opened. The vicarage was restored and blessed by Bishop Turner in 1948. The parish still being without a Vicar, the Bishop moved into the vicarage, which now became Bishopsholme, the old Bishopsholme having fallen to the ravages of white ants. Bishop Turner made the Chapel he called 'Arabia' at the new Bishopsholme, and in November 1953 he blessed a cloistered way leading to it. When Bishop Beardmore moved into Prince's Lodge in 1961, the building once more became St Paul's Vicarage, as it is today.

The Royal Naval Ensign of HMS *Lion* was laid up in the Cathedral in 1962.

Maurice Geen, who had been a schoolmaster in South Africa, was ordained priest at St Paul's on 5 May 1963 by Bishop Beardmore. He moved from St Paul's to St Matthew's parish in November 1965. During his time, in 1964, Mr Charles Clingham completed 21 years' continuous service as Churchwarden of St Paul's parish. The Order of Simon of Cyrene is conferred by the Archbishop of Cape Town on lay people who have given outstanding service to the Church. In recognition of his devoted service, Mr Clingham was made a member of the Order in 1965. His wife, Mrs Iris Clingham MBE was to serve as Honorary Secretary of the Parochial Church Council for 19 years (1963-82).

Another member of the Order of Simon of Cyrene was Governor Sir John Field, who personally restored the memorial tablets in the Cathedral and replaced them on the walls in 1966. Most of these tablets had originally come from the old Country Church.

James Johnson, a St Helenian, later to be the twelfth Bishop, was priested in 1965 in England and returned to St Helena in 1966. He stayed for two tours, until 1971, at first as priest-in-charge and then from 1969 as Vicar of St Paul's. He also looked after St Matthew's parish during 1968-70.

ST ANDREW'S CHURCH, HALF TREE HOLLOW

In 1951 Bishop Turner had the vision to buy from Joseph A. George, known as Blacksmith George, Stone Top Cottage and the surrounding land of more than an acre, in Half Tree Hollow, the steep hill between Jamestown and the Cathedral, which was to become a rapidly growing housing area. Bishop Beardmore turned the cottage into a dual-purpose church and hall. A small apse was built and a very attractive altar made of local stone by a Mr Forster. It now became St Andrew's Church and regular services were held from 1962. In 1971 the Vicar James Johnson raised £700 to replace the flat roof with a pitched roof. A font was made by Mr Douglas Augustus and the church was consecrated by Bishop Capper on 7 August 1971, and registered for marriages in 1984.

Mr Ronald Duncan retired in 1968 after 20 years' faithful service as Cathedral Verger and was succeeded by Mr A. McDaniel.

Fr Johnson exchanged with Fr Duffy on Ascension for a few weeks, early in 1971.

CHURCH OF ST MARTIN IN THE HILLS, HIGH POINT

During his episcopate Bishop Beardmore proposed to build a church at Thompson's Hill, to be named St Martin-in-the-Hills, and had collected £400 from his friends and the Diocesan Association. After Beardmore's death, Bishop Capper decided to build the church as a memorial to Bishop Beardmore. In 1971 the Governor conveyed to the Bishop a site at High Point, amounting to ⅖ acre, for £2. The tiny church, seating about 40 people, was designed by Mr G.A.D. Thornton and built by Messrs Solomon & Co, at a cost of £700 plus £109 for the crushed stone and concrete border. The foundation stone was blessed by Bishop Capper on 29 September 1970 and laid by the Governor, Sir Dermot Murphy. The Church was dedicated by Bishop Capper on 22 May 1971.

The Church Bell was the ship's bell of HMS *Eagle*, of which Bishop Giggall had been Chaplain. In July 1973, Bishop Giggall dedicated a Prayer Desk for St Martin's in memory of Bishop Beardmore. The desk had been made at the Royal Naval Engineering College, where Bishop Beardmore had once been Chaplain. The church was registered for marriages in 1984.

Charles Milton-Smith[36] and his wife Vera spent two tours on the island. He was Vicar of St Paul's from January 1972 to September 1976. He revived the Parish Magazine and produced 30 monthly issues of some 8 pages between May 1973 and September 1976. He included newsletters from the other parishes and from time to time a Diocesan Gazette. Some 400 to 500 copies were produced on the Diocesan duplicator in his study. The issues are packed with news of island people, and the amount of personal news which he gave evidently reflected his pastoral concern. Occasionally one of his comments, or his Baptismal policy, would provoke a reaction, but it is difficult to find cause for anything but praise in his magazine. Charles Milton-Smith died in 1991.

CHAPEL OF S SWITHUN IN THE CATHEDRAL

In 1957 Bishop Turner had dedicated a new Vestry in memory of Bishop Gray, and a new cloister, which joined it to the Choir Vestry, anointing a stone inscribed S Swithun's Cloister 1957. Both vestry and cloister were made by Mr Douglas Augustus and Mr Arnold Peters. It is said that the cloister was built and so named to protect Bishop Turner from the rain when walking in his robes from one vestry to the other!

Bishop Capper wished to have a memorial in the Cathedral to Bishop Turner. He had collected over £500 and planned to convert S Swithun's cloister into a Chapter Room. This proved too expensive a project, but in 1975 the cloister was provided with an outside wall with windows, to convert it into a chapel. This was designed by Mr Idris Davies and built by Mr Douglas Augustus. The chapel furniture was made by Mr Herbert Nicholls. A brass plaque, bearing the names of Bishops Watts, Aylen, Turner and Beardmore, who had not previously been commemorated in the Cathedral, was affixed to the wall.

The Chapel of S Swithun was dedicated by Bishop Giggall on 1 June 1975, in memory of Bishop Turner. He also dedicated a cross and candlesticks given by Mr Leslie Bagley of Vancouver, Canada, in memory of his father the late Mr Robert Bagley; a fair linen cloth made and given by Miss Elsa and Miss Iris Smith (who had previously made the beautiful credence table cloth in the Cathedral); and a chalice and paten given by Bishop Capper and the Diocesan Association in memory of Phyllis Jean Percy and Doris Lucas of Worthing, who had been supporters of the Diocese.

The Chapel was oriented and refurbished in 1984 by the Vicar, the Venerable Andrew Neaum and is in regular use for weekday services.

CHURCH OF ST PETER, SANDY BAY

It will be recalled that services were held in the school-house at Sandy Bay since the time of Richard Kempthorne, and that when he built the school he designed it so that a chancel could be easily added. A verandah was added in 1904, and in 1917, at the instigation of Canon

St Peter's, Sandy Bay (David Bentham)

Walcott, who had been assisting the Bishop by holding monthly services at Sandy Bay, a small stone chancel, with a thatched roof, was added to the school. Bishop Holbech dedicated it to St Peter on the eve of St Peter's Day 1917. The altar was made by Mr Richard Constantine.

The chancel was extended to its present size, at a cost of £150, in 1964. Bishop Beardmore commended Mr Pennell Legg, Mr Kenneth Legg and Mr Reginald Constantine for their help in transporting materials and in the organization of the work, without which expenses would have been higher. In April 1970 Mr Pennell Legg put a new roof on the chancel. The painted East window was given in memory of Mr Fred Graham by his widow. In 1972 the Church Benevolent Society conveyed to the Diocese the two acres of land on which the church stands for the sum of 10 New Pence.

In 1976 a font was made by Mr Douglas Augustus. Ladies of Exeter Cathedral had made a donation, and the Font incorporated a piece of granite from the Chapter House of Exeter Cathedral presented by Mrs Dakers, wife of the Cathedral organist. (Mr Lionel Dakers subsequently became Director of the Royal School of Church Music.) Exeter Cathedral is also dedicated to St Peter, and the arms of that Diocese, the keys of St Peter and the sword of St Paul, are mounted on the stone. St Peter's Church was consecrated by Bishop Giggall on 5 September 1976, after it had been used for church services for over 120 years.

A grey slate plaque, carved by Mr Randolph Constantine, was placed on the south wall of St Peter's Church in 1982 to commemorate Edward Constantine, who had been responsible for building the chancel of St Peter's in 1917. He was a Sidesman (1910-13), Churchwarden (1921-35), Reader (1944-51) and was made a Sub-Deacon in May 1951. He was Head Teacher of Sandy Bay School (1904-60). He died on 31 July 1967 aged 81.

After serving as a Chaplain in the Royal Air Force and with the Chindits during the war (he was Mentioned in Despatches), Angus Macintyre[37] ministered in the Episcopal Church of Scotland until 1968. In 1976, at the age of 62, he came to St Helena, with his wife Eveline, to be Vicar of St Paul's. They were joined for some time by their daughter Anne, who practised on the island as a doctor. Macintyre was a lover of walking and enjoyed taking Holy Communion to distant cottages. He left in May 1979. The parish was looked after by the Bishop from May 1979 until February 1980. In 1979 the Royal Naval Ensign of HMS *St Helena* was laid up in the Cathedral.

An American by birth, but trained for the priesthood in England, Clay Knowles[38] arrived with his wife Jacqueline and two young children to be Vicar of St Paul's in February 1980. The parish changed from the South African Prayer Book to the South African Liturgy 75 in 1980. Fr Knowles showed ingenuity and enthusiasm in arranging projects for the children at the Festivals as well as great care in preparing mentally handicapped parishioners for Confirmation.

A cement screed was laid on the floor of the Cathedral nave and vinyl tiles laid by voluntary labour in 1982 at a cost of £2,500 for the materials. The Cathedral was closed for seven weeks while the work was in progress, and services held at Kingshurst. A Thanksgiving Eucharist was held at its reopening on 1 August 1982.

An aumbry lamp was placed in the sanctuary of the Cathedral in 1982 and dedicated by the Bishop in memory of Reginald Constantine, Churchwarden (1968-80). He was a most loyal and devoted Churchman, and was made a member of the Order of Simon of Cyrene on 6 November 1977. He died on 23 July 1980, during an epidemic of influenza, at the age of 74. The brass for the lamp was salvaged from the *Papanui*, destroyed by fire off Jamestown in September 1911.

The requisitioning of the RMS *St Helena* for the Falklands conflict caused problems of communication: her replacement, the 500-ton *Aragonite* had room for only eleven passengers. Fr Knowles and his family were due to return to England at the end of their tour, and they eventually managed to leave on the tiny tanker *Bosun Bird* going to Tenerife. Similarly, his replacement Andrew Neaum,[39] who came from a parish in Zimbabwe, found himself stuck in Cape Town for six weeks, until he, his wife Margaret and their two sons obtained berths on the *Aragonite* and arrived in August 1982. His father, David Neaum, was already on the island as Vicar of Jamestown and Archdeacon. When David Neaum left in June 1984, Andrew was appointed Archdeacon. It cannot happen very often that son succeeds father as Archdeacon! Their daughter, Elizabeth, was born on the island. Andrew Neaum began a monthly parish leaflet in August 1983, setting an example followed by the other two island parishes.

The Government conveyed to the Bishop in April 1983 about 3,900 square yards of land at the top of St Paul's Churchyard to be used as an extension for the churchyard.

In 1983, cracks began to appear in the chancel arch of the Cathedral. By 1984 these had widened alarmingly and investigation showed that over the years rain had been seeping in, at the top of the wall and where the two roofs met the wall. It was therefore decided to strip the deteriorated plaster rendering, renew it and the lead flashing, and cover the stone coping with lead sheet. The work was done admirably by Messrs Solomon & Co in the middle of 1984, helped by an unusually long spell of dry weather. The work cost £3,500. Tests with a moisture content meter showed the wall to be sodden and time had to be allowed for the wall to dry out before further work could be carried out on the interior. An appeal by the Bishop, Vicar and Churchwardens raised £10,000, thus providing not only enough to pay for the complete work but also a nucleus for a permanent restoration fund. By a happy coincidence, a generous legacy of £1,182 was received at this time from the estate of a St Helenian, the late Mrs Laura R. Francis. The sum was bequeathed to the Vicar and Churchwardens of St Paul's Cathedral parish for the maintenance of the Cathedral fabric.

The Neaums left in April 1985 for Australia. There followed an interregnum of over four months during which the Bishop looked after the parish. In September the Bishop made Mr Michael Crook a non-stipendiary Deacon, to serve primarily in St Paul's parish (see Chapter 2). Peter Cowen[40] arrived to be Vicar of the parish later that month, having previously served in Cyprus as Refugee Projects Officer. He had a great interest in organic farming and he took pains to share that interest with young people, both at St Paul's and later at St Matthew's, whither he moved in October 1986.

Spurred on by the success of the work on the Cathedral, the Church

Council turned their attention to the daughter churches. The little Church of St Martin's needed a porch. With the new generating station, electricity was to be taken to the farther parts of the island, and the Church of St Helena and the Cross needed wiring in preparation and also a tarmac drive. St Peter's needed not only wiring but most important of all, a new roof. The churches were told that as far as possible they must try to raise the necessary money themselves.

St Martin's was the first to be completed. Mrs Ina Benjamin, the Chapel Warden, with tremendous enthusiasm and the help of Saints on Ascension, raised over £2,000 and with some voluntary labour the porch was ready to be dedicated by Bishop James on 14 September 1986. Two stools were also made and presented by Mr Owen Buckley. The Bishop dedicated a new lectern on 27 December 1987.

At St Helena and the Cross the tarmac drive was laid by self-help and the electrical wiring installed by volunteers, ably supervised by Mr Stedson Francis. The newly installed lighting was dedicated by the Bishop on St Helena's Day, 21 May 1987. Peter Cowen preached. One consequence of the electrical supply was that they were able to install an electronic organ in August 1988.

The much needed re-roofing of St Peter's Church was not an easy matter and required professional skill. It was completed in 1989 at a cost of £3,689. St Peter's themselves raised £1,700 and the parish of St John the Baptist, Weston-super-Mare gave £2,100, the proceeds of their Lent giving. It is their custom to give this to the Diocese every other year, and it considerably assists the Diocesan Association in England to pay for the outward fares of the clergy.

Year by year at the Vestry meeting, Mr Charles Yon, the devoted Cathedral Choirmaster, would raise the urgent need of a new toilet at the Cathedral. Sadly, it was only after his death that the new toilet and storeroom was completed by voluntary labour, led by Mr George Thomas. It might not have been done at all without Charlie Yon's persistence!

The Cathedral organ had given good service for 80 years, but now not even the expertise of Mrs Joy George, who had been organist since 1967, could hide its imperfections. The Bishop asked Mr Philip Knights, the Government Treasurer and a very knowledgeable organist, to make enquiries and he recommended a Wyvern York DS40 electronic organ at a cost of £7,000. The Governor gave a very generous contribution from his discretionary fund, and the Organ Fund raised £2,500, helped by £1,000 from the St Helena Association UK (a group of St Helenians in England who raise money for charitable purposes on the island). The organ was dedicated by the Bishop in December 1986.

The Bishop looked after the parish for three months until the arrival of Peter Charles Price[41] and his wife Deanna in January 1988. He had been trained for the ministry in Canada, where he served for some years after ordination. One of his great interests was cycling, which he indulged in even on the steep gradients of St Helena!

On Sunday 19 November 1989, Mr Randolph Constantine MBE received his insignia as a Member of the Order of Simon of Cyrene from the Bishop at the Sung Eucharist in the Cathedral. It was richly deserved. Randy Constantine had been Churchwarden of St Paul's since 1961.

Peter and Deanna Price left for the UK in July 1990, and the Bishop once more took over the parish.

On St Helena's Day, 1989, the BBC World Service broadcast a pre-recorded ecumenical service from St Paul's Cathedral. The address was given by Mrs Lily Crowie, the Assistant Education Officer concerned with Teacher Training, and later to be a Lay Minister. She began:

One of the joys of believing in the Communion of Saints is that never mind how far separated we may be from one another by time, distance or even death, we know that in praying for one another we are one in Christ, and that we have our union in Him.

But in praying for one another it is helpful to know something about each other. So let me tell you something about us.

After an outline of the history of the St Helenians and the life of the Church, she continued:

The Church has always been at the centre of island life – whether it be worship, social or public life, or in caring for those in need. So we feel that our dedication to St Helena is really quite appropriate. St Helena herself was known for her generosity and compassion towards the poor. Here on the island the Church has always been in the forefront of care for those in need …

Another area where it seems appropriate that we are named after St Helena is that she was remembered for building churches on holy sites. And our first church on the island – St James' – was built on that holy and historical site of the first Portuguese church …

But where does all this leave us today? We remain an island and a people free from racial or national prejudice, and are always willing to exercise our ministry of hospitality to anyone who finds us as they sail across the seas. And we are proud to have this opportunity to greet you in the name of the Lord, and we ask that you join with us as we sing of the greatness of God's love for us all.

CATHEDRAL CRAFTSMEN

Many craftsmen have adorned the Churches of St Helena with their work, often given freely, over the years. None have contributed more to the beautifying of the Cathedral and the other churches of the parish than Mr Richard Scott Constantine. He died on 20 May 1953, at the age of 72. He had been Cathedral organist for 44 years. We give a list of the items which he, and others, made and gave to St Paul's, and, where stated, other churches.

BY MR RICHARD SCOTT CONSTANTINE

1905. Teak organ stool (for new 'Positive' organ), Litany desk, Hymn board and Vestry armchair.

1917. Altar for St Peter's Church.

1920. Carved wooden shrine, with list of St Helenians who served in 1914-18 War, in Cathedral porch.

1922. Credence table, carved with motif of grapes and wheat.

1933. Together with his brother, Louis, a complete set of new pews, using metal ends brought from South Africa by the Bishop.

1938. Reroofing of porch as memorial to Gilbert Turner's mother. A roof beam inside porch is inscribed 'O Jesu, remember Frances Turner 1927'.

1945. Altar extended and carved panels, representing St Paul and St Helena added to original reredos of 1901, and reredos regilded.

1946. Diocesan arms on Bishop's Throne, and faldstool.

Altar Cross given by him and his wife as thank-offering for safe deliverance of their daughter who had been in the Channel Islands during the war.

1950. Carved figure of Risen, Ascended and Glorified Christ in memory of his wife. Now in St Peter's Church.

BY MR HERBERT NICHOLLS

1944. With Mr Harry Yarrow, re-roofing of Cathedral.

1952. With his sons, iroko Canons' stalls, in memory of Richard Kempthorne.

1955. Four funeral candlesticks.

1958. Iroko Priest's desk and a pulpit for St Matthew's Church.

1960. Iroko lectern, with Diocesan arms inlaid in island woods, and Bible box to hold Bible presented at Centenary of Founding of Diocese. Dedicated in memory of Miss Mabel Agnes Hartvig, for 10 years a member of the Church on St Helena.

1968. With his sons, complete set of iroko pews, at a cost of £22 each.

(The Governor presented a 'Governor's pew'.)

1970. Teak Priest's stall, at cost of £30.

1975. Furniture for S Swithun's Chapel.

BY MR RANDOLPH CONSTANTINE MBE

1967. Painted sign board with Diocesan Arms for Cathedral.

1982. Slate plaque for St Peter's, to commemorate Mr Edward Constantine.

BY MR DOUGLAS AUGUSTUS

1967. Redecoration of Cathedral, with voluntary help.

1968. Notice boards for daughter churches.

1971. Font for St Andrew's.

1976. Font for St Peter's.

General maintenance of Cathedral over many years.

Space forbids including many others who have contributed.

St Matthew's Parish (1861-1991)

The Parish Ordinance of 1861 made Longwood an Ecclesiastical District until such time as its church should be built, when it would become a parish. Accordingly, on 13 April 1861 Henry James Bodily was admitted by Bishop Claughton to the Curacy of the District of Longwood. The District covered the eastern half of the island. There was (and is) a small centre of population at Longwood, and a smaller, and more isolated, one at Levelwood. The rest of the population live in scattered cottages, with a few larger houses, such as Teutonic Hall and, of course, Longwood House. Bodily was instituted as Rector on St Matthias' Day 1862, the same day as the Church was consecrated.

In 1863 the Parish resolved to provide £50 of the Rector's annual stipend of £200. Two years later they were able to erect a new school to replace an earlier one. Bodily left in 1867 and was succeeded by John Hands. The Reverend Francis Kilvert, in his *Diary*, gives an account of an address about St Helena given by Bodily to an SPG meeting at Hay-on-Wye on 31 August 1870.[42]

John Compton Hands was born in May 1842 and trained at St Augustine's College, Canterbury. He was made Deacon at St Helena in 1868 and ordained priest in 1874. He became Curate of St Matthew's in 1868 and looked after the District while the whole island was one parish from 1871 to 1885, becoming Vicar in 1875.

He married Alice Mary Metcalfe of Willow Bank, the organist at St

Matthew's, on 30 March 1869. They were to have two sons and two daughters. Alice Hands died on 21 July 1905 at the age of 57 after an attack of measles. The parishioners placed a brass memorial tablet behind the organ in memory of her 43 years' service as organist.

The parish was a poor one and in 1872 they had to ask the Hussey Charity to take over responsibility for the running of the parish school, as they were unable to raise enough money. And in 1875, in answer to a question from the Diocesan Finance Board as to whether the parish could increase their contribution to the Vicar's stipend, so that the portion of the SPG grant given to the parish for that purpose could be reduced, the parish replied:

> The Parishioners would not be able to raise any further amounts, being almost without exception farmers who are feeling keenly the bad season, and poor people who live off the produce of their gardens and who already give as much as they are able and therefore, whatever amount the Finance Board decide on deducting ... will cause the Vicar to be the loser thereby.

The result was that at the Easter Vestry 1876 Hands presented a statement of accounts showing a deficiency in his stipend over eight years of £150.[43] Canon Hands became priest-in-charge of St John's in 1886 for one year and then again from 1892 to 1900, for which he received £12 a year. He was made a Canon in 1895.

In 1887 the bell from the Cathedral was installed in the belfry of St Matthew's Church and in about 1898, the Lych Gate was erected by Mr H. B. Morrice, Churchwarden.

A meeting of the parishioners in 1900 was somewhat stormy. Bishop Holmes, recently arrived, evidently wanted to find money to pay a full-time priest for St John's, and proposed to reduce the SPG grant to St Matthew's. It was on this occasion that one of the Churchwardens said that he thought a young man at St James' could easily look after St John's as well, and Canon Hands himself, in the Bishop's presence, said

> that his Lordship seemed to be acting in a very harsh manner, and his knowledge of Diocesan needs was too imperfect to form such a hasty conclusion in withdrawing the SPG [grant], which after so many years service seemed a very spiteful act.

Making changes on St Helena has never been easy, and requires a great deal of tact. One sympathizes with Canon Hands, who was likely to find his stipend reduced if the parish could not make it up. But many of Holmes' successors will smile at his description of the situation:

Canon Hands has been here for 31 years and has never left the Island. At any suggestion as to a change or improvement, he presents the stolid resistance of saying: 'You are new to the island – you don't know our ways, or the people – we have never been used to that' and so on. Of late years I fancied he managed matters for the late Bishop and he resents interference or suggestions.

In 1906 Canon Hands resigned his Military Chaplaincy, which he had held since 1884, thereby losing £60 a year, which the parish were to do their best to make up.

The Church Lads Brigade was formed in the parish in 1905. A lectern made by Mr Arthur Evans was installed in the church in 1906. Altar candles were first used on Easter Day 1907.

On Sunday 5 July 1908 Canon Hands celebrated the 40th anniversary of his landing on St Helena. It was said that he had created a record – no other old student of St Augustine's College, Canterbury, had occupied a single post for so long. In all that time he had only left the island once, for a three month break in South Africa after his wife's death. He resigned in 1910, aged 68, and went to live at Willow Bank. He was much loved by all and continued to help in the parish – particularly when St Matthew's and St Paul's were looked after by one priest – until his death on 25 November 1928, aged 86. He had been 60 years on St Helena. He and his wife are buried in St Matthew's Churchyard.

The Vicarage was repaired at a cost of about £125 in readiness for the new Vicar, Christopher Wood,[44] aged 45, who arrived in April 1911 with his wife and three children. The following year a beginning was made on planting part of the Vicarage grounds with flax, to assist the Vicar's stipend. It is of interest that Wood felt that two Sisters or Lady Workers would be good for the parish.

REBUILDING OF ST MATTHEW'S CHURCH

Wood found the church, which was 50 years old, in a bad condition, most of the wooden uprights had decayed, and the structure was held up by the iron sheeting. It seems that the Bishop was not too keen on the Church being rebuilt. 'I fear', wrote Wood in 1913, 'His Lordship will be a great mountain to get over'. However, in 1915 he began work on a new church. The Church Council were willing for the church to be rebuilt, provided they had no financial responsibility. In the event the work was carried out by the Vicar and a Building Committee, largely financed by friends in England and a grant of £100 from the SPG Marriott bequest. The apse was constructed first and joined to the old church. It was made of local stone with a dome shaped roof. The centre window of three lights, showing the Crucifixion with the Virgin and St John on either side, was the gift of Mr Morrice. The smaller side windows, showing St Matthew and St Peter, were the gift of the 4th Battalion of the Gloucestershire Regiment, stationed at St Helena during the South African War. The teak altar and credence table had been made by the Vicar. The apse and altar were consecrated by the Bishop on All Saints' Day, 1915. The following year work was begun on building the rest of the church. This was accomplished by building a wall 4 feet outside the existing church and when this was complete, removing the old corrugated iron walls. The original metal roof trusses were used in the new church.

The new church was not to everyone's liking. Christopher Wood left in December 1918 and in the *Diocesan Magazine* for March 1919 appeared the following criticism:

It is somewhat disappointing to find that St Matthew's Church is not a good building for sound. The altar is now placed in a deep sanctuary with a round end from which the voice of the priest does not resound, so that it is difficult to hear the words of the prayers ... St Matthew's Church is lacking not only as to sound but as to light. The windows are smaller than in the original building.

There were worse problems. The new chancel roof leaked, and the north wall had been built on inadequate foundations, possibly old graves. By 1923:

The crack in the west wall and the general sinking of the north wall must be attended to. The sanctuary also is in a deplorable condition, resulting in actual mould on the very altar itself, destroying the linen and frontals and making the pavement green; ferns are in fact growing out of the wall behind the pulpit and when the weather is blown against the east wall the water can be seen running off the inside wall and down the pavement.

Mr T. Broadway, of Prospect, a retired Clerk of Works and Church-warden of St Matthew's, wrote to SPG in 1925 asking for 'catalogues for steel or galvanized Churches on wood framing, capable of holding 250-300 persons',[45] but nothing came of his efforts.

In 1924 the chancel arch, a 'pseudo Moorish erection', had become dangerous and was replaced by a simpler one, the sanctuary was roofed with corrugated iron, and the north wall taken down and rebuilt on the line of the north wall of the original church.

A new bell was brought out from England in 1920, the gift of some parishioners.

After Christopher Wood's departure, Canon Hands helped in the parish. The Reverend Sydney Wilson Ruscoe[46] came in May 1920, but

St Matthew's, Hutt's Gate today

had to leave in December of that same year due to ill health. At the Vestry meeting of 1921, Bishop Holbech announced that the Diocese could no longer afford to maintain three parish priests on the island, and that in future there would only be one priest for the two country parishes, who would live in St Paul's parish. He would have a stipend of about £300 a year, instead of £200. Each parish would have its own Churchwardens and Council. It was an arrangement which was to last until 1934, but not one likely to appeal to St Matthew's parish, which had had its own Vicar for 55 years out of the previous 59.

The first Vicar of the two parishes was Frederick Ashworth, who came in November 1921, but at the Vestry meeting in April 1922 announced that 'he had unfortunately had cause to resign'. Sadly, the 'cause' was the difficulty of working with the Bishop. It was not to be the last time that the Vicar of St Paul's and the Bishop had that problem! The Vestry asked the Churchwardens to write to the Bishop deploring Ashworth's departure and asking the Bishop to

take such action as may lead to an alleviation or healing of any breach or differences that may have occasioned the action which has been taken by the Revd. Ashworth in consequence thereof.

Ashworth left and during the next ten years was succeeded by Turner, Lewty and Oxley. St Matthew's Vestry continued each year to make strong representations to the Bishop of their need for their own priest.

The churchyard which had been extended in 1885 was now full. In 1925 Mr H. W. Solomon gave some land for a new burial ground on the lower slopes of Halley's Mount, where in 1676 the young Edmund Halley had catalogued the stars of the southern sky and observed the transit of Mercury.

The church continued to give cause for concern. In 1933 a drain was dug to carry off the water which was soaking the foundations and coming up through the floor. Some of the wooden flooring, now rotten, was replaced by cement. A new roof was put on the vestry and the main roof repaired. The weather side of the church was rendered in an attempt to keep out the wet.

That year the church had a new bell – a gift from St Paul's – and the lighting was improved with a large central brass lamp given by Mr Morrice and six brass lamps sent by Gilbert Turner from South Africa. A new belfry with two bells, designed by Captain Mainwaring of New Longwood House, was erected in 1935.

In 1934, the parish had its own priest once more. Fenwick Hall, who had been made Deacon in England, arrived in May 1934 and was licensed as Curate of St Matthew's. He was priested in February 1935 by Bishop Watts and was made Vicar. Archdeacon B. H. Warner, who had been Vicar-General for a year while Bishop Watts was in Damaraland, wrote in May 1935:

The advent of a new priest for St Matthew's has been a great step forward ... from being one of the most backward and uncouth populations it is beginning to show signs of a return to self-respect and decency.[47]

In April 1937, Fenwick Hall announced that in future Baptisms of children born in wedlock would be held on Sundays, those born out of wedlock on weekdays!

He departed later that year and the parish was looked after by the Bishop until the arrival of the Reverend Percy Clark[48] in 1939. The Tabernacle was placed in St Matthew's Church in 1940 and consecrated by the Bishop. Clark left in 1944.

Fenwick Hall returned for 15 years (1945-61), with a break in 1956/7.

The churchyard was closed in 1953, save for the burial of infants, and all future burials were in the unconsecrated Government cemetery at the Dungeon. (Anglican priests would consecrate individual graves before burial.)

Restoration work on the church was carried out in 1958 and at a Thanksgiving Service in November Bishop Turner dedicated a priest's desk and pulpit, made of iroko by Mr Herbert Nicholls.

Bryan Bartleet[49] came in 1960 as a Deacon and was ordained Priest on St Helena in 1961. He was priest-in-charge of St Matthew's until 1964 when he returned to South Africa.

After a year as Vicar of St James' (1963-4), Fenwick Hall was again at St Matthew's (1964-5), and then he retired and lived in the cottage behind the present St Mark's Church Hall. He was made a Canon in 1966 and in the same year was appointed a Member of the Order of the British Empire. He finally left the island in 1968 and died in Natal in March 1972. A priest's stall in St Matthew's Church was dedicated in his memory in 1975.

After a career as a schoolmaster in South Africa, Maurice Geen[50] was ordained in his years of maturity and came to St Helena in 1963 as a Deacon. He was ordained Priest the same year. At first Curate of St Paul's, he was Vicar of St Matthew's from 1965 to 1967. Geen was followed by Gerwyn Jones[51] who had had a ministry in Wales and had spent five years as a USPG Missionary in India before becoming Vicar of St Matthew's for two tours (1970-75).

ST MARK'S CHURCH AND CHURCH HALL

A Magnetic and Meteorological Observatory had been set up at Longwood from 1840 to 1849. It was one of three (the others were at Cape Town and Toronto) under the command of General Sir Ernest Sabine for making regular magnetic observations. The first Director was Lieutenant J. H. Lefroy RA, who left in 1842 for Toronto, whither the instruments were sent in 1849. Lefroy later became Governor of Bermuda and then of Tasmania.

This former observatory was bought by Bishop Beardmore in 1963 with the help of a grant from USPG. The observatory originally had in front an octagonal room with a dome, but this had disappeared and the building was simply known as the Cottage. It now became St Mark's Church cum Church Hall and was dedicated on Whit Sunday 1963. Services were held there until 1974, when it became the Church Hall.

However, to serve adequately the growing community at Longwood a separate church building was needed and the foundation stone of St Mark's Church was laid by Bishop Capper on 20 January 1973. Contributions towards the cost of the new Church included £1,000 from USPG and £1,280 from the Diocese of St David's. Among English parishes which contributed was St Mark's, Longwood, Yorkshire. The church was designed by Mr Idris Davies and built by Mr Carleton Yon. It was consecrated by Bishop Giggall on 28 April 1974. It was partially furnished with iroko pews in 1979, and with an iroko lectern made and presented by Mr Hugh Gibbs in 1980.

Dennis Mander[52] came from South Africa with his wife Toni and was Vicar from September 1975 to April 1978. He was followed by John Harvey,[53] who spent five months as Priest-in-charge of St Mary's Ascension, before coming to St Matthew's in June 1978. He served two tours in the parish, becoming a member of the Oratory of the Good Shepherd. He left in October 1983 for South Africa.

Hermon Crowie[54] was born in South Africa, the son of a St Helenian father who had lived in St Matthew's parish. He was ordained in England, and came, with his wife Margaret and their daughter, to be Vicar of St Matthew's parish in January 1984. They left in August 1986.

In October Peter Cowen moved from St Paul's. He continued the work which Hermon Crowie had begun on the Vicarage garden and took on a small group of teenagers who enjoyed learning about compost, pruning and grafting. Father Peter became known as Farmer Peter! He boasted that at one stage he helped out Plantation House with squash, lettuce, cabbage, carrots and endive when they were short and had to entertain!

In 1987 Cowen went to South Africa to represent the Diocese at the Partners-in-Mission Conference and the Provincial Synod at Modderpoort. It was the first time that the Diocese had been represented by a priest. One result was the visit of Bishop Leslie Stradling in 1990 to give teaching on prayer.

In June 1988 Mr Matthew Crowie died. His contribution to the Church in St Matthew's parish had been outstanding. He had served continuously as Churchwarden for 49 years and had been Superintendent of Longwood Sunday School for about the same period. He was made a Sub-Deacon in 1963. During his visit in November 1972 the Archbishop of Cape Town, the Most Reverend Robert Selby-Taylor, installed Mattie Crowie as a Member of the Order of Simon of Cyrene, in recognition of his service. I myself would wish to pay tribute to the unswerving loyalty and friendship which he gave me during my own

St Mark's, Longwood (David Bentham)

time as Bishop. There were great numbers of people at his funeral, first at St Mark's Church where he lay in his open coffin, and then at St Matthew's Church where all the clergy took part and church and graveyard were packed with mourners. Peter Cowen preached and recalled how Bishop Johnson had been a boy in Mattie Crowie's Sunday School. The following May his widow, Lily, preached at the BBC World Service broadcast from the Cathedral. She was made a Lay Minister on the Feast of St Matthew 1990.

At the end of October 1988 Cowen left for England and then for Agricultural Chaplaincy work in Central and South America. By the same ship John Ryder[55] arrived from South Africa with his wife Brenda and two small girls. As well as being Vicar of St Matthew's, he was appointed Chaplain of the newly opened Prince Andrew School in succession to Michael Houghton.

St Matthew's parish has always been a particularly damp part of the island, – Napoleon was not enamoured of it! – and the Vicarage has suffered accordingly. Repairs and replacements to windows and chimneys in Ryder's time made some improvement, but the problem of mildew still remains. The electronic organ in St Matthew's also suffered from the damp and was replaced in 1989 by a re-conditioned harmonium from South Africa. The church itself continued to suffer from damp and the subsidence of the walls has caused distortion to the windows, but repairs would cost around £8,000.

The Pamela Williams Memorial Youth Club, founded by Hermon

Crowie, continued to flourish and to make a substantial contribution to church life, led by Gavin Thomas, and when he left the island, by his brother Ian.

The main centre of population in the parish is Longwood. The congregation at St Mark's is two or three times that at St Matthew's, which even today has only scattered houses around. The two churches are less than one and a half miles apart and Ryder became of the opinion that when St Mark's was built the parish resources should have been centred at Longwood, with only one church building to maintain. But one suspects that a proposal to close St Matthew's would meet with considerable opposition. Indeed for a long time there have been discussions whether a Church should be built at Levelwood, which was seen as a stronghold of the Jehovah's Witnesses. For many years, monthly Sunday services have been held in the school. The church has a small plot of ground opposite the school, and a building fund of a few thousand pounds has built up. But the parish has never been able to come to a decision to begin building, and there are conflicting views as to the wisdom of shouldering another maintenance responsibility.

John Ryder, with his wife and children, left for England in September 1991.

Country lane

5
Education and Ecumenism

Education and Friendly Societies (1683-1991)

From the 17th century, education on St Helena was largely in the hands of the clergy, and later was to be, to a large extent, sponsored by the Church.

The East India Company Chaplain, William Swindle (1673-5), was

> to preach once and catechize every Lord's Day and to teach or direct the teaching of children as their Schoolmaster and also as many of the Negro children as are capable of learning. His allowance £50 a year as Minister, £25 as Schoolmaster ...[1]

The school was held in the church. In 1678 a public notice was to be read in church on the next Lord's Day by the minister Mr Wynne:

> These are to advertise all the inhabitants of the Island and earnestly invite and desire everyone that hath children capable of learning, and that can possibly spare them, that they should lay aside unnecessary and frivolous excuses and be so much Friends to their children as to send them to the said school and keep them there as constantly as they may. That they would not be soe great Enemies to their children and to learning as to detain them at home about small or trifling matters, or to send them so seldom and soe uncertainly to the said School as that they should receive little or no profit thereby and so the gratious intendment of the Honourable Company be slighted, the design of this advertisement frustrated, the Minister and Schoolmaster discouraged and the poor children's welfare neglected.[2]

The schoolmaster in 1679 was a soldier, William Melling. He was suspended for a year for many uncivil actions towards one of the children, and was made to apologize upon his knees to the child and her mother; however, in March 1683 he was again permitted to keep a school in the church. Another 'Soldier and Schoolmaster' was the William Clifton who in 1692 put the church registers in good order.

The inhabitants in the Country in 1680 petitioned that they were too far from the Town Church for their children to go to school, and asked for a school of their own.

There is no record of any substantial development in education in the 18th century, and it is not until the first half of the 19th century that progress is made. But it must be remembered that in England it was not until 1882 that education was made compulsory for children even between the ages of five and ten years.

THE BENEVOLENT SOCIETY

A Public Meeting was held in October 1814 to consider proposals for the 'Diffusion of Moral and Religious Instruction among the lower classes'. At that meeting Governor Wilks admitted that some had entertained doubts as to whether it was desirable to extend the benefits of education to slaves and free blacks, but pointed out that similar misgivings in England over the extension of education had been proved wrong. He hoped that many would be prepared to release their slaves for instruction, not only on Sundays but perhaps for two hours on one weekday evening, and assured them that they would be rewarded by the additional value of their labours. However, 'perhaps Sunday alone may, for the present, be advisable, lest we should risque failure by attempting too much'.

The Benevolent Society was formed, financed by local voluntary subscriptions. By 1849 it had established a Town Infant School with 70 pupils, a Town Evening School with 90 pupils, Sandy Bay School (the building so designed that a chancel could be added later) with 45 pupils and Hutt's Gate School with 26. An attempt to begin a school at High Knoll lasted only two years since it was not convenient for liberated African servants in the vicinity.

In 1859 Edward Bennett had

restored the African school which was formerly kept by Jacob Faithful (the African interpreter), but had dwindled to nothing. They attended 4 nights a week, and I prepared 36 for Baptism. I baptized 23 on Sunday October 31st and kept back 13 for 6 weeks, as I was not quite satisfied with them. I now attend the Night School at Red Hill near to Mr Pritchard. I began with 4 Africans, now I have 24. The very fact of these negroes coming between 3 and 4 miles, 3 times a week, to learn to read, and to know more of their duty to God, convinces me that they are in earnest.[3]

The Benevolent Society's Report for 1858 speaks highly of the value of the Savings Bank which it had set up in 1838, but the report on the schools by Archdeacon Richard Kempthorne, Superintendent of the Society's Schools, is disquieting. 'The Bishop of the Diocese [ie Cape Town], when on his visitation here, publicly stated that the Society's Infant and Industrial School was inefficient, and I must add with regret that none of them except Mr Thompson's Evening School is in a satisfactory state.' Kempthorne recommended that they must try to obtain a trained instructor for at least one of the schools. The Society resolved to advertise for a trained teacher from England. As today, it was easier said than done, but by 1861, Mr Goodwin had arrived from England, with a marked consequent improvement in the Town Day School. Thomas Goodwin was to become a Catechist and to be ordained in 1871. In 1867 we read that 'Mr Goodwin, the Catechist, instructs the liberated resident slaves.' To meet the increased expenditure, assistance to Hutt's Gate School was discontinued.[4]

A School at the new Village at Half Tree Hollow was begun in 1860.

In 1864 J.H.Bodily, Vicar of Hutt's Gate, reported: 'I go on Thursdays and teach [the Africans] and examine what Jacob Faithful has been doing with them.'[5] But the same year, Whitehead, recently inducted to Jamestown wrote: 'Last month I surprised a notorious witch doctor, a baptized man, in the midst of his enchantments. He had persuaded his patient that his house was possessed.'[6]

February 1864 saw the fiftieth annual general meeting of the Benevolent Society and the Bishop paid tribute to the only surviving founder member, the Reverend Richard Boys, living in retirement in England.

The Society were anxious to improve the teaching at Sandy Bay School, and engaged a teacher from England, Mr T.R.Wilson, as Master. This was financed partly with a grant from the Government and partly by giving up the small school at Red Hill which had been in operation for a few years.

In 1867 a new Town Day School, with accommodation for 200 pupils, a playground and Master's residence, was purchased for about £950.

In 1874 the Society repaired High Peak School, which had been badly damaged by the weather. This school, which belonged to St Paul's Parish, was given a monthly grant from the Society for one year from 1870.

By 1879, the Society had only two Schools, the Town Day School and Sandy Bay School.

GOVERNMENT SCHOOLS

By 1814 the Government had a Country School near Plantation and, possibly by that date, a Lower School in the upper part of Jamestown. By Rules issued in 1852, these schools were open to all girls and boys between the ages of 6 and 12 years, on payment of 1*d* a week and after that age, 6*d* a week.

The Government Head School (the present Jamestown Community

Centre) was built by local labour and opened in 1825. The East India Company's Arms over the door were cut by a Corporal Galway.

The Head School was open only to boys, and the fees varied from £6 a year for those under the age of ten to £10 a year for those over fourteen. The subjects taught were English, History, Geography, Mathematics, Euclid, Algebra and Latin. Instruction in Greek, French, German, Italian or Drawing was to be paid for as an extra. It was evidently a school for expatriate children, as is further attested by the list of prize winners in 1852: Melliss, Janisch, Knipe etc.[7]

The first Master of the Head School was the Colonial Chaplain, the Reverend Richard Boys. In 1852 the Headmaster and Inspector General of St Helena Schools was the Reverend James Chambers of All Souls College Oxford. His report for 1852 is in the Diocesan Archives. The Reverend George Bennett was Headmaster (1854-63) and (1868-71). He was Inspector Superintendent of Government Schools (1854-63). The Reverend Robert Gray became Headmaster in 1863 but was dismissed three years later for negligence. The Head School was finally closed in 1885.

THE HUSSEY CHARITY

In 1865 Rebecca Hussey left about £22,000 for a Charity for the Redemption of Slaves, to be administered by Trustees in London. The proceeds of the Charity were to be split between St Helena and Lagos. The Local Trustees on St Helena were the Bishop, the Colonial Secretary and four Trustees appointed by the Governor. One of the first Trustees was Eden Baker, father of the first St Helenian priest.

Rules made by the London Trustees for Schools on St Helena under the charity included the provisions that the masters and mistresses were to be members of the Church of England, and religious instruction should be that of the Church of England, but with provision for the withdrawal of pupils, if desired.

The Local Trustees purchased a house in Jamestown in 1866 from Messrs Solomon, Gideon & Co for £850 for use as a Town School, and engaged two certificated teachers from England, Mr and Mrs Hosking, as Master and Mistress of the Town School. They arrived in October 1866, but the Trustees were not entirely satisfied with the success of the school under Mr Hosking and he left in December 1867. His successor was engaged locally.

The Trustees also leased (later bought) Friar's Lodge from the Government, hoping to make it into a residential school for five children, but this did not materialize, and the Lodge was let. It was later sold to the somewhat eccentric Roman Catholic priest, Fr Daine.

The curriculum at the Town School included carpentry and tailoring for the boys and needlework for the girls.

Grants of £15 per year were made in 1868 to the parochial schools of High Peak and Longwood, on condition that a proportion of their pupils were African.

The Governor, 'looking at the exhausted condition of the Local Treasury' in 1870 asked the Trustees to take over the Government Evening School for Liberated Africans.

In 1861 the Church Society required the land on which Hutt's Gate School stood as the site for the new church. The parishioners built another school at a cost of £250, with accommodation for 100 children, on land leased from the Government. At this time, the Benevolent Society ceased their financial support to the school. The parishioners found its financial support an increasing burden and in 1872 the Hutt's Gate School was transferred to the Hussey Trustees. The Vicar, the Reverend J.C. Hands, became the Schoolmaster. Unhappily, in January 1880 we read that Mr Hands will lose £50 p.a. as master of Hussey Charity School, Longwood, since the 'school was unhappily a failure in his hands' and the Committee dispensed with his services.[8]

In 1876 a school was opened in the house 'next to Half Way House' in Half Tree Hollow.

The Evening School was closed in 1896. Mr Algernon Broadway was appointed Master of the Town School.

The Trustees resolved in 1902 to engage a certificated teacher from England for the Town School.

TWENTIETH-CENTURY DEVELOPMENTS

In 1901 there were nine elementary schools on the island, as follows:

GOVERNMENT

Town Boys	90 pupils	
Town Girls	100 pupils	
Town Infants	42 pupils	
Country Mixed	90 pupils	Total 322 pupils

HUSSEY CHARITY

Town Mixed	62 pupils	
Half Tree Hollow }		
Hutt's Gate }	120 pupils	Total 182 pupils

BENEVOLENT SOCIETY

Town Mixed	45 pupils	
Sandy Bay	65 pupils	Total 110 pupils

Canon Porter, who was Inspector of Schools, writing in the *St Helena*

Diocesan Magazine, complains that there was great irregularity of attendance, compared with 40 years previously. However, in November 1902 it was announced that the Ordinance of 1874 which secured compulsory school attendance between the ages of 9 and 12 years was to be enforced. In March 1903 he reported great improvement in attendance. In that year, education was made compulsory for all children between the ages of 6 and 14.

In 1900 no school had any industrial training, except for the Hussey Town School, with its carpentry class.

Most children left school at 13 or 14, whether they could read and write or not, and Canon Porter pressed the need for a more advanced class for those who could profit by it –'But at present this is out of the question, yet one to be considered and kept in mind.'

The Benevolent Town School was in danger of collapsing and was closed for two months in 1901 for repairs. Classes were held instead in St John's School Room above the church, at that time used for Sunday School and Choir Vestry.

The Governor asked Bishop Holmes to make an enquiry into education on the island, and in January 1903 the Bishop presented his report which was forwarded to the Colonial Secretary. Perhaps it was the first of many reports! The Bishop was concerned at the apathy of parents towards the education of their children.

At the Synod in September 1903, Bishop Holmes said: 'The state of Education is a cause for anxiety to all thinking men. Notwithstanding the fact that there are, and have been for many years, 8 or 9 schools on the island. education is at a very low level.'

By 1904 High Peak School had been in ruins for some time and children had to walk 4 miles to the Country School.

The three Government Town Schools had been regrouped into two mixed schools, Junior and Senior, by 1906. The total number of pupils in all island schools was 625, about the same as in 1901, but now 282 in Government Schools and 343 in Hussey and Benevolent Society Schools.

The Superintendent of Schools from 1904 to 1909 was Mr Leslie Tucker. He instituted courses in teaching method for pupil teachers and was evidently a disciplinarian. He is remembered, as Mrs Joan Thomas records in her *Two Great Educationists in the early 1900s*, for his method of punishment for boys. He would put them part way through the window, and pull down the upper sash window on to their backs to hold them in a good position for caning. He introduced Shakespeare as a way of improving diction. Mrs Thomas also records that during his time one of his pupils, Eva Fagan, won the prize, Lord Meath's Cup, for an essay on the British Empire, open to all schools in the Empire. Tucker was succeeded as Superintendent of Education by Canon Walcott. Walcott also held weekly classes in Teacher Training.

Bishop Holbech asked the Hussey Charity in 1906 to build a school at Blue Hill (the present Blue Hill Community Centre). Once built the running of the school was to be in the hands of the Bishop. It became known as the Bishop Holbech Memorial School.

The Benevolent Society Town School was absorbed into the Hussey Charity Town School in 1908.

The Hussey Charity Trustees in 1909 followed the precedent of the Government and the Benevolent Society in charging the pupils at their three schools, one penny a week.

The reorganization of St Helena education in 1941 brought to an end the long history of the Church's provision of schooling. Under the Schools Amalgamation Ordinance, with the agreement of the Bishop and the Trustees of the Hussey Charity and the Benevolent Society, the five Church schools, – the Bishop Holbech Memorial School at Blue Hill, owned by the Diocese, and the schools at Jamestown, Half Tree Hollow, Hutt's Gate and Sandy Bay, owned by the Hussey Charity and the Benevolent Society, were handed over to the Government. Canon Walcott did not approve. Provision was made for right of entry into the Schools by the Bishop or Vicar for religious instruction, and for the attendance of pupils at Church services on Ash Wednesday and Ascension Day. In 1941, education was made compulsory for all children between the ages of 5 and 15.

While the Church might be proud of the contribution she had made to elementary education on the island, the task had become beyond her financial resources. Indeed, in 1935 Archdeacon Warner had reported that 'the state of Buildings and Materials of Church Schools is terribly deficient', and had added that 'the poorest children at the Schools are supplied every day with a small loaf of bread, paid for by funds subscribed by Church people'.[9] The standard of both Government and Church Schools at the time of the amalgamation can perhaps be gauged from the Colonial Report of 1948, even though this was written a few years later.

The average standard of knowledge and attainment in school subjects of pupil teachers now being recruited at the age of 15, is that of an English child at the age of 11. Candidates for pupil teachers are always forthcoming but among many of these there is a regrettable lack of seriousness of purpose and willingness to study; for most, teaching is merely the best-paid and most attractive job available in the Island until a domestic appointment with free passage can be secured overseas.

In 1948 13 local teachers left the Department of Education most of them to take up domestic employment in England. The teacher to pupil ratio was one to 45.

The teachers who did stay laid the foundation for the vast improvement which we see today. Teachers and trainees are well motivated and devoted (although no longer in the best paid jobs). The teacher to pupil ratio is better than 1 to 20. The inauguration of the Secondary Selective School led to the achievement of GCE O-Levels and the first beginnings of A-Levels. The British Government finally agreed in 1984, after some 16 years of pressure from the St Helena Education Department, to build a Central School on Francis Plain, and at his visit in April that year, HRH Prince Andrew graciously agreed to give his name to the school. The Prince Andrew School was officially opened on 5 June 1989 and will provide further opportunities both in the academic field and in vocational training. Tribute must be paid to the splendid work of Mr Basil George, the Chief Education Officer, in his planning and execution of the scheme, ably supported by his staff and by the members of the Education Committee. Tribute is also due to the work of the 'St Helena Link' with the College of St Paul and St Mary, Cheltenham. But these are developments outside the scope of this chapter, which is confined to the contribution to education made by the Church.

Today the clergy visit the schools periodically for assemblies, and in some cases, by invitation, assist with the teaching of religious education, both in schools and to teacher trainees. One of the clergy, first Michael Houghton and then John Ryder, was appointed as School Chaplain to the Prince Andrew School. Peter Cowen and Michael Houghton together with Mrs Exina Thomas, were invited by Mr John Birchall, the first Headmaster, to join him in writing the Religious Education Curriculum. Until 1989 it was usual for the Governor to invite the Bishop to sit on the Education Committee.

Friendly Societies

With no old age pensions, the Friendly Societies were founded in the 19th century to provide sickness, death and old age benefits in return for a weekly subscription. The oldest, the Mechanics, was founded in 1838, the St Helena Poor Society in 1847, the Foresters in 1871, and the St Helena Workingman's Christian Association in 1873. Two Societies

The Children's Benevolent Society annual meeting on Holy Innocents Day

were founded under the guidance of the clergy, the Church Provident Society for Women in 1878, today by far the largest of the Societies, and the Church Benefit Society for Children, with its annual Church Service on Holy Innocents Day, founded by Mr J.E.Watson. The Bishop preached at their Centenary Service in 1987 which was celebrated by a large number with a centenary lunch and sports in the Mule Yard. Today they continue to satisfy a need, and their annual general meetings are preceded by a service in church, to which they parade, with band, banners and regalia.

The St Helena African Benefit Society was founded in 1865 by Mr Thomas Goodwin, but is, of course, no longer in existence.

Roman Catholic and Nonconformist Churches (1819-1991)

THE ROMAN CATHOLIC CHURCH IN ST HELENA

Two Roman Catholic priests, the Abbé Antonio Buonavita and the Abbé Ange Vignali arrived in September 1819 to minister to Napoleon and his entourage. Buonavita was not in good health and he left in March 1821 in the *Orwell*. Vignali administered Extreme Unction to Napoleon and conducted the Burial Service. St James' Burial Register shows:

May 9th 1821. Napoleon Buonaparte, late Emperor of France, he died on the 5th instant at the old House at Longwood, and was interred on Mr Richard Torbett's estate.

Vignali left on 27 May 1821 on the *Camel*.

From 1852 a succession of Roman Catholic priests was sent as Chaplains to the garrison. Fr McCarthy, the first one, recorded the name of a French priest who died on his way back to France. The present church in Jamestown was built in 1852 and in that year Bishop Raymond Griffith, Vicar Apostolic of the Cape of Good Hope, came to administer Confirmation to 33 people. In all there were about 20 RC Military Chaplains. When the garrison was withdrawn in 1906 these Chaplains were also withdrawn. Fr Brendan Sullivan concluded from the Register entries that in this period the ministry of the RC priests was mainly to the garrison and 'little contact seems to have been made with the local people.'

However, this can hardly be true of the last of these priests, the somewhat eccentric Fr J.H.Daine (1891-1906), who, it was said, claimed to be related to the Portuguese Royal family. He lived first at Maldivia and later at Friar's Lodge, which he bought from the Benevolent Society. With a view to improving the island's economy, he carried out experiments in growing cotton, planting about an acre at the Briars, and also in breeding silkworms, in both of which he seems to have been surprisingly knowledgeable. He obtained silkworm eggs from the Roman Catholic Bishop at the Cape and also from France, and planted mulberry cuttings. Fr Daine believed that both projects could become cottage industries, but sadly, like so many other experiments on St Helena, they came to nothing.

For the next 50 years there were only occasional visits by RC priests until in 1957 the RC Archbishop of Cape Town sent the Reverend Jarlath Gough OFM Cap, who stayed for six years. He restored the Church of the Sacred Heart in Jamestown. By 1963, the average attendance at Sunday Mass was 17 on St Helena and 12 on Ascension.

Roman Catholic Church of the Sacred Heart, Jamestown (David Bentham)

Fr Gough was succeeded in 1963 by Fr Kelly SDB (Salesians of Don Bosco) who was to stay for 15 years, until 1978. He had previously spent four years on the Falklands. Fr Kelly continued to visit Ascension periodically, where the changing population meant a fluctuation in the number of Roman Catholics. On St Helena, about ten attended Sunday Mass. In 1977 an RC Matron, Miss Fitzgerald was appointed to the General Hospital, and the Archbishop of Cape Town made her an Assistant Minister of the Eucharist so that she could communicate herself and others, when the priest was on Ascension.

Fr Kelly was succeeded by Fr Peter Paul Feeney OP, who spent a year from August 1979 to 1980. During his time, and that of his successor, there was a growing friendly relationship between the RC and Anglican Churches, and indeed other Churches on the island.

Fr Feeny was followed by Fr Philip Bruggeman MHM (Mill Hill Mission), a Dutchman, who stayed from July 1981 until 1985, with a brief time in the Falklands in 1984. Fr Philip paid five visits to Ascension, spending some 12 months there in all, the number of RCs on Ascension being much in excess of those on St Helena. Fr Philip continued the ecumenical spirit of his predecessor. His manual skills contributed much to the beautifying of his church, and his Christmas cribs were a work of art. He left in February 1985.

A Vatican decree dated 18 August 1986 (the feast day of St Helena in the Western Calendar), designated the three islands of St Helena, Ascension and Tristan a 'mission sui iuris', that is a mission territory not forming part of any apostolic vicariate or prefecture. Previously they had formed part of the Archdiocese of Cape Town. The Mill Hill Missionaries based in London and already working in the Falklands were asked to look after all four South Atlantic Islands. The Apostolic Prefect in the South Atlantic was Monsignor Anton Agreiter MHM, who visited St Helena in 1986.

Fr Joseph Holznecht MHM was based in St Helena from May 1988 to February 1989. He was succeeded in December 1989 by Fr Brendan Sullivan MHM. The relations between the RCs and the other churches continued to be marked by friendship and co-operation.

NONCONFORMIST CHURCHES IN ST HELENA

It was in the 1760s that one Thomas Payne arrived among a fresh batch of recruits to the St Helena Regiment. He was an ardent Methodist, who may well in England have listened to John Wesley's preaching, and he lost no time in seeking to convert his fellow soldiers, holding regular prayer meetings. Although he rose to the rank of Sergeant, he was eventually dismissed the service for refusal to obey orders which he claimed were contrary to his conscience, and was sent back to England. He became a popular evangelist in the North of England and was accepted into the Ministry in 1772 at the Leeds Methodist Conference.[10] When he died in 1783, John Wesley paid tribute: 'he was an honest zealous man; fearing neither men nor devils.'

THE BAPTIST CHURCH

The reader will recall from Chapter 1 the Evangelical Anglican influence among the Service Officers during the time of Napoleon's captivity. There is evidence of a similar Baptist influence among the soldiers, in a letter written from St Helena on 18 September 1817 by J–.N–. to a Baptist minister, the Reverend G.C.Smith of Penzance, Cornwall, and published in 1820 by D.Cox of Southwark under the title *Good News from Calcutta and St Helena*:

On my arrival here, I could find only one man who was a professed Dissenter, and appeared to enjoy the love of Christ in his soul. His name is G–. He was formerly a soldier in the St Helena corps, but he is now free from the army ... You may suppose we soon got acquainted, and determined to do something for Christ on St Helena ... Previous to our arrival, there was no meeting in which to assemble for the worship of God; but as soon as we came, this servant of the

Lord readily opened his dwelling house for regular preaching and praying. I rejoice to say, the house will now hardly contain the number who generally attend; so that we are about to take down a partition, which will throw two large rooms into one, and greatly enlarge our borders. I am sorry, however, to say, that notwithstanding the blessing of the Lord that evidently appears, and the reformation that has taken place in the lives of many on this Island, yet the glorious privileges granted to Dissenters and Methodists in other places under the sway of the British sceptre, are not so fully enjoyed by the civilized inhabitants of St Helena. Those of us in a military life cannot be debarred from them, so that we have abundant reasons for thankfulness to God and respect for our Government. We have lately drawn up a petition to the Governor and Council of the Island, concerning the privileges of Dissenters and Methodists, (in an Act of Parliament passed in 1812 ...) but they declined granting the privileges of licence, &c. as specified in this Act. They did not however forbid our assembling to worship God according to the dictates of our consciences, and as our regiment is providentially divided into three divisions, and stationed in three different parts of the Island, the service of Jesus, the great captain of our salvation, is now carried on in each place, and by each division ... our congregation is chiefly of the lower class ...

The formal Baptist Church on St Helena dates from the arrival of a Scot, the Reverend James McGregor Bertram who came from Cape Town in July 1845 on the *Velox*, the Captain, James Adams, having offered him a free passage. He preached at first in the house of Mr James Morris who was the leader of a small prayer group of four or five people. When it became clear that a larger room was needed Mrs Janisch, a widow, offered the use of her parlour. Her son Hudson Ralph Janisch, later to be the only island born Governor, at first objected to their home being used as a 'meeting house', but was impressed by Bertram's teaching and became a Baptist. (Mrs Janisch's husband, Georg Wilhelm, had been on Hudson Lowe's staff in Germany and later in St Helena, where he bought Miss Mason's house and renamed it Teutonic Hall.)

In September 1845, helped by another offer by Captain Adams of a free passage, and a collection by local people, Mrs Bertram and her two children were able to join her husband.

The Baptists purchased a Mission House in 1846 for £550. In 1848 Bertram welcomed the Reverend Jonathan Wade and his wife, of the American Baptist Board for Foreign Missions, for a three month visit. It was during their visit that the first public baptism by immersion took place on 2 April 1848 and on that day Hudson Janisch was ordained a minister and became co-pastor with Bertram.

By 1849 there were four 'preaching posts' – Jamestown, Sandy Bay,

Rose Bower and Longwood. There were also Sunday schools at Jamestown, Sandy Bay, Half Tree Hollow and Levelwood, and Day schools at Jamestown and Sandy Bay.

Colonel Trelawney, the Governor, was sympathetic to Bertram, and Captain Mapleton, the Chief Magistrate, invited him to preach at Sandy Bay, where Mr and Mrs Lambe allowed him the use of their house. But there was also considerable opposition. It will be recalled that even in 1816, the East India Company, anticipating the changed situation with the increase of the military, had written to Sir Hudson Lowe:

We cannot but contemplate the great change which is about to take place ... in the ... varieties of religious persuasions, as fraught with the most serious consequencies ... The subversion of the Established Church we should consider as an evil of incalculable magnitude.[11]

One can only regret Bishop Gray's reaction during his first visit in 1849:

Unfortunately for the first time schism began in this island two or three years ago, by an emissary from the Cape, and I find him now in full confidence of success. He has started a church of his own and is an Anabaptist on principle. His success is chiefly with the poor, and he is a thorn in the side of the Church.

The reader may recall the appalling moral and social situation in Jamestown in the 1840s, recounted by Kitching (see Chapter 1). Kitching went on to write:

Knowledge of these conditions was not, of course, confined only to St Helena, and it is not a matter for surprise, therefore, that the Island should have come to be regarded as a fruitful field for spiritual endeavour. In 1845 ... a Baptist Minister arrived and his work was very soon to shake the Established Church to its foundations.[12]

There was, indeed, an enormous field for ministry to the deprived, and Bertram soon attracted numbers of the poor to the Baptist Church by his preaching and ministry. There was so much to be done, that it is sad that the sectarian temper of the age did not encourage co-operation rather than confrontation.

The American Presbyterian Edwin Hatfield, writing in 1853 an account of Bertram's ministry is scathing of the Anglican clergy.[13] Their preaching was 'destitute of power and life, if not of godliness.' He speaks of the people of Sandy Bay,'the poor neglected population of this remote valley, for whose spiritual welfare none had cared ... all at once they [the Anglicans] made the discovery that there were souls to be

Baptist Church, Jamestown (David Bentham)

cared for in the secluded valleys of St Helena.' This is not entirely fair. (It is not clear whether the sentiments are those of Hatfield or Bertram.) It is indeed likely that the two Anglican clergy had not been able to provide adequate care for the scattered population in the remote areas, but Kempthorne had designed the school at Sandy Bay so that it could be used as a church and by 1849 the Benevolent Society had schools at Hutt's Gate as well as Sandy Bay. Some missionary work was done among the Africans and by the time of Bishop Claughton, a considerable amount. However, writing of St John's, Claughton admits: 'I have a great many negroes landed some years ago for whom nothing was done (as we are trying to do).'[14] But by 1860 there seems to have been a decided improvement in relations, and Claughton could write 'I have every reason to be satisfied with the spirit in which I have hitherto been met by all classes, not excepting our Dissenting brethren.'[15] And the following year, when he had been preaching in Jamestown in the open air, he was 'much gratified ... by the Baptist preacher posting himself at my side'.[16] This surely refers to Bertram.

Bishop Welby felt the growing pressure of Baptist influence more acutely and wrote to the Archbishop of Canterbury in 1867 that he could not attend the Lambeth conference because 'the number of clergymen at present on the island being insufficient for the work, a large share of parochial duty devolves upon me', and to attend would 'leave one parish ... exposed to be seduced from our Communion by the Baptists, who are numerous and influential on this island.'[17]

Bertram was Pastor until 1868, save for the two years, 1850 to 1852, when he travelled to the Cape and to America to raise funds. Amongst other works of mercy, Hatfield pays tribute to Bertram's concern for the released slaves in Rupert's Valley.

The story of the Baptist Church up to 1957 has been told by the Reverend Wilfred Edmunds, in his book *An Isolated Family*[18] and will only be summarized here. However, the present Baptist minister, the Reverend Andrew Coats, has kindly pointed out to me that when Edmunds gives the membership in 1870 as 352, this figure actually refers to the 352nd baptism by immersion to have taken place, and the correct number of members that year was 205, to fall to 118 by 1871.

Hudson Janisch died on 19 March 1884 and his memorial can be seen today in the Baptist Knollcombe cemetery. Bertram's successor, W.J. Clother, left the following year, and an appeal for help was sent to the great Baptist Charles Spurgeon. He replied that he would try

to send out a suitable man to you. It may be that I can only send a brother for a year, but, in that case, I will bear the charge of passage for another at the end of that time.

In 1899 the Church was affiliated to the Baptist Union of South Africa.

In 1900 the first Boer prisoners arrived, with their Chaplain, the Reverend J.R. Albertyn of the Dutch Reformed Church. The Baptist Minister, the Reverend Thomas Aitken, welcomed him and invited him to preach in Jamestown. Some of the prisoners were Baptists. When many Boers died following an outbreak of typhoid, the Baptists offered them a piece of their own ground at Knollcombe, just below the

Baptist Church, Sandy Bay (David Bentham)

Baptist Chapel, as a cemetery. Thomas Aitken left in 1905 and became Baptist Union Secretary (1919-35) and was President in 1917.

There were 12 Pastors between 1845 and 1918, but when the Reverend W.D. Morris left that year, there were not enough funds to invite a successor and for the next 40 years the Church was led by Lay Pastors. Alfred Nicholls, who had come to St Helena in 1904 as an Army Sergeant, and who later became Police Superintendent, offered to become a self-supporting Pastor, and continued as such for 20 years until 1938. In 1934 he was awarded the MBE, and in the same year the South African Baptist Union made him an accredited Minister. A St Helenian, Mr William Benjamin served faithfully as the Pastor from 1939 to 1958. The first South African minister, Eric Hayward, came with his wife in 1958 for three years. Since then the Church has been served almost continuously by Pastors from overseas. From the welcome the present writer and his wife received when they arrived on the island in 1979 from the Reverend Michael Longstaff and his wife Norma, it was evident that over the years the Churches had grown closer together. It remains, however, largely determined by the individual clergy.

Today the Baptists number about 50. They have four attractive stone Churches, but the raising of money for their maintenance and repair is not easy. One is in Jamestown by the Manse; Knollcombe was built in 1875; Sandy Bay is the most isolated, in an area of barren rock, which has a beauty of its own; and Head-of-Wain Chapel was built in 1918.

THE SALVATION ARMY

The Salvation Army[19] on St Helena dates from 5 May 1884 when HMS *Opal* called. Some sailors led by one Jack Bashard, who had themselves been recently converted in Cape Town, held an open-air meeting. Mr Thomas Woodman,[20] a former soldier and a Baptist, who had married and settled on the island and had been holding evangelistic meetings, offered them his house for cottage meetings. There followed a whirlwind mission, led by these sailors, and when they left the island five days later, 59 people had accepted Christ.[21] Eight months later a British Army soldier, who was a Salvationist, landed on the island and found Salvation Army meetings being held in many parts of the island. Thomas Woodman became the first corps sergeant-major with oversight of the corps at Half Tree Hollow. He continued to be an active Salvationist until his 'promotion to glory' in September 1895, at the age of 60. About 500 people, including the Governor, attended his funeral, at which the combined Salvation Army and St Helena bands played. He was buried in the Salvation Army cemetery, near St Paul's. The first Salvation Army property, the Victoria, Ladder Hill Corner, Jamestown, was bought by him in 1892.

Evidently once again Bishop Welby was far from welcoming, for in 1885 he wrote to SPG that

he was sorry he was unable to take advantage of the *Opal* to visit [Tristan] ... in consequence of the strenuous exertions made by a recently organized Salvation

Army, at first with some prospect of success, to draw off people from the Church, and the need of the utmost exertion to resist this attack.[22]

The Captain of the *Opal* later wrote that it would have been too rough for Welby, at the age of 84, to land anyway.

The first Officers to be appointed to the island were Captain and Mrs Harris, who arrived with their two children in November 1886. At six o'clock in the morning they were marched by Woodman and the delighted Salvationists from the wharf to the market place for an open air meeting![23] On one occasion, Captain Harris hired the market for a day, and no less than 1,000 people heard the Gospel.

Two women Officers, Captain Wilcox and Lieutenant Evans, were appointed in 1888. Sarah Wilcox was only 21, but had had experience of work in the East End of London, and was surprised to hear the Cockney dialect on St Helena, probably brought by seamen and St Helena Regiment recruits. She found her work was not only among the poor, but also among 'the rough sailors who came ashore from passing ships and the soldiers of the British Garrison'. Her visits to distant cottages were by donkey. After a posting to South Africa, she returned to St Helena in 1896 as Mrs Wallace Holt. In 1944 she broadcast on the BBC an account of her memories, later to be published in a book of *Travellers' Tales*.[24]

The written records of the Army on the island begin only in 1927. In that year a new Penitent Form was made and given by Corps Treasurer R.C. Quinn. Each year Solomons would give 15 pounds of bullock for distribution to poor Salvationists on Christmas Eve. We first read of the annual Self Denial, a worldwide appeal, and the local Silver Tree appeal, in 1930. The Silver Tree envelopes were printed by Canon Walcott. That year the Army asked the Government Secretary if they could hold an Armistice Service at the Cenotaph at 5 pm. Permission was given, since it would not clash with the Anglican service! Happily, by 1935 the Cenotaph service was a combined one with the Salvation Band playing. Seven Salvationists were on the Roll of Honour; Percy Broad and Cavalla Grey with the Australians, Edward Clifford with the South African Infantry and James Graham with the Heavy Artillery, George Scipio with the London Regiment, and Richard Scott and Edwin Joshua.

The young persons' treat on Francis Plain was first recorded in January 1931. In addition to the Sunday School, there were the Life Saving Sunbeams and Life Saving Chums for the younger children, and the Guards and Scouts for the older ones. Twenty Songsters were commissioned that year, and with the Band have been a source of evangelism and enjoyment ever since, as well as a training ground for musicians and singers. In August, four Officers received Long Service Badges. CSM J.Benjamin had been commissioned in 1896, RS Mrs J.Benjamin in 1901, Treasurer R.C.Quinn in 1908 and CS Mrs Fuller in 1923.

The Salvation Army was concerned with people living all over the island and as early as 1887 there had been five centres. A Home Company was launched at Blue Hill in 1933, and in 1938 a Home League, separate from Jamestown, was formed in Half Tree Hollow.

There was an important development in 1935 when Adjutant Townsend was invited to be a member of the Local Relief Board. He was also invited in May of that year to be the Defence Counsel in a murder trial. In thanking him the Governor said that it was due to his advocacy that the sentence had been reduced to four years, (later to be further reduced). This work as Counsel and as acting Probation Officer was to continue.

There have been a number of visits by Senior Officers. The Divisional Commander, Major Siebrits, visited with his wife in the late 1920s. In 1930, Commissioner J.de Grook conducted a Revival Campaign. In 1933 Commissioner and Mrs Turner led an island-wide campaign for eleven days. This was supported by Mr A.Nicholls, the lay Baptist pastor, who gave them the use of the Baptist Chapels and by the Bishop. Commissioner Turner obtained an annual grant from headquarters of, at first, £100 for work on the island. In 1936, Brigadier and Mrs H.C.Norman, Divisional Commander, came for a month to carry out an inspection. They stayed at the Consulate Hotel for 30 shillings a week, without board.

The 100th anniversary was celebrated in March 1984, with the visit of Colonel and Mrs Dinsdale Pender, the Salvation Army's Territorial Commander for Southern African Territory. A good number of clergy and members of other Churches accepted the warm invitation by the Commanding Officer, the American Captain Denis Strissel, to partici-pate. 'Look at the Bishop clapping his hands!' one woman observed in amazement. Colonel Pender's maternal grandparents Adjutant and Mrs Harry Widdowson were Salvation Army Officers on St Helena from 1900 to 1903. The next Territorial Commander, Commissioner Stanley Walter, and his wife visited the island in 1989. The welcome meeting was in St James' Anglican Church, the Women's meeting in the Jamestown Baptist Church and the Ministers' Fraternal in the Salvation Army quarters![25]

In 1980-82, there was no Officer for 21 months and the work was led

Salvation Army meeting in the country (Charles Frater)

by Corps Secretary Rebecca Fuller, who is commemorated on the 1984 Centenary stamp issue. Similarly Corps Secretary Gwen Yon was in charge for several months in 1984 and again in 1985 and 1990.

Today the Salvation Army on St Helena follows the teaching of its Founder, General William Booth, with a strong emphasis on Evangelism combined with a great concern for social work, especially with the aged and young people. The benefit of its work is felt far beyond its own members. It organizes a meals-on-wheels service, with some assistance from other Churches, and has a holiday camp at Rock Rose. Its centres are at Jamestown, Half Tree Hollow and Deadwood.

SEVENTH DAY ADVENTIST CHURCH
Some of the Boer prisoners were Seventh Day Adventists, but it was not until 1949 that the Cape Field Mission of the Seventh Day Adventists in Cape Town sent Pastor Hilgard P. Camphor and his family to St Helena. The church in Upper Jamestown was built in 1950. Since then there have been eight Pastors – the longest serving being Basil Kriel (1980-89); the present Pastor is Charles Chalmers. The Hall was completed in December 1988 and used for worship while the sanctuary was being repaired. Extensive alterations and enlargement to the

Church were completed in September 1990. Membership from 1957 to the present day has varied between 55 and 80.

Some members of the New Apostolic Church arrived on the island from Cape Town on 24 February 1989.

Other religious groups on the island include the Baha'i and the Jehovah's Witnesses.

In 1980 a Ministers' Fraternal was begun, meeting on the basis of a common acceptance of Jesus Christ as Lord and Saviour. Anglican, Roman Catholic, Baptist, Salvation Army and Seventh Day Adventist ministers have met monthly (with some gaps due to comings and goings), to share in fellowship, for Bible Study, to discuss matters of common concern on the island and to grow together in Christ. We may thank God for the change in the relationship from earlier days. There were large ecumenical services at St James' at Pentecost 1986, the BBC World Service broadcast from St Paul's on 21 May 1989, and also at St Paul's on 1 April 1990 before Bishop Stradling left.

Part II

Ascension (1815-1991)

Ascension Island from Green Mountain

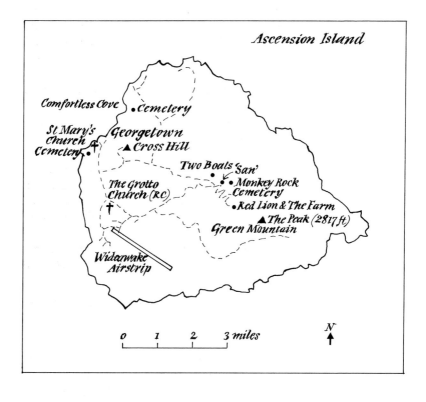

Ascension Island lies about 700 miles north-west of St Helena. Its area is 34 square miles, and except for Green Mountain, which rises to 2,800 feet and whose top is covered with trees and vegetation, the island is barren rock and ash, with 44 major craters and six large lava flows. The Wideawake or Sooty Tern breeds in large numbers every ten months, the females laying their eggs on the bare rock. The Green Turtle, which lives off the coast of Brazil, swims every two to four years over 1,000 miles to Ascension, where, after mating offshore, the females lay their eggs on the beaches, before returning to Brazil. When they hatch, the baby turtles scurry down to the sea, and swim or drift on the current to Brazil.

The island was named 'Concepción' when it was discovered by Joao da Nova Castella in 1501; the name Ascension was probably given by Alphonse D'Albuquerque in 1503. For over 300 years the island was not occupied, except by visitors and castaways, but in 1815 it was garrisoned by the Royal Navy and Royal Marines to prevent the French from using it as a base from which to attempt to rescue Napoleon from St Helena. After Napoleon's death in 1821, the garrison continued, but now its function was to victual the naval ships engaged in suppressing the West African slave trade and to receive any fever victims from their crews.

Naturally with a Service establishment, Sunday worship was regularly held, at first in the open air. According to the diary of General Simon Fraser RMLI:

On Sundays, we all assembled in the veranda of the barracks, that being the largest, and the Commandant or Adjutant read prayers and a sermon. Just before we left, however, the foundation of a Church was laid.

The barracks mentioned is the present Exiles Club. The cornerstone of the church was laid on 6 September 1843 by Mrs Dwyer, the wife of the Commandant; the occasion is commemorated by a brass plate in the church porch. The first Royal Naval Chaplain, the Reverend George Bellamy, arrived in 1844 and found problems over the building of the church due to alterations in the plans by the authorities. In 1845 the Commandant was instructed by the Admiralty to 'cause the Church now in progress at Ascension to be enlarged by advancing the walls eight or ten feet at the entrance end and to proceed with its completion as soon as possible.'[1] It is not clear whether this was complied with by adding the 7 foot 6 inch long porch at the west end, or by lengthening the nave to its present 61 feet. Some of the materials had been used to roof the school house, which was being used as a church, and there was delay until more materials were received from England. But by 1847 the main body of the Church was completed, making it the second oldest existing Anglican Church in the Diocese, second only to St James' on St Helena. By 1852, contingency plans were laid in the event of an episcopal visit: 'It would be proper in the case of any Bishop of the Protestant established Church visiting this island to receive him with a salute of eleven guns on landing.'[2] Whether Bishop Claughton received such a salute when he arrived in April 1861 in HMS *Buffalo* is not recorded, but he certainly wrote appreciatively of his reception by the Commandant, Captain W. F. Burnett.[3]

Claughton consecrated the Church of St Mary the Virgin on Ascension Day, 9 May 1861. It is clear from the Petition for the Consecration and the Deed of Consecration[4] itself that the land on which the church stands was granted by the Lords Commissioners of the Admiralty for ecclesiastical use to the Bishops of St Helena, and indeed this would have been a necessary requirement before the church could be consecrated. The church site, together with the burial grounds and possibly the Vicarage, are the only pieces of freehold land on the island.

Claughton's comment on the church – 'although it is not a very ecclesiastical edifice, it shows very creditably among the white houses of the Garrison'[5] – perhaps reflects a Victorian idea that only English church architecture is really suitable, even on a volcanic island. Mrs Gill, wife of the astronomer David Gill, visiting in 1877, made a similar comment: 'There is little of the ecclesiastical in its exterior, except it be the primitive belfry, containing a single unmelodious bell which is rung in rather a primitive way by pulling the clapper. The outside walls are of an ochre yellow, flecked with green jalousies, which shade the glassless windows.'[6] Perhaps it was the colour that seemed unecclesiastical? The writer once heard its architecture described as 'Toy Town Gothic' which, to the modern eye, seems remarkably apt![7]

It was during this visit that Claughton consecrated the cemeteries at Dead Man's Beach, Georgetown, and at Monkey Rock on Green Mountain.[8] He wrote that he went up the Mountain in a cart drawn by two mules and that Cape Periwinkle was growing in profusion.[9] Monkey Rock was the cemetery for the Hospital – the 'San' – completed in 1867 and now the Administrator's residence. Claughton also consecrated the 'Bonetta' cemetery at Comfortless Cove. This last cemetery dates from about 1838, when HMS *Bonetta* brought cases of yellow fever to the island and they were quarantined at what was then named Comfort Cove. The victims were left to look after themselves,

St Mary's Church (Reverend Richard Davison)

food being left for them and a musket fired as a signal. In 1865 HMS *Archer* brought yellow fever victims and the Chaplain, James Robinson noted in the Burial Register that he was not allowed to attend the burials because of the strict quarantine. Five victims were buried at Monkey Rock by Dr Cowen and two at the Bonetta cemetery by the Commandant, Captain Martin. Chaplain Alwyne Rice noted in the Burial Register in 1894 that HMS *Phoebe* arrived with 120 fever cases after coming from the West Coast of Africa where she 'had been engaged in a campaign against native tribes'. The hospital, schoolroom and Commodore's cottage were full, but only six burials on the island are recorded.

The Georgetown cemetery, with its rows of graves each covered with a heap of barren lava rocks, has a grim dignity of its own, but the Bonetta cemetery, hidden away in the middle of a completely barren lava flow, is a salutary place to visit.

Some years after the Bishop's visit, a doubt appears to have arisen as to whether a portion of Georgetown cemetery amounting to 19.8 poles had been included in the ground consecrated by the Bishop. Chaplain James Robinson accordingly measured the cemetery and showed that it had indeed all been consecrated.[10]

Georgetown Cemetery

Robinson complained that the church was ill-designed for a tropical climate. It accommodated only 250 people, which was too small for a community of about 500. The Commandant, Captain Bickford, forwarded his complaint to the Commander-in-Chief, who, as might have been expected, declined to recommend any further expenditure.[11]

There followed a period of repair and embellishment of the church. Chaplain G. E. Waller recorded:

In 1872 the Revd J. T. Westroff removed the old Pulpit and Reading Desk and replaced them by a Lectern (the new Reading Desk was added, I believe, by the Rev W. A. Richmond). Mr Westroff also removed the old pews and replaced them by the present open seats. The Altar, altar rails etc. were also then added by him. To this work, which was in progress when I joined the island as Chaplain in August 1872 I added the seat in what may be called the chancel, at present used by the Lieut of Marines, and the front which separates this part of the Church from the rest.[12]

This could imply that the 'chancel' was a portion of the nave, suitably separated, although the reference to the Lieutenant of Marines is obscure.

A Cambridge Paragraph Bible (still in the church), together with a Prayer Book and a large Hymns Ancient & Modern, all bound in

Comfortless Cove 'Bonetta' Cemetery

Russian leather, were bought in 1874. Two brass three-candle standard lamps, made in the Bronze Statue Foundry, Thames Ditton, Surrey, were purchased by the Island Fund in 1876, together with 18 spare glass shades, at a total cost of £13 14s 6d, including £2 for a zinc-lined case. A further four candle standards were bought in the following year.[13] Some of the spare shades are still in the church vestry. It would be interesting to know the present whereabouts of the six standards. Possibly they were removed when electric light was installed in 1924.

Chaplain H. W. Millett fixed an alms box in the porch in 1877, and also a brass plate commemorating the laying of the foundation stone, which had been accidentally discovered. He designed a mahogany pulpit which was made by a marine carpenter. He also fixed 20 bracket candle lamps, of which eight have survived.[14]

Another brass plate in the porch records: '1879-80 This Church was restored and chancel built'. There is no record of this restoration or the building of a chancel in the parish or diocesan records, and unfortunately the plan originally attached to the petition to have the church consecrated is missing. The Deed of Consecration gives the dimensions as 32 feet by 71 feet. The present external lengths are: chancel 11 feet, nave 61 feet and porch 7 feet 6 inches. The porch is probably original, since the small tower and spire are built over it, and there is no mention of their subsequent construction. We have seen that it was in existence in 1877. It may also be significant that decorative mitres are fixed to the roofs of the porch and nave, but not to the chancel roof, suggesting that the chancel may have been built later. Since nave plus porch measure only 68 feet 6 inches, it is possible that the original Church had a small recess at the east end to accommodate the altar, but this is speculation. A photograph in the Ascension Historical Society Museum, showing the interior of the church decorated for Christmas, and possibly dated 1879 or 1880, shows a chancel with an altar, but the depth of the chancel cannot be judged.

The Registers contain a touching personal note concerning the Chaplain John MacGregor, who on 24 July 1880 took advantage of the visit of F. A. J. Gace, Chaplain of HMS *London*, to marry Miss Anne Halifax. One wonders how long they had had to wait![15]

The tessellated pavement in the sanctuary was laid in 1895 and the brass eagle lectern bought in 1896. The old imitation stained glass in the east window, consisting of a coloured transparent design sandwiched between two sheets of glass, was replaced by genuine stained glass, of a geometrical design, in 1899.[16] The oak litany desk was given on Christmas Day 1899 by Mrs Arthur Dawson, presumably the Chaplain's mother. The stone font was presented by the congregation on Easter Day 1900, and the brass ewer was given by children of the island in July.[17]

Another major restoration occurred in 1901 when a concrete floor was laid. In addition, 'The walls having been badly built at first, salt water having been used, were always breaking out and looking dilapidated ... A large portion of the interior surface was removed and the whole thickly covered with good cement.'[18] The salt water still causes trouble, and has affected some of the marble tablets. There are 24 mural tablets commemorating personnel of the Royal Navy and Royal Marines who died between 1836 and 1909 (see Appendix B).

For 61 years, from 1844 until 1905 the Garrison was served by a succession of 21 Naval Chaplains. From 1861 these Chaplains were licensed by the Bishop of St Helena and referred problems and matters of ecclesiastical discipline to him. These could be various indeed. Thus John Cavanagh in 1885, in a letter concerning Baptism returns, refers to two men of the Merchant Service 'murdered by the Captain of their ship'.

Cavanagh had a somewhat sardonic sense of humour. The American organ was giving trouble.

For year after year, the tuners (bandsmen from visiting ships), who as a rule visited the island once a year, regretfully but firmly declined to touch the organ … pleading … that they knew nothing about these modern American organs. This was honest on their part, if disappointing to us. They knew they would but make matters worse … We had a melancholy illustration of this truth in July 1885. The *Boadicea* called here … The tuner … came on shore to tune all the pianos on the island … I asked him to do something for the American organ in the Church and after making many excuses … he at last … said 'he'd have a look at it.' He had the look but alas for the organ the note on which he concentrated all his powers of eye and hand has been silent ever since. Its just as well the *Boadicea* left before he had time to have a second look, as a 2nd look would have doubtless been fatal to a 2nd note.

Accordingly, Cavanagh opened a subscription list and ordered a 15-stop Alexander harmonium catalogued at £50. While they were waiting for the harmonium to arrive, the Admiral visited the island. At lunch, Mrs Cavanagh, who was the organist, asked him if they might expect a subscription from him.

He at once replied that he would be most happy to subscribe etc. etc … I forwarded a copy [of the subscription list] to the Admiral reminding him of his promise and asking him to remit his subscription to the Chaplain of the Fleet to save time. To this communication I received no reply, but I have heard indirectly that in a private letter to Captain Napier the Admiral was good and liberal enough to say that he felt in no way called upon to subscribe to our harmonium but that if there should be a deficit, it was to be supplied from the Island Fund. The deficit has been supplied from the Offertory … and when I suggested to the Captain that this amount (£2 13s 6d) should be given from the Island Fund to the Offertory he disregarded the suggestion, being of the opinion that the offertory should be expended on the Church and objects in the Island, instead of going to support two excellent charities (Service Orphan Schools at Devonport and Portsmouth) to which it has been in great part devoted for some years past … But this only shows the value of a promise. 'Put not your trust in Princes' – Psalm 146.

Cavanagh goes on to give the Admiral's name. It is sad to learn that there was opposition to such money going off the island. Captain Napier had used money from the Island Fund to erect a salt water fountain of doubtful value in Georgetown. Cavanagh concludes by commenting:

Captain Napier having taken it into his head to erect a fountain in Garrison, and having unfortunately the sole management and disbursement of the Island Fund, lavishes it on his font to the utter neglect of everything connected with the Church.[19]

The new harmonium eventually arrived in 1888 in time to be placed in the church on Sexagesima Sunday. The old organ was sold for £5 and the money used to buy an alms dish.

Cavanagh's successor, Arthur Hill, also found himself at odds with Captain Napier. Napier claimed the right to take services himself in St Mary's in the absence of a Chaplain, just as would the Captain of a ship, but Hill maintained that the Chaplain must be asked on each occasion. Hill wrote to Bishop Welby asking for a ruling. Perhaps it was coincidence that in July 1889 Napier wrote to Hill that he had informed the Commander-in-Chief that: 'Mr Hill has not in my opinion been in all respects an influence for good on the Island.' However, Hill remained as Chaplain until December 1890, and in March 1890 he was able to write to the Bishop thanking him for his help: 'As regards the performance of Divine Service there is no longer any dispute – the matter was settled in accordance with your Lordship's letter.' Whether Captain Napier would have expressed it quite in that way is questionable![20]

The celebration of Holy Communion on Green Mountain 'in any fit and convenient room or building' was authorized by Bishop Welby in March 1889,[21] and such celebrations have continued up to the present time. Services had, however, been held on Green Mountain since at least 1865; a minute of that year states: 'whenever the Chaplain is not present at the Mountain on Sunday the Chief Gardener is to lead Morning Prayers ... should he be a Roman Catholic the next in seniority is to perform the duties.'[22]

Labour on the island was provided by Kroomen from the Gold Coast and liberated slaves from West Africa, and a Confirmation by Bishop Claughton in May 1861 had included 34 African labourers, servants and cooks. Claughton's pastoral care is shown in his dealing with some Africans who had been taught by Wesleyans in Sierra Leone, which led one of them to say, 'I was taught by Wesleyans, and am a Wesleyan; but I wish to belong to the whole Church and to be confirmed. I shall tell the Wesleyans this when I go back.' It is good to see the evidence that the Naval Chaplains were concerned with this aspect of their ministry. Bishop Welby wrote to SPG in 1882 that the Naval Chaplain George M. Sutton had been carrying on his interesting work among the Kroomen employed by the Admiralty and had baptized nine of them. But Sutton lamented the departure of most of them in consequence of reduction in the Admiralty establishment.[23] Cavanagh baptized 12 Kroomen in 1887.[24] It is evident that some St Helenians were working on the island in 1890, since Chaplain Arthur Hill in a letter refers to his

Roman Catholic 'Grotto' Church (1980)

servant Alexander Duncan and his friend, both from St Helena and who both come to Holy Communion and are in the choir. As a result of an insurrection of the Kroomen in 1921, more St Helenians were brought in to replace them.

Chaplain Thomas Austin had his knuckles rapped in 1893 by the Commander-in-Chief for presuming to interfere with the allocation of pews, which was the prerogative of the Captain in charge. However as a result, we have a copy of the seating plan for that year, ranging from the Captain's pew at the front to the Kroomen and Prison Warder at the back, and providing for every individual, including the island washerman and his family.[25]

The Reverend H. P. Dawson, writing to St Helena in 1900, described life on Ascension:

The whole population – 445 men, 12 officers, 19 women, 30 children – are on the books of the Admiralty, and all of them receive their rations of meat, vegetables, milk, etc. per diem. Everything goes by the sound of the bugle ... We have a nice little Church holding about 350 people. Prayers are said every day at 9 o'clock. We have a Celebration every Sunday and Saint's Day, and the Services are hearty with plenty of congregational singing. We also have a school presided over by a Sergeant School Master and his wife ... We are earnestly looking forward to a visit from the Bishop, as there are a considerable number of candidates waiting for Confirmation, both white and coloured people. We hope after the War to get the Bishop here in a man-of-war. We are getting quite a number of lads from your island. I think we have five now.

Bishop Holmes landed at Ascension in 1902, on his return journey from England. He consecrated an addition to the cemetery and held a Confirmation.

With the reduction of the Garrison to about 120 men, women and children, the last Chaplain, Dallas Brooks, was withdrawn in January 1905. In addition to the Royal Navy there were seven members of the Eastern Telegraph Company, which in December 1899 had landed a submarine cable from the Cape at Comfortless Cove. It was the beginning of the growth of Ascension as a communications island.

Bishop Holbech visited Ascension in November 1905 and licensed the Commanding Officer, Captain Reginald Morgan RMLI, and the Assistant Paymaster, Oswald Carter, as Readers. In a letter to the Chaplain of the Fleet, the Bishop accepts that it would not be wise for him to send a civilian priest who would not be under Naval discipline to such a small community and urges that there should continue to be a Naval Chaplain. Alternatively, he would hope to visit Ascension himself twice a year, and asked if the Admiralty would bear the cost of his passage which amounted to £15 a visit. The Admiralty agreed to pay, but could not send a Chaplain. Writing a year later, the Bishop reports that regular Sunday services were held by the Readers, and the Church was in good repair and order.

For the next 60 years, until 1967, this was to be the pattern of Church life – no resident priest, twice-yearly visits by the Bishop and regular Sunday worship led by lay people licensed by the Bishop. Bishop Holbech left a record of all his visits. Each time he spent a night on the Mountain, with an evening service and Holy Communion the following morning.[26]

In 1912, when Captain George Carpenter was Commandant, the slate roof of the Church was replaced by one of 'uralite', paid for by the Admiralty. A brass tablet in the porch commemorates the work.

In 1922 the Royal Naval Garrison was finally withdrawn, and the members of the Eastern Telegraph Company were now the sole residents. The Bishop's visit in 1923 coincided with that of Admiral Grant, the Managing Director of the ETC. An agreement was reached that the Company should continue the Admiralty custom of providing a free passage for the Bishop and entertaining him free of cost. The Company would also make such repairs as may be necessary to the church building. Accordingly in 1924 the church was renovated and electric lighting installed.

There continued to be occasional visits by RN Chaplains; P. C. Gough in HMS *Dublin* in 1925; Archer Turner in HMS *Birmingham* in 1928; HMS *Lowestoft* in 1929; and Harold Beardmore, later to be Bishop of St Helena, in HMS *Dorsetshire* in 1934. British and American Chaplains visited Ascension during the Second World War.

In 1942 the Americans constructed the 'Wideawake' airfield, named after the Wideawake Terns. It was at this time that some American Roman Catholics erected what Fr John Kelly SDB called 'a cave-like structure', later to be called the Grotto, in the middle of a lava flow, which they used for Mass. After the war this fell into disrepair, but the altar and also a Madonna which had come from America remained. Fr Kelly repaired and extended the Grotto in 1964, to make it into an open-air chapel, which he named 'The Grotto of Mary Help of Christians'. This was further restored and developed in 1983 and a Mass of Thanksgiving was celebrated by Fr Philip Bruggeman MHM on the Feast of the Epiphany 1984. The preacher was the Reverend Michael Hawes, the Anglican RAF Chaplain. The tabernacle was given by Mr Gerry Peake in memory of his wife Mary. Today the Grotto is used for Mass, when there is a visiting RC priest, and when there is not, for a Communion service, led by a lay Eucharistic Minister.

By 1947 the Americans had left and Cable & Wireless, successors to the Eastern Telegraph Company, were the sole inhabitants, with a population of under 200. The Americans returned in 1956, to track test missiles fired from Cape Canaveral on the Missile Testing Range. Today the Americans are still there, but save for the Commanding Officer and a Sergeant, all are civilians. They were joined in the 1960s by NASA, who left in 1990. The BBC came to establish their Atlantic Relay Station in 1964 and the South Atlantic Cable Company sent a few South African engineers. In 1964 the St Helena Government appointed an Administrator.

This influx of people, together with the St Helenians employed by them, gave a fresh impulse to the life of the Church. People of different nationalities and different Church allegiances combined to worship God. The Anglican Church of St Mary now had a congregation which included members of other Churches, and who were invited on to the Church Council.

But until 1967, and after that during intervals between Vicars, the services were still taken by lay people. It is encouraging to note the number of people, sent to Ascension to do a job of work, who were equipped and prepared to lead worship. Between 1940 and 1959 Bishop Turner issued 20 Reader's licenses for Ascension, a tribute to the calibre of Cable & Wireless personnel. As well as the Sunday services, Readers conducted funerals, but civil marriages were performed in Court by the Resident Magistrate. Baptisms and Confirmations had to wait for the half-yearly visit of the Bishop. Among the Readers we may mention in particular James R. Bruce, now in retirement in Haywards Heath. He first landed on Ascension in 1936 (when the Senior Reader was N. T. Bramble assisted by N. W. Barnes) and after instruction by Bishop Aylen, Bruce was appointed a Reader. He left in 1939, returning in 1955 as Assistant Manager and JP when Bishop Turner renewed his licence. He left in 1958 and returned in 1961 as General Manager of Cable & Wireless on Ascension and Resident Magistrate, and this time it was Bishop Beardmore who renewed his licence! It was due to Mr Bruce that in 1963 much of the present furniture, altar, choir stalls and pews were made by Mr Bertram Williams, a St Helenian, known to most as 'Little Willie', under the supervision of the Clerk of Works E. Schirn. As Senior Reader he trained John E. Packer, who was licensed in 1957 and who later wrote his invaluable handbook on Ascension. In 1963 in recognition of his outstanding service, James Bruce was appointed to the Order of Simon of Cyrene by the Archbishop of Cape Town. He was the first person in the Diocese to be appointed to the Order.

Later other organizations were to provide Readers. Geoffrey Guy, later to be Governor of St Helena, was a Reader while he was Administrator. For 20 months, in 1978/9, Mrs Valerie Allen, a Methodist Local Preacher and wife of a member of the BBC, was licensed by the Bishop and was responsible for worship in St Mary's Church.

An altar bookstand in oak was given by Mr and Mrs F. B. Stevens of Cable & Wireless and blessed by Bishop Turner in January 1955.

With the increase in population, Bishop Beardmore decided to appoint a resident priest, and in October 1966 the foundation stone for a Vicarage was laid by Sir John Field, Governor of St Helena.[27] The first Vicar, John Crawford,[28] arrived in 1966, just in time to take the Christmas services. The Vicarage was somewhat slow in building, and at first he lived in a tent at English Bay. The completed Vicarage was blessed by Bishop Capper in October 1968. USPG contributed £180 per annum towards his stipend. During his time services were begun on the American base.

Interior of St Mary's

By 1968 it became evident that repairs amounting to £4,000 were necessary on the Church, but by the time he left in May 1969, John Crawford had collected £3,000 towards this, including £1,500 from USPG and donations from the Diocese, the Royal Navy and the Royal Marines.

Thomas Duffy[29] came from South Africa in July 1969. He had previously looked after St James', Jamestown, for four months early in 1966. Soon after his arrival he formed a choir. Under his inspiration, many young people came forward for Confirmation each year. Finding that it was difficult for some St Helenians to make their Communion in the mornings because of work, he began monthly evening Communions with good results. Indeed, he was regularly attracting congregations of 100 to his evening services. In 1971 Duffy exchanged parishes with James Johnson of St Paul's for about four weeks.

During Duffy's time restoration work on the church was carried out, involving the replacement of the roof tiles with copperoid sheeting, the replacement of the sheeting on the spire, resetting of the coping stones and making of louvred windows.

He left in July 1973 and for the next two years services were taken by Readers, Mr J. K. Donald and Mr G. C. Guy.

The Reverend David Bowles[30] became Vicar in July 1975. A regular monthly Eucharist at the 'Red Lion', at the top of Green Mountain, was revived. The 'Red Lion', built as new quarters for the Royal Marines in 1843, is today occupied by the St Helenians who work on the Farm. Bowles left in September 1977.

The Reverend John Harvey was priest-in-charge from December 1977 to May 1978, *en route* from England to St Helena. After his departure there was another gap until January 1980, covered by Mrs Valerie Allen. At the end of 1978, Padre Andrew Couch of the Royal Army Chaplains Department came with his wife and children for several weeks to take Christmas services. Padre John Slegg RAChD visited for two weeks with a Combined Services exercise in August 1979.

Very heavy rain in 1978 caused damage to the church and the Bishop appealed for £2,500 for restoration. £1,000 was given by USPG, £500 by the Diocese and £450 by the Royal Navy. Sudden torrential rain and consequent severe flooding, undermining roads and causing much damage, is a feature of Ascension from time to time. Packer mentions 9 inches in a day in 1859, and both he and Mr Bruce write of flooding in 1934 and 1963. A similar rainstorm in 1983 flooded Two Boats and the newly constructed RAF domestic site, and caused damage to the cemetery in Georgetown, but not to the church.

The next Vicar, Richard Davison[31] arrived with his wife Margaret and their three children in January 1980 and was collated as Vicar when the Bishop visited in July 1980. He introduced the South African 'Liturgy 75' for the 9.30a.m. Sunday Sung Eucharist.

The Church was rewired in 1980, floodlights installed outside the west end, and repairs made to the tower and the roof. The Vicarage garden was fenced and planted.

The British Task Force came through in April 1982 on its way to the Falklands. From that time there has been a continuous British Service presence. An RAF station was set up and the domestic site at Traveller's Hill completed in December 1983. The work on that site and on the airfield produced employment for a limited period for a large number of St Helenians.

For their last three months, the Davisons ministered to a population considerably increased by Servicemen, and the work of both Richard and Margaret Davison was greatly appreciated. They left in July 1982 and from then until April 1984 both civilian and Service people were ministered to by a succession of Royal Air Force Chaplains, living in the Vicarage. Their ministry was very welcome, but had the disadvantage that – like the majority of the Servicemen – none stayed longer than four months. Furthermore the Chaplains' Branch had its own manning problems, and in April 1984 it again became possible to appoint a civilian Vicar.

George Bradshaw[32] had been Vicar of Wittering, Peterborough, for 18 years and also Officiating Chaplain to RAF Wittering, receiving his Commander-in-Chief's Commendation. He became both Vicar of St Mary's and Officiating Chaplain to the new RAF station. His ministry was marked by an energetic programme of improvements to the church.

Two small stained glass windows were installed in 1984 in the east wall on either side of the chancel arch, representing on one side the Virgin and Child and on the other, St Michael. These were given by an anonymous donor in England, in memory of those Servicemen who passed through Ascension in 1982 and lost their lives in the Falklands. These were dedicated by the writer in July 1984, as was an electronic organ.

The same month the sanctuary was refurbished, the altar resited, and the East window of 1899, which was in a dangerous condition, replaced by frosted glass. In 1985 a War Memorial outside the porch was dedicated, a Yamaha organ was given by ss *Uganda* on her way home, a new bell given by ss *Maersk*, and two ceiling fans installed.

One of George Bradshaw's Confirmation candidates was John Ford, 30 year old cook on the ss *Maersk*, a tanker anchored off Ascension. High seas often make landing at Ascension hazardous or impossible. So it proved on the night of the Confirmation. Showing remarkable determination when the ship's boat could not come alongside the wharf, John put his clothes in a plastic bag and swam the last 100 yards to his Confirmation!

Bradshaw returned to England in June 1985 due to ill health.

For the next year, RAF Chaplains paid periodic visits. The present writer and Mrs Cannan spent a week on their way home and took the Christmas services, and Michael Stark, Chaplain of Exeter Prison, came for Easter 1986. Bishop Johnson visited from 28 April to 24 May. Tom Duffy returned at his own expense to minister for three weeks in June.

The next Vicar, Ronald Cottingham,[33] arrived on 4 July 1986. (The writer recalls his momentary surprise at the size of the apparent celebrations on the American base for his arrival when he landed on 4 July 1980!) Ronald Cottingham was to do two tours on Ascension.

The Bishop visited for a few hours on the shuttle of the RMS *St Helena* in May 1987 and took a Confirmation. His next visit was for a fortnight in April/May 1988 on his way to Lambeth. In August 1988 the sanctuary arch was strengthened and the sanctuary redecorated.

The Vicar of Ascension rarely sees other clergy, and it was good that at the end of 1988 Ronald Cottingham was able to exchange parishes for two months with Michael Houghton, Vicar of St James'.

Cross Hill behind Georgetown was given its name because of the wooden cross erected in the eighteenth century as a guide to shipping. Although this function had been replaced by more sophisticated equipment, a new illuminated cross was dedicated by the Bishop in 1989.

Mr Cyril Leo, a St Helenian, had for some five years been in charge of the Sunday School, which met in makeshift accommodation. Mr Leo found this so unsatisfactory that he decided, with the help of voluntary labour, to build a suitable hall himself. Materials, money and offers of help came from unexpected quarters, including one man who had been looking for a project on which to spend his personal tithing account, and the result is a well equipped building which any parish would be delighted to own. When the Sunday School was finished Mr Leo built a garage for the Vicarage.

Due to a shortage of clergy on St Helena, Cottingham left in October 1990 to take charge of St James' parish, Jamestown.

Once more RAF Chaplains stepped into the breach with periodic visits. The writer, accompanied by his wife, looked after the parish from late February to mid June 1991, and was appointed an Assistant Bishop in the Diocese during that period. The 1899 stained glass window, which, by courtesy of the RAF Commanding Officer, had been flown to England, was repaired in the workshops of Salisbury Cathedral and reinstalled in the East window of the church, thanks to a donation of £1,000 by the Royal Marines. It was re-dedicated at the St George's Day parade, attended by the Scouts and Guides. A tabernacle from St Stephen's College, Broadstairs, was given by the Sisters of the Community of St John the Baptist, Clewer in 1991, when they closed the school, through the good offices of Fr Michael Houghton.

Bishop Ruston paid his first visit in July 1991, stayed for five weeks and on 25 August instituted Nicholas Turner[34] as the next Vicar and licensed his wife Ann, a Deacon, as a Non-Stipendiary Minister. Turner had been Tutor at St Stephen's House, Oxford, and then Vicar of a parish in Leeds.

In addition to the perennial problem of the salt content in the walls, it has been discovered that the ceiling is asbestos, and will need replacement. The parish proposes to issue an appeal for £25,000 in September 1993, the 250th anniversary of the laying of the foundation stone, so that a complete renovation of the Church may be carried out.

There has never been a permanent community on Ascension. Everyone is an expatriate, on contract to do a job. Many have their families and there is a school and a hospital, but there are no old people. It is conceivable that one day it will once more be uninhabited. In this artificial situation, the Vicar (and, if married, his wife) plays a very important part in the life of the whole community. The Church and the Vicarage are almost the only places on the island which are not connected with a particular organization. Ascension Day every year is a public holiday when a Fair is held to raise money for the support of the Church.

St Mary's Church, built by the Royal Marines 140 years ago, is a continuing symbol and reminder of the continuing concern of God and His Church for that unique community.

Part III

Tristan da Cunha (1811-1991)

The 1961 volcano on Tristan da Cunha still smouldering a few years later (Patrick Helyer)

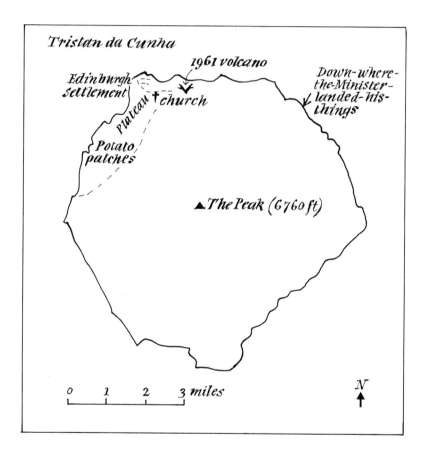

Tristan da Cunha lies some 1,300 miles south-south-west of St Helena. A volcanic island, about 20 miles in circumference, conical in shape, it rises to a summit of 6,760 feet. The only inhabitable part is a narrow plateau on the north west, about four miles long and a mile wide, 100 feet above sea level. Two other islands in the group, Inaccessible and Nightingale, both uninhabited, both lie 20 miles away. The island was named after the Portuguese navigator who discovered it in 1506. It was not inhabited until 1811, when an American, Jonathan Lambert arrived with a few companions and declared himself its king. Only one of his party was left by 1816, when a small British garrison arrived to prevent the French from using the island as a base from which to rescue Napoleon. The garrison was withdrawn a year later because of food problems, but a Scotsman, Corporal William Glass, elected to remain with his family, and was joined by a few others. Glass was a religious man, of some education, and held daily prayers, and on Sundays read a printed sermon.

When the sloop *Duke of Gloucester* called in 1824, one of the passengers, Augustus Earle, came ashore for a day to paint. Unfortunately a storm blew up, the ship could not pick him up, and he had to remain on Tristan for eight months!

Since my arrival, I have been unanimously appointed chaplain; and every Sunday we have the whole service of the Church of England read, Mr Glass acting as my clerk.

Earle commented on the 'clean and orderly state' of the congregation, the children in their best, and all paying great attention. He also taught the older children who were 'pretty forward in reading' and whose parents were anxious for their education.[1]

By 1826 the little population had increased to fourteen. Captain Simon Amm of the sv *Duke of Gloucester* was asked to find some wives for the five bachelors and returned in 1827 with five women from St Helena.

William Glass himself conducted at least one marriage service. The first page of the Tristan Marriage Register reads:

I, William Glass, do certify that on the 26th day of May 1837, the undersigned William Mills Daley and Elizabeth MacTarvish Garnley Glass came before me, there being no lawful minister, nor magistrate in the place, and I being the oldest and principle [sic] inhabitant, and were joined together in marriage by me; I using for that purpose the forms of the united Church of England and Ireland. In witness whereof I have drawn up, and they have signed, this certificate, this 26th day of August 1851, in the presence of the Reverend William F. Taylor, now Chaplain to the British residents on this island; I having neglected to make certificate of the same at the time.[2]

The first clergy to visit were missionaries *en route* to the East. In October 1835 the Reverend T. H. Applegate landed on his way to India and baptized 29 children. In October 1848 the Reverend John Wise, an SPG missionary going to Ceylon, came ashore and baptized 41 children. An account of his visit was published in the SPCK *Monthly Report* and Bishop J. Chapman, first Bishop of Colombo (he was succeeded by Bishop Claughton), wrote to SPCK: 'A speck only in the wide Atlantic, it is not too small or too remote to be beyond the reach of your benevolence'. As a result SPCK made a grant of books and SPG undertook to find a priest.

Mr William Frederick Taylor offered himself, was ordained Deacon and Priest in 1850 and arrived on Tristan on 9 February 1851. The following Sunday, in the largest room of William Glass' house, all the 80 persons on Tristan gathered for worship. The first celebration of Holy Communion was on Easter Day with eight communicants.

Taylor became concerned that the population was outgrowing the resources of the island and made representations to Bishop Robert Gray, since by now Tristan was in the Diocese of Cape Town. The Bishop interested Sir George Grey, Governor of the Cape Colony, in their plight and in March 1856 HMS *Frolic*, with the Bishop, was sent to investigate. The Bishop reported:

We landed on Tuesday, in the Holy Week. We found Mr Taylor living, as you may suppose, in a very primitive way. For the greater part of the time he has been here he has lived in a small stone building, which has been his prophet's chamber, school, and house of prayer ... The men are English, American, Dutch, Danes. Their wives have come for the most part from St Helena. The children are fine, healthy, active, modest, young men and women. These have been nearly all under Mr Taylor's instruction ... The houses are about equal to an English labourer's cottage; the furniture ... more scanty. At evening prayer we had about 50 present ... Their reverence and devotion impressed us all ... Mr Taylor has prayer in his Chapel, morning and evening throughout the year.[3]

On Good Friday the Bishop confirmed 32 persons, leaving only two people above the age of 15 unconfirmed. He agreed that the poverty of its resources made the island unsuitable for its present numbers. Later that year Fred Taylor left with about 40 islanders to become Rector of Riversdale in the Cape Province. It is said that some descendants of the Tristanians still live there. Taylor died in 1903 at Mossel Bay, aged 79. In 1856 SPG and SPCK published his book, *Some account of the settlement of Tristan d'Acunha*.

Tristan was now without a priest for 25 years. William Glass had died in 1853 and the next 'Headman' was Peter Green, a Dutchman wrecked on the island in 1836. In 1859 Tristan became part of the new Diocese of St Helena. Bishop Welby's efforts to find a priest were unsuccessful until 1880 when Edwin Dodgson volunteered.

John Milner, Chaplain on the frigate HMS *Galatea* which was taking the Duke of Edinburgh on a world cruise, went ashore with the Duke on 5 August 1867, and Milner baptized 16 children who had been born since Fred Taylor's departure ten years earlier. He offered to marry any couples who wished, but no one took advantage of the opportunity. It was in honour of the Duke's visit that the settlement was named 'Edinburgh'.

By 1880 the population had risen to 102. Mrs Cotton, a St Helenian wife, used to read Prayers and give Religious Instruction at her home every Sunday.[4] Is this an indication of the teaching she had received as a girl on St Helena from the later East India Company Chaplains?

The Reverend Edwin Heron Dodgson, the younger brother of C. L. Dodgson (Lewis Carroll), was Tristan's next Chaplain. Born in 1846 and trained at Chichester College, he was ordained priest in 1874 and became Principal of the UMCA College, Zanzibar in 1878-80. SPG, who provided a stipend of £100 a year for Dodgson, had difficulty in finding a ship to take him to Tristan. Eventually he left England in January 1881 for St Helena, hoping to find a ship there, possibly one of the American whalers returning to Tristan after leaving its cargo of oil at St Helena to be sent to America. But by the time Dodgson arrived the whalers had all left for that year, and Welby wrote to SPG, suggesting that they ask the Admiralty if a ship bound for Australia could call at St Helena.[5] However, by chance an English schooner, *Edward Vittery*, called looking for a cargo of oil, and finding none, offered to take Dodgson to Tristan for £35, a voyage of 10 to 12 days.[6]

Dodgson arrived on 25 February 1881. Unfortunately, after he was put ashore, the schooner ran on some rocks and was wrecked. Almost all his luggage was lost, although some of his clothes were washed ashore, and proved repairable. The case with the Communion vessels was saved, as was a stone font, but a harmonium he had brought out was lost, as were all his books, save for 100 copies of the *Mission Hymn Book*.

Nevertheless, he wrote optimistically the next day to SPG. There seemed to be quantities of bullocks, sheep, pigs, geese, fowl, potatoes, cabbages, apples and dogs. The population numbered 105. The younger children were being taught by Mrs Cotton, although the older children had run wild.[7]

To Bishop Welby, he wrote that since it was so long since they had received Holy Communion, he had used Lent for a course of instruction before celebrating for the first time on Easter Day. He had followed the Bishop's advice and invited the people to renew their Baptismal vows on Easter Eve. All the people came to Church on Sundays and about three quarters of them for Evensong and an address every weekday. He held school every day, with 48 pupils.

I found the children at first utterly undisciplined and with very few exceptions utterly ignorant, but by the combined use of patience and cane I have got the school into tolerable order, and though the children have very little idea yet of using their minds, they seem very fond of school, and as they are naturally bright, they are getting on very well.

The Admiralty diverted HMS *Diamond* to Tristan in 1882, at the request of SPG, to deliver books, school materials and a harmonium. In a letter of thanks, Dodgson wrote that they had been reduced to a few slate pencils, about an inch long. The harmonium had suffered damage – one of the bellows split and notes unshipped – but he had repaired it. 'I have been able to supply everyone on the island who can read with a Bible, Prayer book and hymn book.' They now have daily choral matins and evensong, with an average congregation of 20 adults plus children. The total number of communicants is 26, of whom 13 are unconfirmed. The Sunday services are attended by 'pretty well everyone on the island'. School attendance is 50 by day and 20 at night.[8]

Dodgson shared with Bishop Welby his problem with regard to those couples who were living together without having been married in the presence of a priest. The Bishop showed his pastoral attitude by replying that 'under their peculiar circumstances' Dodgson should, after morning prayer, take the marriage service from Psalm 67. This only involves prayers and a blessing – their exchange of vows being accepted as already constituting a marriage.[9]

Writing to SPG in January 1884, Bishop Welby said:

I have not had an opportunity of hearing from Mr Dodgson for the last ten months and I see no prospect at present of being able to visit him. I cannot go whaling for an uncertain time with the chance of being landed at Tristan d'Acunha, and then having to wait for a long time until the return of the only season in which whalers again touch there to get back to St Helena. No ships of war are now sent there from the Cape – the Admiral on this station told me that my best way would be to go to England and get a passage by some ship of war going out to the East: but if I could do this I must either go on to Australia or China or be left at Tristan d'Acunha for many months.[10]

Early the same year a letter from Dodgson to SPG shows that, although 'The people are still as kindly as ever, and I am well provided for in board and lodging,' he is becoming despondent about what he calls the 'mindlessness of the children', which he attributes to their isolation – 'It has been for a long time my daily prayer that God would open some way for us all to leave the island.'[11] He wrote to his brother Charles in the same vein. Welby gave Dodgson permission to return to England, after learning from Dodgson's letter and a report from a whaling Captain of his 'very depressed state of mind'.[12] Dodgson arrived in England in February 1885, after four years on Tristan, having paid for his own passage and suffering from concussion sustained by an accident on board ship. He endeavoured to persuade the Government to arrange for the Tristan community to be moved elsewhere 'before they are actually starved out by the rats which are over-running the island and eating all the produce', but he was unsuccessful.

Later that year, in November, tragedy struck when 15 men, who had put out in rough seas to intercept the sv *West Riding* for provisions, were drowned and never seen again. Only three adult men were left on the island. Hearing of this loss, Dodgson offered to return. As the Government will not repatriate them, 'I think it is my plain duty to throw in my lot with them and minister to their souls.'[13] He sailed in HMS *Thalia* which carried stores sent out by the British Government, arriving in August 1886.

Dodgson, in poor health, was invalided home in December 1889 by the doctor of HMS *Curacao*. He had given eight years to the islanders, becoming more and more convinced that the only hope was for them to be resettled elsewhere. Tristan was to be without a priest for the next 16 years. After a year at home, Dodgson served five years at St Vincent, Cape Verde Islands, and then from 1896 to 1898 was Vicar of St James', St Helena. He wrote to SPG in 1898 at the age of 52, that he 'did not feel equal to much locomotion' as his legs and back had been affected by ague in Zanzibar, but he was willing to go back to Tristan. However in 1901 the Doctor told him he could not go as he had damaged his spinal cord. He hoped 'to try a galvanic battery' and if cured would see a specialist. He died at Guildford in 1918.

Bishop Welby, at the age of 82, sailed to Tristan in HMS *Raleigh* in March 1892. Unfortunately, although the ship stayed for 24 hours, bad weather prevented the Bishop from landing. However he confirmed three young men, three young women and one widow on board, together with three young sailors presented by the Naval Chaplain W. Highmore. The population of Tristan was down to fifty, with only nine young men fit to row a boat. Thirteen islanders, including four children, were taken to the Cape in HMS *Raleigh*.[14] Later that year the barque *Italia* was wrecked on Tristan and two of its crew, Andrea Repetto and Gaetano Lavarello decided to stay.

Peter Green, on behalf of all the islanders, wrote to Bishop Welby in 1898, asking for a clergyman who could also act as doctor and schoolmaster:

> We are very poor and plain people, but we are thirsting for the Lord, and our children need education. We would do anything to make life as comfortable as possible for any clergy who felt inclined to come among us.[15]

Commander Rollestone of HMS *Racer*, who visited in 1893 reported that the 52 islanders – 15 men, 18 women and 19 children – were in good health and did not wish to leave. They had 450 cattle and 200 sheep in good condition. In the fine season, October to February, the island was visited by four or five whalers with whom trade was conducted by Andrew Hagan, an American ex-whaling Captain, who owned 250 cattle. The only schooling was given by Mrs Swain, a St Helenian widow.[16] However, the Captain of a whaler which called on Christmas Day 1900 reported that of the 18 families on the island, many would like to leave. Their problem was that, were they to do so, they would become paupers, since all they possessed was their homes and livestock. Mr Peter Green, the Head Islander, still took services and taught the children.

Peter Green died in 1902 at the age of 94. Bishop Holmes wrote a pastoral letter to the inhabitants of Tristan, dealing with the problem of spiritual loneliness and their life of prayer and worship in the absence of a priest.

In December 1905 Bishop Holbech was able to write to Andrea Repetto that he was sending, for the first time, a married priest, John Graham Barrow. In her diary[17] Mrs Barrow tells that Graham's mother, as a girl aged four, was a passenger on the *Blenden Hall* when she was wrecked on Inaccessible Island in 1821. The passengers were eventually rescued by William Glass and the islanders. In gratitude, Graham Barrow, an Evangelical Churchman, and evidently with private means, offered to go to Tristan as Chaplain at his own expense.

Graham Barrow, his wife and their servant Ellen arrived at St Helena in December 1905, hoping for an American whaler to take them to Tristan. None being expected, they went on to Cape Town and after a month found a ship which would take them on the understanding that if the weather was too rough to land on Tristan, they would have to go on to Buenos Aires. They arrived at Tristan on Palm Sunday 1906, bringing with them a bell given by Graham's old parish of St Andrew's, Polbrook, Malvern Common, and Rob, their collie. The sea, however, was too rough to land their luggage at the settlement and it had to be landed at a beach on the north-east coast. Hence the origin of one of Tristan's memorable place-names: 'Down-where-the-Minister-Land-his-Things'! His things included stores, books, and a harmonium from the SPG Chapel in England which had been 'floating in the sea but being in a zinc lined case took no harm'. They found 75 people on the island. On that Good Friday there was a congregation of 74, and on Easter Day 12 at the 8 am Holy Communion. Andrea Repetto wrote to the Bishop that they were all delighted at his arrival and the women very much appreciated the presence of Mrs Barrow.

The Bishop gave Barrow a letter of detailed if conventional advice to take with him. Concerning alms he wrote: 'Even if there be no money current, the people should be trained to make offerings to Almighty God in some suitable way.'[18]

The Bishop replied to a letter from Barrow in 1907 that he thought him too severe in telling his people not to trade with passing ships on Sundays. Since ships pass rarely and the people need supplies, it is on a par with 'leading your ox or ass to watering'.[19]

The Bishop wrote in May that he could see little prospect of being able to visit Tristan, and Barrow should admit to Communion those who had been instructed, even though they were not yet confirmed.

The Barrows left Tristan for the Cape in a whaler on 1 April 1909 with the firm intention of returning. With the Bishop's approval, Andrea Repetto was appointed Reader, to take services in Barrow's absence. But it proved impossible to find a passage back to Tristan. The Barrows waited in Cape Town for 15 months with no success. They returned to England and then went to Buenos Aires to try from that direction, but after waiting there for some months they had finally to return to England. Tristan was again to be without a priest for 13 years.

HMS *Yarmouth* called in July 1919 and the Chaplain, the Reverend Archer Turner stayed a night on the island. At a service at 10 pm he blessed ten marriages which, since Graham Barrow's departure, had been contracted before Robert Glass. Next morning 23 men and 18 women received Holy Communion, and 15 children were baptized. The population had risen to 111, in 22 families, living in 18 houses, which Turner commented 'are very superior to the Crofters' houses in the neighbourhood of Scapa Flow, Orkney'. He noted that there had been only one illegitimate birth, which was definitely condemned by the Islanders, who maintain 'a very high moral standard'.

The Reverend Henry Martyn Cheselden Rogers AKC, aged 42, parish priest of Alexton in Rutland, and his wife Rose Annie, aged 17, answered an advertisement placed in *The Times* and the *Guardian* in February 1921 for a priest for Tristan. His letter to SPG expressing anxiety about the moral state on the island, whether there was lawlessness and asking 'was it a place to take a lady to?',[20] makes one realize the courage of those who volunteered to go to an island about which so little was known and whose communications were so erratic. After waiting a year for a ship, the Rogers managed to get to Tristan on a Japanese vessel, arriving in April 1922. They brought with them a small pre-fabricated wooden bungalow to serve as the Parsonage, but it was not really adequate to the Tristan gales and they had to move into an island house within twelve months. The wood was used in the building of the church. A lively insight into their ministry, and the general conditions of daily living and Tristan customs, was given by Rose Rogers in *The Lonely Island*, published in 1926 after her husband's death.

Martyn Rogers started the 1st Tristan da Cunha Scout Troop, which was registered at Imperial Headquarters on 11 July 1921, with a Penguin Patrol, and also organized cricket and football. Rose Rogers listed as additions to their functions as missionaries those of Postmaster, Schoolmaster, Scoutmaster, Medical Adviser, Dispenser, First-Aider, Architect, Journalist, Meteorological Observer, Entertainments Organizer, Magistrate and Universal Umpire. Their son Edward was born on Tristan on 21 September 1922 and baptized in the font brought out by Edwin Dodgson. The Reverend Edward Rogers has kindly allowed me to quote from his mother's diary:[21]

When Edward was born the entire population flocked outside our house, and begged to see the baby. My husband, in his cassock, carried the three-hour old babe to the door. From my window I had a vivid impression of the women in brightly coloured Victorian dresses and the coloured 'kerchieves on their heads, the weatherbeaten faces of the fishermen and numbers of small children. They all knelt down on the grass and said the general prayer of thanksgiving together. Then they sang a hymn after which presents began to arrive, sea shells, hats and wee socks. Carpenter Tom Rogers had made, out of precious washed-up redwood, a quaint little cot of an old Norwegian design. Edward was soon one of the richest islanders, for he was given half the coin of the realm on the island – a half crown, a shilling and a threepenny bit!

On 24 October Mrs Rogers wrote in her diary:

Today, the Christening of Baby Edward was a red-letter day for the island. Every house was decorated with flags ... At the 3p.m. service in the church school room, Edward had three Tristan Godfathers, Tom Rogers, John Glass and Fred Swain, and one Godmother, Mrs Frances Repetto ... After the service all the adults, about one hundred of them, came round to the Parsonage for the party. After shaking hands they drank the baby's health in tea. Owing to a shortage of flour and raisins, and the difficulty of getting milk, the baptismal cake was so very small that there was barely a taste for the Godparents and ourselves. Everyone else was promised a piece of cake when the mail comes.

Edwin Dodgson had prepared a quantity of stones to build a church but progress was so slow that he had ordered the stones to be used for a cemetery wall instead. Martyn Rogers determined to build a church, and was able to use some of the stones prepared by Dodgson. Foundations were laid for a church 50 feet by 14 feet and at the laying of the foundation stone a tin box containing small silver coins was buried beneath it.

Work was begun in October 1922 and Rogers was able to persuade every man on the island to share in the work, with the result that the church was ready to be dedicated on Sunday 8 July 1923. The Lectern Bible had been brought by Barrow. The altar had seasonal frontals and a crucifix from Oberammergau. In a letter to the *Church Times*,[22] Martyn Rogers had begun: 'Some of your readers will, I am sure, be interested to know how we endeavour to uphold the Catholic Faith in our remotest island', and had ended: 'I only wish I had incense and a set of Stations of the Cross; perhaps someone at home will help us for the love of Jesus and Our Lady.' At least in one respect his wish was granted, for the new church was furnished with Stations of the Cross.

The Church was not, however, finished in time for Bishop Holbech's visit in March 1923. The Admiralty had arranged for HMS *Dublin* to take a large quantity of stores to the island and offered the Bishop a passage. Writing from Cape Town on 12 March the Bishop lists among the stores: 96 tins of Huntley & Palmer's biscuits, 3,600 boxes of matches from Bryant & May, 5,000 cigarettes and 50 lbs of tobacco, together with 6 bales of clothing, and wood and iron for the roof of the church – altogether some 25 tons of stores. Queen Mary had donated money for flour. HMS *Dublin* left Cape Town on 19 March and arrived at Tristan a week later on the Monday in Holy Week. The Bishop held a Confirmation that night, spent the night on the island, celebrated the Eucharist next morning and held another Confirmation. Altogether 76 people were confirmed, out of a population of 127. On Tuesday afternoon the Bishop returned to the ship which left on Wednesday.

Captain Hugh Shipway of HMS *Dublin* sent a report to the Commander-in-Chief Africa Station which was forwarded to the Secretary of the Admiralty. On his list of stores, the Captain notes 'One case of PORT WINE was not landed at the request of the Reverend Mr H. M. Rogers and will be returned to the donors'! Reports by the Medical Officer and by the Chaplain, N. B. Kent, were enclosed, the latter covering a wide range of welfare topics and including:

The regard which the Inhabitants have for their Clergyman ... was expressed to me many times by word of mouth. His influence shows itself in a variety of ways. The housing problem has been successfully tackled and every family now has a home. The Cemetery has been walled in and an attempt has been made to put it in order and keep it decent. Work has been undertaken on the roads and paths which are continually being washed away by rains and can never be good ... Education has been systematically organized so far as it is possible. Young men and boys are taught to 'play the game'.

These are no mean achievements. His religious ministrations are also appreciated ... On Sundays two services are necessary in the forenoon to accommodate all those who wish to attend and I was told that the people often arrive an hour or more before the beginning of the afternoon service to ensure getting a seat. Perhaps the most striking evidence of their active interest in Religion which came to my notice was vouchsafed to me by Mr [John] Hagan, a former inhabitant of the island who took passage in the *Dublin* to visit his kinsfolk. Their first action on his reaching the house was to kneel down and give thanks to Almighty God for bringing them together again. The singing at the Bishop's services was good and the behaviour of the congregation was without exception reverent. Mr Rogers' ministrations, religious and secular, are appreciated and have made their mark on the life of the people.

7 June 1924 was Rose Rogers' 21st birthday, and it was celebrated by a public holiday. Everyone was invited for dinner, for which nine sheep and two pigs were killed and 40 Tristan potato puddings cooked. On 7 January 1925, Rogers wrote to SPG:

There is now no person on the island who has not been baptized and received into Church. [We have] Scouts, Sunday School, Choir, MU and King's Messengers.

We have only moderate health as food is very poor. We are long out of flour, sugar and such things. Dispensing and ambulance work has been a regular part of our work here. Alas! that soap has given out and tea is at its limit. But these are minor ills. We have had much to thank God for.

I feel the greatest thing has been the building of the Church. When we first came we used a large room in the Hagan's house, which was overcrowded and unsuitable as it had at other times to be given over to all manner of secular uses. A gift of wood and zinc came on HMS *Dublin*. John Glass acts as Parish Clerk, as he did for Barrow, and remembers Dodgson.

St Mary's Church (courtesy Allan Crawford)

Interior of St Mary's Church, note the painted decoration by the Reverend A. G. Partridge (courtesy Allan Crawford)

There has been no mail for fifteen months, and it is many months since we have even sighted a ship in the far distance – about eight I think. The livestock is getting few in number, poor, often diseased. Milk is insufficient for the needs of the people.[23]

The Rogers left in February 1925. In a wireless message to the Cape Argus from the ship, he said:

My wife and I left Tristan da Cunha ill, due to bad feeding. The islanders are in a state of semi-starvation. For many months they have been short of flour, meat, groceries and clothes. Practically the only food on Tristan da Cunha today consists of sea-gulls and eggs. Tristan's food shortage is due chiefly to the failure of the last potato crop – a very serious event, as potatoes are the main food of the islanders.

He was to advocate strongly the removal of the whole population to the mainland.

Martyn Rogers offered to return for a further tour of three years, or less if health and supplies failed, and asked SPG to guarantee to pay their passage home. He also asks:

Would SPG find the stipend as before, or increase it from £100 to £150?
Would SPG give assistance to fresh outfit of stores?
Could SPG secure passage on warship next March?
Could SPG consider me as a missionary on furlough and allow a stipend of £100 pa?[24]

These seem all eminently reasonable conditions, but for some reason Bishop Holbech was very reluctant to accept the offer. On 1 July 1925 he wrote to Rogers:

The conditions for your possible return to Tristan which you have written to SPG they will answer; to me they seem to demand impossible guarantees.

I thank you and Mrs Rogers very sincerely for your courage in going to Tristan da Cunha, and for the work you have done there; the people have had the advantage of the ministrations of the Church for three years, with schooling for their children, benefits for which I have no doubt they are grateful to God and to you. But I do not think it desirable that you should return to the island; such work requires gifts which you do not possess. Therefore I accept your resignation, and send you the Letters Testimonial required in passing from one Diocese to another.

Please remember me kindly to Mrs Rogers, I hope that after her brave adventure she is enjoying England.

Rogers persisted, backed up by representations from Mr Douglas Gane, a London solicitor who had formed the Tristan da Cunha Fund to raise money for relief work on Tristan. It seems that the Bishop was upset by Rogers' telegram to the *Cape Argus*, and objected to his efforts at getting publicity for Tristan, which he felt encouraged begging. 'The *Quest* brought me a letter from Mr Rogers – much shorter than those to the papers', he complained.[25] He considered that Rogers' work lacked 'system', and 'he is casual and untidy … in his personal dress and appearances'.[26] There exists a photograph of Bishop Holbech on Tristan, to our eyes incongruously dressed in episcopal apron and gaiters. When one realizes the traditional ethos to which Holbech would have been accustomed on St Helena – over 40 years later a successor was rebuked by one of his junior clergy for attempting to attend a sports day without benefit of clerical collar – perhaps it is not surprising that Holbech would have found it difficult to understand the way of life on Tristan. As Douglas Gane pointed out, the only personal contact Holbech had with Rogers was his brief visit to Tristan in March 1923. It must be realized that the visit of HMS *Dublin* may not have been anticipated, that the Bishop was only on the island for 24 hours, and Rogers had to organize two Confirmations involving 76 people as well as hosting the Bishop. The Rogers received a multitude of letters from the islanders, begging them to return. Eventually the Bishop reluctantly agreed 'to accept Rogers if no one else was available, otherwise the Salvation Army or some Church will take advantage,'[27] but sadly by that time Rogers had died, leaving his young widow in straitened circumstances with two small children. SPG raised over £700 to help, and George Allen and Unwin, publishers of Rose Rogers' book *The Lonely Island*, gave all the profits from the sale to a Memorial Fund for her benefit. In a letter of condolence to Mrs Rogers Bishop Holbech wrote:

I am truly thankful to your husband for his work at Tristan da Cunha; he will be remembered amongst the line of good priests who have served there, Taylor, Dodgson, Barrow, Rogers.

In a tribute of a different kind, the Flightless Rail (*Atlantisia rogersi*), found only on Inaccessible Island, was named after Martyn Rogers, who had sent the first specimens to the British Museum.

The Reverend Robert Pooley, of St Mary's, Waterloo, Liverpool, next volunteered to go to Tristan. Being single, he asked that he should be accompanied by a lay assistant. Philip Lindsay, a young man born in Pietermaritzburg, with five years' experience in the Army in India, then training at St Boniface Missionary College, Warminster, was chosen and licensed as a Reader. Pooley had had some medical training which was to stand him in good stead. They arrived on Tristan in March 1927, taking over 40 tons of stores, including flour and blankets from King George V and Queen Mary, tools, Bibles, wedding rings and a gramophone. A wireless transmitter and receiver unfortunately proved not to be sufficiently powerful.

Pooley wrote to Bishop Holbech soon after his arrival that there were 62 Easter communicants out of a population of 151 and 51 pupils at school. On 15 May brass memorial tablets were dedicated in memory of Dodgson and Rogers. Pooley revived the informal meeting of Heads of Families, introduced by Rogers, and in March 1928 he wrote, by the first ship for 11 months:

At our parliament for all heads of houses, I stopped gradual starvation by common sense. Mongrel dogs were killing lambs by dozens, hence flocks have dwindled steadily for 30 years. All dogs except one per family, in special cases two, were humanely destroyed. Now flocks increase.

The islanders had built a house for the two men and were building a new school, 30 feet by 12 feet, behind the church. The church was repainted and a new floor laid. Both Pooley and Lindsay made visits to Inacccessible and Nightingale Islands. They owned 18 sheep, two cows and many hens. Lindsay wrote that on his birthday his presents included 58 pairs of hand knitted woollen socks, 10 dozen hens eggs and a load of firewood from each of the 13 Scouts!

At this time the financial responsibility for the priest on Tristan, his recruitment, passage and stipend, etc, were borne by SPG, and sometimes there would not be time for the Bishop of St Helena to be consulted. Hence, when it became necessary for Pooley to leave the island because of ill health, SPG were able to act speedily, enabling Pooley to leave on the ship which brought his successor, the Reverend Augustus George Partridge in March 1929. Lindsay stayed on for another year.

Partridge had served with the British Red Cross during the first World War and had been a Missionary in South Africa and Brazil. He arrived in March 1929 on the tourist ship *Duchess of Atholl*, with stores including a wireless set, half a ton of flour from the King and a harmonium from the Queen. With more honesty than tact, Partridge wrote a letter of thanks:

Your Majesty,
The Islanders of Tristan da Cunha desire me to express their cordial thanks for Your Majesty's kind gift of an organ for their Church of St Mary.
    It was indeed a kindly and gracious gift but unfortunately there is no one on the island able to play and the Church is so small that room cannot be found for it. When Your Majesty realizes that the whole building measures but 41 ft by

10½ ft and every man, woman and child to the number of 154 souls attend church regularly Your Majesty will understand that there is no room even for your kind gift.

The organ is therefore kept in the house of Mr Tom Rogers and will be preserved from the terrible damp and wind.

Your Majesty will be sorry to learn that the potato harvest has utterly failed and the Islanders will have a very hard winter indeed.

They send their loyal greetings and are overjoyed to hear of the recovery of His Majesty for whom they pray every day.

Readers will not be surprised to learn that this occasioned a flurry of correspondence between the Colonial Secretary and Douglas Gane. 'I hear Her Majesty is much disappointed at receiving Mr Partridge's letter. What can I say in reply to the Private Secretary?'

Unfortunately the wireless set also was not satisfactory. The dry batteries did not last long enough and the Leclanche cells were found to be broken.

Partridge continued the 'Parliament' of Heads of Families, but it is with some surprise that we read in his letter to Mr Gane of 20 January 1930:

Crime. On two occasions punishment has been given for crimes committed during the year ...
... taking Mollyhawks without permission – twenty lashes.
... stealing potatoes and cabbages and lying – one lash each from each member of 'parliament' (33 lashes), and deprivation of stores for a year (this may be commuted on good behaviour).

Partridge lengthened the church ('stretched it' to use a local phrase), which had become necessary due to the increased population. He painted the East End in bright colours, still a feature of the church today.

Bishop Watts wrote in 1931 that he was entirely happy to leave the matter of the Chaplain on Tristan in the hands of SPG. He visited Tristan in January 1932 in HMS *Carlisle*, the first ship to call for 13 months. The purpose of HMS *Carlisle*'s visit was to report to the Colonial Secretary on the spiritual, mental and physical condition of the islanders. The Bishop reported:

(1) Wholesale evacuation of the islanders is quite unnecessary and would be cruel. There is no starvation in sight and, as a rule, the people are well fed. During the winter times are hard.
(2) The people are hardy and show little sign of degeneration.
(3) The Islanders as a whole are unanimous in their desire to remain on the island.

(4) If possible some of the younger ones should be taken away. In 10 years time the cultivable land will be insufficient for the needs of the people.

However,

(a) Certain stores, amounting to £150 per annum must be supplied.

(b) A strong, sympathetic and capable missionary must be permanently resident.

(c) A ship must visit at regular intervals.

The Bishop spent several days on the island and confirmed 36 candidates. Partridge returned with the Bishop on HMS *Carlisle* after a ministry of three years.

The following year, 1933, the British Government asked Partridge to return to Tristan and appointed him Magistrate, to be there during the projected 18 month visit of a Brazilian Scientific Expedition. The Expedition did not materialize, and Partridge stayed for only seven months. In contrast to Bishop Watts' assessment, he wrote after his return: 'As matters stand I can see no future but inevitable starvation and progressive degeneration of the people.' Before he left, Partridge set up an Island Council with Peter Repetto as the Head Man and his mother, Frances Repetto, as the Head Woman. Partridge was made a Member of the Order of the British Empire in the Birthday Honours List. He wrote a booklet of his experiences, *Tristan da Cunha: The Isle of Loneliness*, published by SPG in 1934.

As well as Bishop Watts, a Roman Catholic priest, Fr L. H. Barry, was also on HMS *Carlisle* when she visited in 1932. In the 27 January 1932 issue of the Roman Catholic newspaper *The Southern Cross* he claimed that: 'One thing is quite certain about Tristan da Cunha, the islanders are no more Church of England than the rest of His Majesty's dominions.' He paid tribute to the work of SPG 'but it is time it became known that more than half of the population of 163 on the island are of Catholic stock'.

To suggest that half the islanders were of Roman Catholic stock was, to say the least, something of an exaggeration! What had happened was this. In 1908 three islanders who had been to the Cape returned to Tristan with their brides, three Irish sisters. These sisters, together with their children born in the Cape, were Roman Catholics. One sister returned to the Cape, one died, and Joe Glass, the husband of the youngest, Agnes, died in 1915. Agnes Glass then married William Rogers, a native of Tristan da Cunha, and they had six children.

According to Partridge, for three years Agnes attended the Church services, was churched after childbirth, and brought her children for

Baptism, but did not receive Holy Communion. Fr Barry, learning from Rose Rogers' book *The Lonely Island* that there were two Roman Catholics on the island, came on the *Carlisle* to minister to them. However when Partridge returned to the island in May 1934, he was somewhat disconcerted to discover that Fr Barry had baptized all Agnes' children, even though, as he pointed out in a letter to the Bishop, some of them had been confirmed by Bishop Watts that morning.

One can appreciate Fr Barry's dilemma in the different ecumenical climate of those days. He was cut off from advice from his ecclesiastical superiors, he was only on the island for a few days, and he could not know how long it would be before another Roman priest would call. But equally, one can appreciate Partridge's feelings!

Although SPG were themselves in some financial straits, they resolved to recruit and support another Chaplain. The Reverend Harold Wilde MC,[28] volunteered and arrived on Tristan by the Royal Mail liner *Atlantis* in February 1934, bringing with him another 'powerful' wireless set!

Harold Wilde was a bearded, extrovert priest with a bluff manner. He was a man who liked to 'get things done'. Shortly after he arrived Amy Repetto wrote that the children 'are never so happy as when playing football or going swimming with him.' He repaired the harmonium sent by the Queen in 1929 and played it in church. In his reports he writes of the need for renovation of the church and for school materials, but is delighted with the way in which he has been able to teach the Islanders to drop into the church during the day for private prayer. He also wrote of problems caused by a plague of rats in 1936.

Under the guidance of Mrs Agnes Rogers the Roman Catholic Church grew until by 1940 it had about 50 members. Both Professor Peter Munch and Mr Allan Crawford, who were on Tristan with the Norwegian Scientific Expedition in 1937, suggest that the reason for part of the increase may have been dissatisfaction with the way in which the Anglican Church had been run.[29] Perhaps Wilde was a little too extrovert for some of the islanders! Allan Crawford writes that when he returned to Tristan in 1942 he felt that:

Rivalry in so small a community would have split it dangerously in two, which nobody desired. Islanders concerned about the situation confided in me and, guided by island elders, I visited the dissidents to hear their grievances. Eventually I was successful in bringing many of them back to the Anglican Church ... When the new Naval padre arrived in the next ship he found a considerably enlarged congregation.

It is good to know that on his next visit to Tristan, Crawford found once more harmonious relations between the Anglicans and Roman Catholics.

Bishop Aylen visited Tristan from 28 February to 3 March 1937, in HMS *Carlisle*, whose Chaplain Harold Beardmore would himself one day become Bishop of St Helena. The population was 183. All appeared healthy although one man was mentally defective. Harold Wilde had had a storehouse built, which helped to conserve supplies. 'The panic rumours of rats and starvation are the irresponsible reproductions of sensation mongers and bear no relation to the facts ... The idea of evacuating these people would be more than cruel – it would be silly.' But the Bishop stressed the need for outside support of stores and more regular ships. During the visit he confirmed ten male and nine female candidates.

Harold Wilde returned with the Bishop to St Helena, and preached in the Cathedral before going to England. He was appointed a Member of the Order of the British Empire, receiving his award from the King at Buckingham Palace. The Bishop of St Helena wanted to offer Wilde a Canonry, but SPG advised against it, on the grounds that he had already been sufficiently 'lionized', and they had to consider their other missionaries![30] Wilde returned to Tristan later in the year, and finally left in 1941, having served the island for seven years.

Wilde was probably the most ebullient and controversial Chaplain to serve on Tristan and there have been conflicting views on his ministry. The SPG *Year Book* for 1937 reported on developments at Tristan with some optimism:

They [Bp. Aylen and the crew of HMS *Carlisle*] found that wonders had been done by the Reverend H. Wilde, Chaplain since 1933. He had organized supplies, cultivated new ground on Inaccessible Island, improved the health of the people and provided a 'hospital' of two beds in his own house, but above all, had infused a new spirit of vigour and happiness, based on a simple Christian faith and centred in daily worship in the little island Church. Not only the Bishop, but the whole ship's company were deeply impressed by the good work of which they found such evident proof.

Wilde sailed on *Carlisle* for furlough, made Tristan front page news all over England, and returned in autumn [of 1937] with a Norwegian scientific expedition.

But it must be admitted that Wilde's scheme to grow potatoes on Inaccessible Island failed after two years and had to be abandoned. Perhaps without Wilde's drive the project just lapsed, or perhaps after all the conditions were not really suitable!

In many ways the war years marked a watershed in the life of the Tristan community, even more important than their evacuation after the volcanic eruption of 1961. Until 1942, virtually the only 'expatriate' had been the Priest and his family. All islanders had been equal; there was virtually no administration or organization, and no money. From then on, however, there was to be an increasing number of expatriates, a fishing industry providing employment, rising standards of living and of medical care, and eventually an Administrator and a Constitution. Already in 1938 an Order in Council had made Tristan a dependency of St Helena.

It puzzled me, when I was on St Helena, that the Diocesan Archives were completely silent about Tristan during the war years. I was indebted to the Reverend Gordon Taylor and his book *The Sea Chaplains* for first clearing up the mystery. A secret Meteorological Station was set up on Tristan, manned jointly by the Royal Navy and the South African Air Force, and the staff included a doctor and a Royal Naval Chaplain, who also ministered to the Islanders. The SPG publication *The Tristan da Cunha Newsletter* for August 1945 revealed that SPG had paid half the stipend of the Naval Chaplain but because of the secrecy of the appointment could make no appeal for funds during the war. The establishment was known first as HMS *Job 9* and from 1944 as HMS *Atlantic Isle*, and part of its function was to maintain communication with the Cape for the benefit of Allied ships and aircraft.

The first Naval Chaplain was the Reverend Cyril Percy Lawrence, who arrived in May 1942 in HMS *Cilicia*. He had the ideal qualities for such a post. He was skilled in carpentry and building, and as well as continuing the tradition of the priest teaching in the school, he made much of the school furniture. As it happened he had been trained at St Boniface College, Warminster, as a missionary. He returned to Tristan in 1948 as a civilian leader of a combined commercial and scientific expedition, and the present economic viability of the island owes much to Lawrence, to whose vision the inception of the crayfish industry is due. He died in 1967.

David Luard, another Naval Chaplain, succeeded Lawrence in 1944. Luard had spent some years as a teacher in China. He joined the RNVR in 1942 in which year he was Mentioned in Dispatches. He wrote two articles on Tristan, published in *Corona*, the Journal of the Colonial Service,[31] and also an unpublished book on his time on the island, kindly lent me by his widow. One extract must suffice:

'In my young days,' Mrs Repetto is fond of saying, 'things was different.' Mr Dodgson and Mr Barrow often used to make me feel degenerate! In our time there were quite a few families who had altogether given up attending Church, except at Christmas, when everybody came. Other people had become irregular ... The Church is a remarkable and lovely building. It is made of stone lined with wood, like other island houses, but it has a tin roof instead of a thatched one. It is very narrow, only 12 feet wide and about 70 feet long. Inside it is far more brightly coloured than is customary with Anglican Churches, but this is suited to the congregation. The sanctuary in particular is most elaborately decorated with geometrical designs which must have taken weeks of patient work to execute. There is a harmonium, a French instrument, presented by Queen Mary. The bellows had been eaten by rats, but my versatile predecessor had mended them with the leather of an old shooting jacket ... They still regard Sunday as a day on which no ordinary work such as digging or fishing should be done, but it is allowable to make a boat trip if it is fine ... The men still sit on one side, the women on the other ... The building is scrubbed through every week. It is a very easy place to pray in.

Since some of the Naval personnel had their families with them, a Queen Alexandra Royal Naval Nursing Service Sister arrived in 1942. Her successor, Margaret Reynolds, was posted to HMS *Atlantic Isle* in 1945. David Luard married her on their return to England.

David Luard was succeeded by a civilian, Alec Edward Handley, accompanied by his wife Marjorie. Born in Yorkshire, he went to sea as a youth and served in the Royal Army Medical Corps during the first World War, experiences which were to serve him well on Tristan. He emigrated to Canada where he was ordained and had seven years of parish life on the prairies, before returning to England. They arrived on Tristan in 1946.

After HMS *Atlantic Isle* closed, only three expatriates remained, Mr Allan Crawford, who had returned to take over the Weather station, and his two assistants. The Handleys moved into the wooden bungalow built for the Naval Chaplains. In his report to SPG Handley wrote that no one under 21 had been confirmed, because of the lack of a Bishop's visit, but he was preparing 25 youths and girls for receiving their Communion. Mrs Handley was a qualified teacher, sponsored by SPG. On Tristan, assisted by her husband, she taught 15 juniors and 14 seniors. In addition there was an afternoon infant class of 20. The little church was jammed full for the Midnight Eucharist on Christmas Eve 1947.

January 1st, being the Feast of the Circumcision, we thought there would be the usual 'faithful few' at Church this morning, with perhaps one or two extra. We got a very pleasant surprise; the Church was crowded and nearly all present made their Communion. I had intended taking a plain celebration but we had a Sung Eucharist instead.

Sadly on 6 February 1948, the day when Lawrence's expedition arrived, Handley had a seizure; he died three days later. His widow decided to remain on the island until the arrival of the new Vicar, and she continued her work as schoolmistress, as well as the many other duties normally performed by the Vicar. Today Mrs Handley modestly says she had no choice because there was no ship anyway, but this does not detract from her devotion to the islanders.

At Lawrence's suggestion, since he wanted someone who knew the island to have charge while his expedition was on the island, SPG invited Luard to return as the civilian priest, which he did in January 1949, when he was appointed Administrator of Tristan by the British Government. Unfortunately he had to resign after three months due to his wife's illness in England.

When Mrs Handley returned to England at the beginning of 1949, SPG sent out Miss Ethel Harvey, Headmistress of Gooderstone School, Norfolk, to run the school during 1949. Mrs Handley then volunteered to return as Schoolmistress, which she did in January 1950.

The island was without a priest for some six months in 1949, until the arrival of the Reverend Dennis Wilkinson,[32] accompanied by his wife and two daughters aged 2 and 7. Another Yorkshireman, he had served as Chaplain to the Forces (1942-6). He assisted Mrs Handley in the school, and ran the Scout Troop. He extended the Church on the south side, using cement pillars to support the roof. The work, which was carried out under the direction of the Development Company's engineer, Mr Pickel, was completed by 8 July, the date on which the original church had been dedicated by Martyn Rogers. A carpet was given by a branch of Toc H and an altar cloth by Mrs Handley's mother. Mrs Handley left in November 1952, taking with her Valerie Glass, for further education in England.

By the time Wilkinson left in 1952, the crayfish industry had been well established by the South African based Tristan Development Company; the island had had a full time Administrator since 1950, Mr Hugh Elliott, who with his wife Elizabeth gave much support to the church; and the island had its own stamps, due to the enthusiasm of Mr Allan Crawford. In terms of church history, 1952 saw the transfer of Tristan from the Diocese of St Helena to the Diocese of Cape Town, with whom it had far easier communication links. Its priests continued to be sponsored by SPG until 1981.

The next Chaplain was David Neaum.[33] A Derbyshireman and a trout farmer before ordination, he came to Tristan with his wife Dorothy and three young children in HMS *Actaeon* in October 1952. He was accompanied by Wilfrid Parker, retired Bishop of Pretoria, who confirmed 26 candidates. David Neaum could turn his hand to most things, and he added an extra bedroom to the Chaplain's House and built a stone fireplace and chimney. He and Dorothy were musical and improved the singing in church, Dorothy being the organist. Strict in matters of church attendance, if a ship came in on a Sunday, Neaum would declare Monday or Tuesday to be Sunday that week!

By now there were many expatriates and their families, including the Administrator, a Postmaster and Agriculturist, Meteorological Officer, Electrical Engineer and a Doctor and Nurse, as well as the Fishing Company Manager, Engineer and Storekeeper.

At the end of 1952 SPG appointed Mr and Mrs R.J.Harding to run the school. Financial support for Mr Ron Harding was to come from the Crayfish Company, and for Anne, his wife, from the Colonial Office. Until they came, and when they were on leave in 1955, Neaum ran the school. Throughout his time as Chaplain he taught Religious Knowledge on four mornings a week. By 1953 Mr Harding reported that the school had 65 children, aged 5 to 15. Considerable improvements were made to the school building in 1954. The main schoolroom was fitted with a new floor at a cost of £100, mainly met by contributions of £1 each from the men of the island and the sale of the Chaplain's cow! The wood was imported from South Africa. Neaum supervised the work, assisted by eight islanders. Other furniture was made, 50 desks were imported from the Cape and text books supplied by SPG. Trina Glass was appointed as the first pupil teacher.

The Archbishop of Cape Town, the Most Reverend Geoffrey Clayton, visited in HMS *Magpie* in October 1955 and confirmed 19 children. He later wrote, after referring to the deterioration of the islanders' teeth:

Gradually the Islanders are becoming like other people, which is not necessarily an improvement. But they are still most attractive and hospitable people ... so far as I could judge there is a great deal of genuine and simple piety. It remains to be seen what will be the effect upon this of the increased association with the outside world which modern conditions have brought; and at the present time it is very important that the succession of faithful pastors should be continued.

David Neaum agreed to extend his tour by one year and the Neaums finally left in February 1956.

They were succeeded by the Reverend Philip Harold Bell,[34] who had some experience in agriculture. He arrived with his wife, Dilys, and three young children in 1956. Another baby, Christopher, was born on

Children outside the school building

the island on 26 June 1957. Mr and Mrs Harding left in April 1957.
Bell wrote:

Mr Harding's whole-hearted and full-time devotion to the children and school
... the whole school has been splendidly revolutionized and equipped during
his headmastership, so that it is now a good deal better in furniture and stock
than many a Church school in the countryside in England.

Dilys Bell was a qualified teacher, and she and Philip, assisted by Trina
Glass, staffed the school, until the arrival in November 1957 of the new
Headmistress, Miss Rhoda M. Downer, recruited by spg. When the
Chaplain was sick early in 1959, Miss Downer took Matins and
Evensong for several weeks.

Ever since the church was widened, there had been trouble with rain
leaking through the roof, and in 1958 the Chaplain launched an appeal
for £1,000 for its renovation. A Paschal candlestick had been made
locally by Mr Watt and Mr Pedersen:

The four legs are of oak, the stem is turned from part of a longboat oar, and the
drip catcher is part of the echo-sounder wrecked in the Bisco gale, and the
candle fits into a removable holder made from a brass engine fitting. Nothing
could be better, and I value this more than the most expensive model we could
have bought.

The worst gale on the island since 1931 occurred in August 1958, but the Chaplain's house escaped damage, being the best sheltered on the island.

In February 1959, HMS *Lynx* brought the Governor of St Helena, who invested the Head Islander Mr William Repetto with the MBE which he had been awarded in the New Year's Honours. Also on the ship was Bishop Roy Cowdry, Assistant Bishop of Cape Town, who confirmed 11 children, including the Chaplain's eldest daughter, Gillian, at the first Evensong of Candlemas. Communion next morning was at 5.30a.m., 'All the congregation brought their own candles,' the Bishop wrote, 'filling the dark little building with a really heavenly light. I shall not quickly forget it.'

The Bells were on furlough from April to October 1959 and their place was taken by the Reverend Percy Clough from Cape Town. The Bells returned with pews and an altar which the Archdeacon of London had secured. SPG later provided four frontals for the altar. Her Majesty presented a harmonium to replace the one given by Queen Mary. The church was connected to the new electric generator, together with the hospital and the Prince Philip Hall, the foundation stone of which had been laid by HRH the Duke of Edinburgh in 1957.

In May 1960, HMS *Puma* brought two priests, the Reverend Robert H. Mize, later that year to be consecrated Bishop of Damaraland and the Roman Catholic Fr Freeman to visit his 24-strong flock.

Philip Bell was succeeded in the spring of 1961 by Charles John Jewell,[35] with his wife Phyllis, and their three young children. They were accompanied by Miss Ethel Bennett, the new schoolteacher. They could hardly have anticipated the calamity which was to occur only six months later. From August onwards the island experienced increasingly strong earth tremors and on Sunday 8 October a fall of rocks and earth blocked the water supply. Returning from praying for safety in church, they found that doors and windows would not shut. The islanders decided to move to the western side of the settlement which seemed as yet to be safe. Jewell baptized one baby, Margaret, at 11.30 that night, as her mother was understandably worried and felt happier when her baby had been made a member of Christ. The next afternoon a bubble of earth rose about 300 yards east of the village, and the Administrator, Mr Peter Wheeler, who with his wife and three children had been on the island about six months, decided to evacuate everyone to the potato patches two miles away for the night. That night the bubble grew and burst and began to throw out lava. Fortunately the two fishing vessels, the *Tristania* and the *Frances Repetto*, were both at

Tristan and were able to evacuate everyone to Nightingale Island. The Naval Headquarters at the Cape had been alerted by radio, and HMS *Leopard* was despatched. It would take her several days, so it was providential that the Dutch liner *Tjisadane*, which was due to call at Tristan the following day, could be diverted to Nightingale to pick up most of the islanders. The Administrator and a small party remained on the *Tristania* to wait for HMS *Leopard*. The day after they arrived at Cape Town they gave thanks for their deliverance at services in St George's Cathedral (conducted by Bishop Cowdry) and the RC Cathedral.

The British Government brought the islanders in the *Stirling Castle* to Southampton, where they were greeted by Bishop Trapp, Secretary of SPG, amongst others. They were taken to Pendell Camp, a disused Army camp near Merstham in Surrey. The Camp was excellently run by the WVS, assisted by the British Red Cross and St John's Ambulance Brigade. Mr Wheeler and Jack Jewell were there and their old Tristan teacher, Miss Downer, came to teach in the school. The parishioners of Bletchingley, led by the Reverend R.A. Brownrigg, offered their friendship and hospitality, the County Guide Commissioner came to the camp and children were invited to local Guide and Brownie meetings. The local Rotary Club gave their assistance. But the islanders were not really happy. In January 1962 they were moved to the old RAF married quarters at Calshot, on Southampton Water. Here at least they were near the sea. The WVS had prepared the camp and looked after them. Jack Jewell was with them until he became SPG Area Secretary in Ireland in May, when the Reverend Noel Brewster, Rector of Fawley, took over their pastoral care. The Diocese of Winchester bought a chapel at Calshot for their use. Many of the islanders took jobs locally, but it was hard for them to adjust to the pace of life, and to working for a boss and clocking on. They yearned for Tristan. In September, twelve islanders left for Tristan, six to fish with the Development Company which was anxious to re-establish the fishing industry and six to assess the possibility for return and to begin repairs to the houses. Lars Repetto held services for them in the church each Sunday.

At a secret ballot held by the Colonial Office in December, 148 islanders voted to return to Tristan, and only five wanted to stay in England. Thus an advance party of 52 arrived on the island in April 1963. SPG recruited the Reverend Keith Flint,[36] who had recently returned from nine years on St Helena, as the next Chaplain and he went to Calshot to live with the remaining islanders, sailing with them on the *Bornholm* in October. With them went the harmonium given by Queen Elizabeth in 1960 and which had been salvaged by the Royal Navy in two halves in 1961. The Queen asked the organ builders N.P. Mander Ltd to repair it and it was used at Calshot from Easter Sunday 1962. They also took back with them a banner. Tristan was perhaps the only community where all the Anglican married women were members of the Mothers' Union and they had been invited to many events by the Winchester Diocesan MU. The Diocese had an MU banner made for them to take back to Tristan. It was blessed in Winchester Cathedral by the Bishop of Southampton at the Diocesan MU Festival service in May 1963 and presented to the headwoman Martha Rogers and two married women bearers.

On returning to Tristan, they discovered that only one house had been seriously damaged, and the lava flow, although it had covered their beaches, had created the possibility of a small harbour. To the islanders it was coming home; to Keith Flint it was all new. He wrote of the Church:

The Church is a real delight and though its homely island character is a bit physically cramping it can claim some really good vestments and ornaments, and is a holy happy spiritual home ... Within a couple days of landing we had started a daily Eucharist and not much later Reservation was restored – both with great joy. Our Administrator, Peter Day, whom I find a very good friend, is to be admitted to the office of sub-deacon.

From now the teachers were to be appointed, not by SPG, but by the Government. The first was Mr J.H. Flint, no relation to the Chaplain. In *The Fortunate Island*, still in typescript, he indicates that Sunday observance was still an important part of Tristan life. 'Under normal circumstances no Tristan will work on the day of rest, unless such work is essential. Thus milking the cow is acceptable, whereas digging a potato patch is not.'

The church roof was repaired with canvas and bitumastic paint to make it waterproof. Bishop Robert Mize of Damaraland visited in 1964. 'The Bishop put us on to the idea of building a belltower with a generous contribution. A team of men got busy at once'.[37] The bell came from the *Mabel Clark*, which ran aground in 1878. Once a year Flint would bless the fishing 'longboats', those traditional boats with wooden frames covered by tightly stretched and painted canvas. He left Tristan in 1966 and died in December 1990. His ashes are interred at St David's Cathedral.

Paul Davies[38] left his Rectory of Llandrinio in March 1966 for Tristan. Soon after his arrival he wrote that he found the islanders:

Father Keith Flint and Bishop Robert Mize

naturally very devout and friendly people. But they were badly upset by their exile in England, and have a strong sense of being different from 'You English', which came as a complete surprise.[39]

He was the first Welsh Chaplain and not surprisingly encouraged church music and singing. He made a detailed survey of the population, which he sent to USPG. The population was now 252, including 23 non-islanders. Those were years of increasing prosperity and, after Davies left in June 1968, there was a strike by the fishermen who demanded, and received, an increase on the price that the Company were paying per basket of crayfish caught.

Angus Welsh[40] was the next Chaplain. He served on Tristan from 1968 to 1971. Bishop Stanley Pickard, the Provincial Executive Officer, visited in September 1970 and confirmed 21 children. It was the first episcopal visit for six years. In 1970 USPG gave the Church a new corrugated aluminium roof. Every man, including Roman Catholics, gave his services free. The job was done in a day, and the rain held off until the new roof was in position. The weather could change unexpectedly, and Angus Welsh recalls the anxiety when fishing boats would go out at first light in good weather, only to find themselves in great danger when a storm blew up.

The leader of the Roman Catholic community, Mrs Agnes Rogers, died in 1970. She had been sent a Papal Medal by Pope Pius XII in 1950 in recognition of her devotion in leading the Roman Catholic services in her own home for so many years. They were to be carried on by her son, Cyril.

Welsh left on All Saints Day 1971, and looking back on his ministry he wrote:

I thoroughly enjoyed Tristan and got on with the islanders very well indeed. I was very happy among them. They laugh a lot, they think a lot, and they brood a lot. They are cautious and conservative, but will often act on impulse and emotion. They very often come to a common mind without anybody seeming to have taken the lead. They are a courteous people. They usually accept and act upon established authority. But they always resent it, and sometimes utterly reject it. They remember that central authority is a comparatively recent innovation. Individual liberty has always been cherished on Tristan.

The islanders are now living through a time of crisis, halfway between new ways and old ways. As long as the economic basis of their lives remains firm and favourable, they could easily enjoy the best of both worlds, but there is a real danger that they will end up with some of the worst features of both. Spiritually they are at the crossroads. They could maintain their old life of faith. They could possibly lose their belief in the Providence of God, and the living power of prayer, and sink into the life of unbelief and indifference so characteristic of the England they all lived in for almost two years. Sometimes they are very generous indeed. Sometimes they seem to love money very dearly. They are in great need of wise, sympathetic and above all, patient administration officers, factory managers and chaplains, to help them through this time of change and crisis.[41]

Who better, then, could come than Jack and Phyllis Jewell who returned just 10 years since they had left so precipitately. Andrew their eldest son, was now working at USPG House, but they brought their four younger children. They found a new pre-fabricated wooden Chaplain's house just waiting to be erected. Work on renovating St Mary's Church, to celebrate the 50th anniversary of its dedication, was soon under way. Giving their services free, men removed the rotting floorboards and laid a concrete floor, covered with marley tiles. They

Spinning

made new window frames and replaced the old sanctuary ceiling with masonite. The old ceiling had been made of mail bags, and Jack Jewell sent one to the Post Office in London for their museum! Roy Folgate and Stanley Swain rewired the church and replaced the fittings. Jewell started a Church Maintenance Fund from gifts received, but Tristan did not forget needs beyond their shores and the Church took up a USPG scholarship to help a child polio victim in Tanzania. Jewell was also appointed the official meteorologist for the island.

The Reverend Kenneth Giggall called in 1973 on his way to be consecrated Bishop of St Helena and brought for laying up in the Church, a White Ensign, which HMS *Magpie* had presented to the Island on her visit in 1955. Jewell had rescued it from the Church when they left in 1961 and deposited it with the Admiralty for safe keeping.

After the Jewells left in 1974, the island was without a priest for over a year. However, Prebendary Edmund Buxton[42] had just retired to Hampshire at the age of 66, after 41 years' ministry in England. He explained to me in a personal letter:

When Jack Jewell wrote in the *Church Times* appealing for a priest for Tristan I thought there was a chance of further travel and adventure and ministry, and I offered ... USPG thanked me for the offer but replied that they were really looking for a younger man ... However we were accepted and commissioned at a service in which our son, Francis, was also commissioned as Chaplain to Vellore Hospital in South India.

Edmund Buxton and his wife arrived in Tristan in October 1975. The journey from Cape Town had taken 17 days, since they were nine days off Gough Island waiting for a calm sea to offload men and supplies for the Weather station. In the interregnum, the services had been taken by the two Lay Readers, Lars Repetto and Eddie Rogers. Their very accomplished organist was Pamela Lavarello, who had been playing since she was 14, having been taught by Mrs Joy Thompson, wife of a previous Administrator. Attendances at the Sunday services were 50 to 100 at 8a.m. Holy Communion, almost 100 per cent at the 10.30 Children's Church and two or three dozen at Evensong.

In 1977 Leslie Stradling, retired Bishop of Johannesburg, visited and confirmed 20 candidates. The Mothers' Union flourished under the guidance of Mrs Katharine Buxton. The Bishop attended an MU Admission Service for five new members:

Pam [Mrs Pamela Lavarello, the Enrolling Member] said I was the first Bishop to attend an MU meeting on Tristan and presented me with a pair of Tristan socks, made of wool grown, spun and knitted on the island. White with coloured rings around the top.[43]

Buxton was asked to take meteorological readings and report them daily to Gough Island for a few months. He used the payment to buy a carpet for the Chaplain's house. When USPG said they had some money earmarked for Tristan, he asked for a hardback Good News Bible for each household. The Buxtons came to love the island and its people and enjoyed walking and bird-watching. They never reached the top of the mountain, unlike the energetic Christine Stone, who came out to join the school staff, and among many other innovations, introduced the Duke of Edinburgh's Award Scheme. She was a very good Christian influence among the young people. The Buxtons left in 1978, to be succeeded by Patrick and Mary Helyer.[44]

Patrick Helyer had been a Missions to Seamen Chaplain in Glasgow and in Australia. He had served in the RNVR (1942-6) and in the Royal Australian Navy (1952-61). After two parishes in England, he was Rector of Christchurch Cathedral, Port Stanley, Falkland Islands (1971-5). He left England for Tristan in November 1978, with his wife Mary, a qualified nurse. Mary brought her New Zealand spinning wheel, which she had used in the Falklands. This was smaller than those used on Tristan and much easier to work, so copies were made by a carpenter and became popular.

The arrival of the *Queen Elizabeth II* in February 1979 caused much excitement on the island. The fishing vessel, MV *Tristania II*, in March brought the Franciscan Fr Matthew to minister to the Roman Catholics. He accepted Helyer's invitation to say Mass in St Mary's and preached at the Anglican Evensong. On Easter Day, Helyer dedicated a Yamaha electronic organ, a present for the church from his son, Nicholas, a Commander in the Royal Australian Navy, and on 21 December Helyer celebrated the 40th anniversary of his ordination to the priesthood.

The church roof was painted green by the Public Works Department, courtesy of the Administrator, in April 1980, and a new safe arrived for the church, sent by a retired Naval Commander whom Helyer had met in Cape Town. Throughout their tour, Helyer taught in the school and was Vice-President of the Island Council. Mrs Mary Helyer was able to give valuable assistance in the hospital during emergencies and epidemics and during the illness of the doctor. She wrote of the islanders' faith in the power of prayer and how they, and she, believed that their prayers had cured a serious eye complaint from which Mary suffered. Archbishop Bill Burnett of Cape Town wrote of 'the way in which you both gave devoted service to our Lord and His people on the island.'

The Helyers left in November 1980, Patrick being the last priest to be recruited for Tristan by USPG in England. Future clergy were to come from South Africa. He published a very useful diary of their time there and an exhaustive bibliography of books and articles on Tristan.

At Easter 1981, during the interregnum, many of the men were on Nightingale Island, including Lars Repetto, the Lay Minister. On Easter Day, Lars held a service for them there. And on Good Friday on Tristan, because Lars was away, some people joined the RC service in the new Roman Catholic church.

This new church was dedicated to St Joseph in September 1982 by Fr Frank Gouveis from Cape Town. As a schoolchild aptly remarked, both island churches were dedicated to one of our Lord's parents. Dereck Rogers was the Eucharistic Minister and services were held every Sunday morning at 8.30 and on Holy Days of Obligation. Services were also led by Anne Green, an island teacher.

There was a seven month interregnum at St Mary's until the arrival in June 1981 of Michael Edwards,[45] with his wife Elizabeth and four children. They had many varied and useful skills. Michael was a keen radio amateur, photographer and weatherman. Elizabeth, a trained nurse, helped in emergencies and taught the island nurses. Their daughter Ruth, born on the island, was handicapped, and was loved not only by the family, but by all the islanders.

In a newsletter, the Edwards described their first island funeral:

As soon as the person dies, all work stops on the island until after the funeral, and the flags are at half mast ... The funeral takes place as soon as the coffin can be made ... We were very moved by the way the funeral service is done here. There is very much a sense of the whole island grieving ... Michael, led by the Lay Minister as crucifer walked over to the hospital where the family was waiting. After saying prayers over the body, the Lay Minister and Michael led the Landrover as a hearse, with the family walking behind back to the Church. After the service the procession winds its way slowly down the hill to the cemetery which is in a field overlooking the sea. Everyone walks in complete silence and there is no one, neither animals nor children around. Everyone who is not at the funeral stays indoors until it is over.

A pulpit, given by St Dunstan's, Ashurst Wood, East Grinstead, was brought out by the Denstone College Expedition to Inaccessible Island in 1982, under arrangements made by Patrick Helyer. The Edwards left in September 1983.

In January 1984, the new Treasurer's wife, Mrs Edith Alexander, brought consecrated hosts from the Cape for the Roman Catholics, who were able to receive Holy Communion again after a gap of 15 months.

James David Pearson[46] arrived in February 1984 with his wife Mary and their three young children. Born in Cape Town, he had been a Probation Officer before ordination. He brought with him for the Rectory a new gas heater, lounge suite, typewriter and washing machine provided by the Diocese.

28 November 1985 was the 100th anniversary of the tragic occasion when 15 of the 18 men on the island had been lost at sea trying to intercept the sailing ship *West Riding*. The anniversary was commemorated by the dedication in St Mary's Church of a commemorative plaque which Mr Allan Crawford designed and had engraved in Tunbridge Wells, and by an issue of postage stamps. The Mothers' Union Headquarters sent a framed document of sympathy with the names of the bereaved women.[47]

The RMS *St Helena* had now begun to call at Tristan once a year on its way from St Helena to Cape Town. This enabled the Most Reverend Philip Russell, Archbishop of Cape Town, who had visited St Helena to enthrone the new Bishop, to call at Tristan in February 1986. It was the first archiepiscopal visit for 31 years. The Archbishop confirmed 47 candidates.

The Roman Catholic authorities in 1986 asked the Mill Hill missionaries, based in London, to add the islands of St Helena, Ascension and Tristan to their care. They were already working in the

Falklands, where the Apostolic Prefect was Monsignor Anton Agreiter of the Mill Hill Fathers. In future it would be possible to have an annual visit by an RC priest.[48]

The Pearsons left in October 1986, and for over a year, services were held by Lars Repetto, assisted by Edward Rogers. In October 1987, the Reverend Trevor Tyers, Vicar of St Barnabas, Cape Town, volunteered to come for three weeks during the visit of the SA *Agulhas*. Then once again it was a retired priest who responded to the need. Philip Jourdan[49] had been Chaplain at Addington Hospital, Durban and then at Groote Schuur Hospital, Cape Town. Both he and his wife Mary were qualified counsellors, Mary specializing in helping the hard of hearing. They arrived in January 1988 for a year. Jourdan's counselling experience led him to encourage the islanders to improve their self-image. He tells how, at the age of 72, he was asked to play in an island cricket match. He knocked up a good score and was delighted to overhear an islander say: 'Padre tells us to walk tall and claim our space, and he goes in and does just that.'

The Jourdans left in February 1989. Their replacements were Bill and Olive Skipper who arrived in May, hoping to stay for three years. William Stanley Skipper[50] was born in Bloemfontein in 1930 and became a chartered accountant.

In February 1990 Bishop James Johnson of St Helena visited Tristan on his way to an Episcopal Synod in Johannesburg and confirmed ten candidates. He brought consecrated hosts from the RC priest on St Helena for the RC community.

An increase in numbers on the island to over 300, again brought a need for the church to be extended. Members of the Church Council, assisted by volunteers, extended the church to the east, and re-roofed the whole building. Bill Skipper was able to celebrate Easter 1991 in the enlarged church. The intricate painting at the east end, carried out 60 years earlier by the Reverend A.G. Partridge, was integrated into the new decoration.[51]

In concluding this chapter, we recall the words of Angus Welsh in 1971. 'Spiritually they [the islanders] are at the crossroads.' It will be for a future historian to show which road they took, but the news of the extension to the Church is an encouraging sign.

Part IV

The Falkland Islands (1764-1991)

Port Stanley, Falkland Islands, showing Christchurch Cathedral

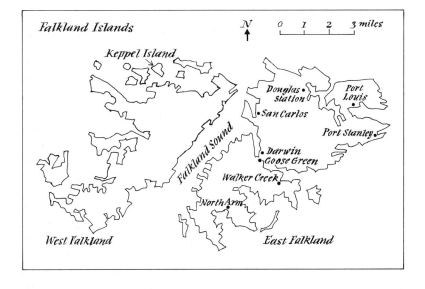

In 1984, when I was Bishop of St Helena, the telephone rang. It was Terry Waite, ringing from Lambeth. The Archbishop of Canterbury was asking whether on my next visit to Ascension, where I had to stay 5½ weeks while I waited for the ship to return from England before I could return to St Helena, I could spare the time to fly to the Falklands on his behalf for an episcopal visit.

Delighted with the opportunity, I borrowed a pair of long johns from the Purser of the RMS *St Helena* and flew in an RAF Hercules, having the thrill of seeing from the cockpit our mid-air refuelling from a Hercules tanker. I received splendid hospitality from the civilian Chaplain, Harry Bagnall and his wife Iris, and Harry insisted I should wear his own cloak and hat, since I had flown from the heat of Ascension to the depths of a Falklands winter. Although they had had the opportunity of leaving, Harry and Iris had insisted on staying in Port Stanley with their flock throughout the Argentine occupation. His book of their experiences *Faith under Fire* is well worth reading.

A great problem of internal communications confronts the priest. There are about 100 small farms, ranging from single family farms to those comprising perhaps 100 people, scattered over the two islands with a total area of some 2,600 square miles. It takes over a year for one priest to visit them all and means for the most part using either a ship or the unscheduled flights of the Government light aircraft. One telephoned to say where one wished to go next day, and then listened to the radio that evening to see if it was possible. One day Harry Bagnall took me to Darwin. We listened to the broadcast the evening we arrived and were a little put out to discover that our names were not on the return flight next day, especially as we were due to dine at Government House! Since there were no telephones outside Stanley, we had to wait for the radio schedule next morning to make our plea. Fortunately, all was well! There was of course the same problem for education, until recently solved by the use of itinerant teachers. I pondered that if these problems of communication still existed in the 20th century, the earlier settlers must have found great difficulties.

The Falklands were uninhabited when visited by John Davis in the *Desire* in 1592. For the next two centuries there were disputes over sovereignty between the British, French and Spanish, but only small settlements were involved. The French settlement was established by de Bougainville at Port Louis on the East Falklands in 1764. Three years later, they handed over to the Spaniards, who renamed the settlement Port Soledad and stayed for some forty years.

Meanwhile at Port Egmont in the West Falklands there was also a

British settlement, which carried out a survey of the islands from 1766 to 1774. The Naval Officer in charge conducted Divine Service on the Sabbath, which was 'kept in a decent manner'.

The Spanish settlement came to an end by 1810 and a period of disorder followed. The harbours in the Falklands continued to be used by sealing and whaling ships, mostly English and American. The United Provinces of the River Plate laid claim to the Falklands but the British flag was hoisted at Port Louis in January 1833. Five years later, we find the Naval Superintendent, Lieutenant Robert Lowcay conducting a marriage, a baptism and a funeral.

Lieutenant Richard Moody was installed as the first Lieutenant-Governor in January 1842. By 1845 the settlement had moved to what is now Port Stanley. Chaplains of visiting Naval ships exercised a ministry, thus we read of David Casson, Chaplain of HMS *Daphne*, conducting several baptisms in 1844. At other times the Governor conducted Sunday Services and baptisms and funerals until the arrival of his brother, James Leith Moody, as the first Colonial Chaplain in October 1845. In October 1847 the Church was given the use of a room in the barracks. The second Governor, George Rennie, enlarged the church by including a part which had been used as a hospital.

James Moody did not have an easy task. The settlement consisted of about 100 inhabitants, of very mixed origins. Rennie reported in 1849:

It is scarcely possible to conceive a greater apathy, destitution and drunkenness than is found among the lower classes, more particularly the English and Scotch. Irish and foreigners are less addicted to intemperance but equally devoid of industrious habits.[1]

It is not surprising that Moody's efforts met with little success. However, Port Stanley found itself on a busy shipping lane and was a haven for ships passing round Cape Horn, and by 1851 Rennie writes that he is impressed with the energy of the people.

James Moody was succeeded in 1855 by Henry Martyn Faulkner. In 1856 the Governor, Thomas Moore, moved the Church into the east wing of the Exchange building, and made the west wing into a school. In 1862 the church was named Holy Trinity and Governor Moore transferred responsibility for it to the Churchwardens. However, they were unwilling to bear the expense of its maintenance and in 1865, under Governor Mackenzie, the responsibility for the building reverted to the Government. Faulkner died in April 1859 and the colony was without a resident clergyman until Charles Bull and his wife arrived on 29 December the same year. He wrote in March 1860 to Bishop Tait, who as Bishop of London was responsible for all Colonial Chaplains:

I cannot speak favourably of the religious state of my people. There was a complete state of indifference displayed ... only 7 or 8 communicants ... the school is taught by a Pensioner. The late Chaplain thought it his duty to refuse to visit the schools unless he had full control over Religious Instruction. I accepted the offer of Inspector of Schools ... most Roman Catholic children attend my catechetical class.[2]

The mention of 'a Pensioner' refers to one of the 30 soldier pensioners from Chelsea and Greenwich who were brought out in 1849 and given a wooden cottage and 10 acres of land each. They were asked to do some garrison duty and provided with rations and fuel.

Bull gives the average Sunday Church attendance: 80 in the mornings, 33 in the afternoon and 56 in the evenings. This probably includes 24 soldiers who attend on Parade each Sunday, for which Bull receives £25 a year. In addition Mrs Bull runs a Sunday School. The Church will contain 88. There are 540 inhabitants, including 210 children.

Meanwhile a quite different and unconnected work of the Church was beginning on Keppel Island, at the northern end of the West Falklands. Commander Allen Gardiner had resigned from the Royal Navy in 1826 at the age of 32, to become a missionary, and in 1844 he founded the Patagonian Missionary Society. It was his intention to establish a Mission station on the Falklands, which could be used as a base for missionary work in Tierra del Fuego, 'The Land of Fire', at the southern tip of South America. Charles Darwin, who had visited them on his voyage in the *Beagle*, wrote of the native Indians: 'These poor wretches were stunted in their growth, their hideous faces were bedaubed with white paint, their skins filthy and greasy, their hair entangled, their voices discordant, and their gestures violent ... If attacked, instead of retiring, they will endeavour to dash your brains out with a stone.' What did he expect them to do, when they lived on the edge of starvation? Darwin thought it was useless to send missionaries to such savages, but in 1869 he handsomely admitted that the Missionary Society had proved him wrong and sent them a cheque for £5. Gardiner made two expeditions to Tierra del Fuego, the second in 1850, when he was landed on Picton Island. Supplies did not reach him, and when in October 1851, a ship eventually arrived, it was to find him and every member of his party dead of sickness or starvation. When the news reached England, the Reverend Pakenham Despard, Secretary of the Society wrote to *The Times* of his firm resolve that 'with God's help the Mission will be maintained'. A schooner was built, named the *Allen Gardiner*, which sailed from Bristol with a catechist, Darland Phillips, a Surgeon, Dr Ellis and two builders.[3] They arrived on the uninhabited Keppel Island in 1855. The Governor allowed them to buy 160 acres and to lease the rest. In 1856 Despard joined them, with his wife and an adopted orphan, Thomas Bridges. Also on board was the Reverend J. Furniss Ogle. However, on arrival at Stanley, Mr Ogle was reluctant to accept Despard's invitation to proceed to Keppel since he felt that his physical powers were 'unfitted for the labour of digging peat and hewing stone', and he wanted to get to grips with missionary work on the mainland. Finding himself at odds with Despard, he paid a brief visit to Patagonia by himself, and then returned to England early in 1858. Meanwhile, under Despard's leadership, trips were made to Tierra del Fuego and a few Indian families invited to visit Keppel, where a Mission Farm was established. Then in November 1859 came another tragedy, when eight of the workers, including Phillips, were massacred at Woolya on Navarin Island and the ship pillaged. Despard returned to England in the ship which was to be refitted, but Bridges, aged 19, asked to remain on Keppel, together with the Farm Manager, Mr Bartlett, to look after the few Fuegians there.

The Reverend Waite Hockin Stirling, who had succeeded Despard as Secretary of the Society in 1857, arrived with his wife and family in January 1863 to be the new Superintendent on Keppel. The Mission was to prosper under his leadership. Soon after his arrival, Stirling, accompanied by Thomas Bridges, who had used his time to become proficient in the language of the Yaghan Indians, sailed for Woolya. It was a brave act, but Bridges was able to talk to the Yaghans in their own language and assure them that there was no thought of punishment. Some of them returned with Stirling to Keppel.

Mrs Stirling died in 1864 and in 1865 Stirling took four young Fuegians to England for a four-month visit. The same year the Patagonian Missionary Society became the South American Missionary Society (SAMS).

When he first arrived Charles Bull had been critical of the work on Keppel and had written to the SPG:

Patagonian Missionary Society. The practice of gathering natives from Fuegia to Keppel Island will never do, it is like kidnapping them ... taken away from their wigwams, a shock is given to the only redeeming feature in their character, love of home and of their children ... Instead one missionary and 6 other craftsmen should settle on Woolya, at the very place where Capt. Fell and poor Phillips and crew of the *Allen Gardiner* were murdered.[4]

The Mission House, Keppel Islands

Perhaps this was too hasty a judgement, for less than five months later he was asking if SPG would aid a native school for Stanley, 'I think young Fuegians might be brought to Stanley for education.'[5]

In fact, Stirling was himself keen to set up a Mission on Tierra del Fuego, taking back some of the natives from Keppel. It was a courageous decision and in July 1867, Charles Bull, now also the Honorary Secretary of SAMS in Stanley, wrote to the Bishop of London that

few men could do what he is doing; few men are so endowed with grace as to be able to do it.[6]

So in January 1869 the *Allen Gardiner* took Stirling to Ushuaia, on the north side of the Beagle Channel in Tierra del Fuego. He was installed in a wooden hut which he had brought from Stanley, on his own, apart from some of the natives who had accompanied him from Keppel. Here he stayed for seven months. Winona Hardy says that one of the best memorials to his work there is contained in some words on an Admiralty chart of 1927:

The natives living South of Beagle Channel are friendly and most of them speak English. They can be trusted to assist shipwrecked mariners.

A great change has been effected in the character of the natives generally, and the Yaghan Natives can be trusted.[7]

Thomas Bridges left Keppel at the end of 1868 for England where he was ordained in St Paul's Cathedral on Trinity Sunday 1869. He returned, with his new bride, and in December 1870 he sailed for Ushuaia, where he succeeded Stirling and where he laboured for nearly 20 years. In 1886 Barbrooke Grubb, who was to be a famous missionary in South America, arrived at Keppel at the age of 21, where he stayed until he left in 1889 for missionary work in Paraguay. The history of the SAMS Mission to Tierra del Fuego is a story of men and women of great faith and heroism, but it is outside the scope of this book. It has been well told in the books listed in the Bibliography.

The Mission Farm on Keppel, named Cranmer Farm, prospered under its Manager, Mr Bartlett and his staff. It was primarily intended as a training farm for the Fuegians, who would then return to their homes, having been taught the Christian faith, English and practical farming. However as it expanded with sheep, cattle and vegetables, it was able to supply fresh provisions to the crew of the *Allen Gardiner* and the Mission on Ushuaia, as well as feeding its own staff. The surplus was shipped to Stanley, where its sale provided an income for running the Mission.

As yet there had been no Confirmations and no visits by a Bishop. In 1860 Bull wrote: 'I have not heard from the Bishop of St Helena who had promised the Bishop of London, under whose jurisdiction I am, to hold a Confirmation here if he could get from Monte Video to these islands.'[8] This is of interest because when the Diocese of St Helena was founded in 1859, it was assumed that the Bishop would carry on the pastoral oversight of the English congregations on the coast of South America, which had been exercised in theory by the Bishop of Cape Town, and money had been raised in Montevideo towards the endowment of the See. The Bishop had included Charles Bull in the list of clergy of the Diocese in his return to SPG. In the event, the Bishop of St Helena did not visit the Falklands -at least not for another 100 years or more!

In November 1867 the General Committee of SAMS passed a Resolution: 'It has become necessary that a Bishop for South America be appointed as early as possible.'[9]

Evidently this recommendation was taken seriously in England and on 15 September 1868 a letter signed by 54 people of Stanley was sent to the Bishop of London, expressing 'joy at the news that W. H. Stirling BA has been nominated as first Bishop.'[10] So in August 1869, the *Allen Gardiner* returned to Ushuaia to summon Stirling to England for his consecration. In South America the news was not received quite so joyfully. The See was to include all the Anglican congregations in South America, except for British Guiana. These were ministered to by Colonial Chaplains nominally responsible to the Bishop of London, but who was unable to exercise any effective oversight. While I do not think that there was any personal objection to Stirling, whom they would not have known, they may not have wanted any closer episcopal supervision. Some may have felt that they might find themselves under the influence of a missionary society to which they did not belong. Such would seem to be implied by letters written by the American Bishop of Honolulu, after his visitation of the congregations in South America. He wrote to the Archbishop of Canterbury from Buenos Aires in June 1869:

I feel it due to your Grace that you should know that the idea of Mr Stirling being placed over them, Clergy and laity, as their Bishop, is received with an unanimous expression of discontent ... The Falkland Islands are quite unsuitable for a See. I have left no stone unturned to get there ... but all in vain. For 4 months, from May to September they are unapproachable owing to currents, winds and fogs ... Scarcely a ship ever calls there...and [the Bishop would be] 1,000 miles from ... his chief work.

The SAM Society having now got their clergy ordained, and having, as Mr Kirby informed your Grace, no need of my help for Confirmation ... have no immediate wants to be supplied and at least can afford to wait for further ventilation of the subject.

My own idea is a Bishop of South America would be a very mischievous thing, from all I have heard and seen, distasteful to the majority of the Consular Chaplains, Clergy and people, unnecessary, productive of collision with the Spanish Republics ever alive to proselytism; likely therefore to embarrass the Government ... it has been my aim to render the SAMs every help while here ... all I say concerns the welfare of the Society as much as the Church in general.

If a retired Bishop without territorial jurisdiction could take a Chaplaincy, say for health reasons, on the coast, and every 4 or 5 years visit other places to confirm, it would answer every purpose.[11]

And on 4 October 1869 he wrote from Panama:

From the statement everywhere expressed by the laity as well as all the clergy, whether Consular or of the SAM Society, I regard Mr Stirling's nomination as the greatest disaster that could have occurred ... it is regarded by the Clergy (chiefly old fashioned Churchmen) as the enthronement of the above Society over them in ecclesiastical things ...[12]

All this was a little late, since Queen Victoria had on 19 June 1869 issued her Licence to Archbishop Tait to consecrate Stirling, and he was duly consecrated in Westminster Abbey on 21 December. The Bishop of Honolulu had evidently also written to the Prime Minister and in September 1869 Gladstone wrote to the Archbishop:

I have rec'd a letter from Bp. of Honolulu complaining on the part of the Brit. residents in S. America about the proceedings of Mr Stirling who appears to have been appointed Bishop of the Falkland Islands ...

He also pointed out that 'Govt. declined to give a territorial title or jurisdiction.'[13]

This was indeed the case, and the Licence to consecrate which was issued, not by Letters Patent, but under the Queen's Sign Manual and Signet, contained no mention of the Falkland islands but was 'to Consecrate Our Trusty and Well-beloved Waite Hocking Stirling, Bachelor of Arts, to be a Bishop, to the intent that he should exercise his Functions in one of our Possessions Abroad.' This was to cause Stirling some embarrassment, and in October 1870 the Archbishop, responding to a letter from Stirling, wrote to the Earl of Kimberley at the Colonial Office pointing this out and asking what Stirling's precedence would be on the Island. The answer was that:

although Colonial Regulations Chapter VI does not in strictness apply to Bishops not appointed by Letters Patent, I have told the Governor of the Falkland Islands that the Bishop is to have precedence as presented in the Regulations as a matter of courtesy.[14]

Bishop Stirling did not arrive on the Falklands until January 1872 when he was brought by HMS *Cracker*. He was enthroned on 14 January by Charles Bull in Holy Trinity Church. Stirling wrote to the Archbishop of Canterbury in May 1872 speaking well of Bull's work:

The Rev. C. Bull, lately of St Anne's Soho, and since then for more than 12 years Colonial Chaplain, recently sailed for England on leave of absence ... he has had to face some animosity in a small community. If he returns, as a mark of respect I shall make him Archdeacon.[15]

Bull did not return, and in December 1872 Henry Coulson Lory came out as Bull's locum. He had offered to come for one year. In the event, because no replacement was forthcoming, and Lory was loath to leave his flock without a shepherd (the Bishop presumably being in South America), he had to stay for three years. Thus, in September 1874, he wrote to the Archbishop:

I came out as Locum for Charles Bull for 1 year on ½ Colonial Chaplain's salary = £200 + £25 from Admiralty, at the recommendation of the Secretary for SPG. My time as locum expired last December. Bull resigned 2 months before.'

He had asked for the full stipend but the Government had declined. He also asked to be relieved without delay and

my passage home paid, as I had to pay half my passage out, Mr Bull paying the rest. I have a wife and 3 little boys in England. My wife is ill and will never recover. I had hoped to better myself not to be ruined.[16]

In October 1875 the Government agreed that he might receive the full salary, from the previous 1 January.[17] When he finally left, Lory was given a testimonial, signed by the Bishop and 100 inhabitants and a purse of 72 guineas. The Colonial Secretary was still in despair of finding a replacement.[18]

In his letter of September 1874, Lory gave some useful statistics.

	Adults	Children	Total	C of E	RC	Pres.	Others
E. Falklands							
STANLEY	267	242	509	360	93	40	16
OUTSIDE STANLEY	159	125	284	77	26	174	7
W. Falklands	113	65	178	111	8	31	28
TOTAL	539	432	971	548	127	245	51

The high proportion of Presbyterians was due to the Falkland Island Company bringing out Scottish shepherds and their families. The Roman Catholics were probably mostly Irish, in some cases Pensioners.

As had been the case in 1859 with Bishop Claughton of St Helena, the Anglican clergy in South America were undecided whether their loyalty lay towards Bishop Stirling or the Bishop of London. In 1874 Lord Derby issued a Foreign Office circular to all the South American Consuls informing them that 'the spiritual superintendence hitherto exercised by the Bishop of London over Ministers and Congregations in certain countries in South America shall henceforth devolve on Bishop Stirling.'[19] Perhaps it was a pity that the circular had not been sent four years earlier!

The next Colonial Chaplain, who came in March 1877, was Lowther E. Brandon. He was to stay for 30 years and the Church in the Falklands owes much to his energy and devotion. Mrs Cawkell describes him: 'An Irishman, short sighted, deaf, none too robust, but with a forceful and redoubtable personality.'[20]

Brandon set up highly organized Sunday Schools in Stanley, and supplemented them with a Children's Library, under the care of Mrs

Brandon, a Penny Savings Bank and regular sports and activities. For older people there were reading circles and a Night Schools.

Brandon waged war against the drunkenness which had plagued the Colony since early days. He set up Abstinence Societies for the adults and a Band of Hope for the children. He was especially conscientious in his visitations of the farms in the Camp, as the land outside Stanley was called. This involved great exertion and hardships, as his aim was to visit all the houses once a year, no mean feat. His magic lantern shows, which he took with him to entertain children and adults alike were a byword, both in the Camp and in Stanley.

Stirling had declined to consecrate Holy Trinity Church since it was in a shared building. Brandon, with Stirling's support, was anxious for a new church to be built. In 1882 a Church Building Committee was formed and in 1884 the Government granted a site near the stone jetty. However in August 1886 a disastrous peat slip occurred. A whole mass of peat bog above the town moved downhill, causing considerable damage, and pushing in the back wall of the Exchange building, which had to be demolished. The Building Committee asked for, and were granted, the site of the Exchange building together with the stone from the demolished building. In November 1888 the Bishop issued an appeal in the UK for the new Cathedral. The design, for a church to seat 250, had been given by Mr John Oldred Scott. The estimated cost was at least £6,000, of which the Colonists (now numbering 2,000) had undertaken to raise £3,000, 'a large sum considering many of the population are Presbyterians and RCs.' The Bishop's aim was to raise the other £3,000. He had already obtained half 'from the great kindness and liberality of friends. Some of the very first contributors, and most generous, to the fund were captains of merchant vessels visiting Port Stanley.'[21] The Bishop's son-in-law, Mr W.F.Robinson was the driving force in England. Subscribers included Her Majesty Queen Victoria and the City of Canterbury.

The foundation stone was laid on 6 March 1890. The original design proved too expensive and the Cathedral was built to a design by Sir Arthur Blomfield. On 21 February 1892 Bishop Stirling consecrated Christ Church as a Cathedral and for use as the Parish Church. The cost had risen to nearly £9,000, and it was not until 1902 that the tower was completed by Austrian stone masons. Stirling appointed Brandon as Dean and the Reverend Arnold Theophilus Pinchard of Buenos Aires and the Reverend George Adams of Rosario de Sante Fe as Honorary Canons.[22] HMS *Cleopatra* gave an American organ, and from Keppel Island came an altar book of 1856. In 1893 the stained glass West window in memory of George Markham Dean was dedicated.[23]

Christchurch Cathedral

From 1892 until 1935, there was a Dean at the Cathedral. together with an assistant clergyman, and money had to be raised to provide a house for him. Brandon resigned in 1907, and C.H. Golding-Bird succeeded him as Dean and as Inspector of Schools. However, with Brandon's retirement the office of Colonial Chaplain was abolished and the Government grant of £400 per annum was reduced to £200, but only provided the clergy undertook some educational work. Since 1935, the Bishop has been the Dean, and the resident priest has been known as the Senior Chaplain.

A note about the involvement of the clergy with the schools may be of interest.[24] From the beginning of the colony the Chaplains had some concern with the running of the school. A schoolmaster and a schoolmistress who was the widow of the murdered catechist Phillips arrived in 1860. Since there was only one school, the Governor naturally ruled that care must be taken not to offend the religious feelings of non-Anglicans. However two years later the Governor went further and forbade Bible reading in school. Bull protested strongly but in vain, and in 1865 resigned as Inspector of Schools. It was not until 1871 that a new Governor allowed Bible reading and reinstated Bull. Brandon acted as Schoolmaster for some 18 months from the summer of 1879, when the schoolmaster left at short notice, and in 1882 became Inspector of Schools. After schools had been opened by the Roman Catholics and Baptists, the Government, in 1895, abolished religious instruction in their own school. In 1912 Bishop Blair protested to the UK Government regarding this lack of religious instruction, but to no avail, and from 1916 the post of Inspector of Schools was no longer held by one of the clergy.

The activities of the Bishop were naturally mainly directed towards the mainland of South America, a tremendous task in itself. Indeed, in 1882, when the Archbishop of Canterbury suggested that Stirling might take over British Honduras as well, the Secretary of SAMS, R. J. Simpson, wrote to the Archbishop that he

cannot advise such a course ... the Bishop has a very large and responsible charge and has never yet been able to superintend the Amazon Mission, though situated within the South American continent.[25]

Stirling resigned in April 1900 and became Canon and then Precentor of Wells Cathedral and Assistant Bishop. He died in 1923. In 1927 a new East window of stained glass and an oak chancel screen, paid for by public subscription, were installed in Christ Church Cathedral and dedicated by the Dean, F. S. Vaughan, in memory of Bishop Stirling.

Since they contributed £300 to the stipend of the Bishop, SAMS were invited to submit some names for consideration for the next Bishop. In 1902, Stirling wrote to the Archbishop: 'of the names submitted by SAMS the first choice is E. F. Every.'[26] Edward Every was consecrated that year. He wrote to SPG that, since most of the South American mail steamers stopped at St Vincent, the Bishop of London has made me his commissary with power to licence clergy etc. for Chaplaincy of St Vincent, Cape Verde Islands. I was pleased to have this slight link with the SPG.[27]

In 1910, on the advice of Bishop Every,[28] the Diocese was divided into two, with Every remaining Bishop of the Diocese of Argentina and Eastern South America (until 1937), and L. F. D. Blair appointed to the Diocese of the Falkland Islands. The See was vacant from 1914 to 1919, when Norman Stewart de Jersey was appointed. He was Bishop for 15 years, residing at Valparaiso, since the Diocese included Western South America. He tendered his resignation to Archbishop Lang as from April 1934, on the grounds of age and ill health, and recommended that his successor should be unmarried, since he had much travelling to do, and should be a good sailor!

His successor, consecrated on 29 June 1934, was John Reginald Weller, who had been a missionary in India and a Missions to Seamen Chaplain. In 1937, Bishop Weller was translated to the other Diocese of Argentina and Eastern South America, but retaining supervision of the Diocese of the Falkland Islands.

In January 1945, Weller wrote to Archbishop Fisher, pointing out that the division into two Dioceses in 1910 was made before the Panama Canal was opened, when there were many ships sailing between the west coast of South America and the Falklands. Now there was a problem of travel by sea, and also by land, since the Argentinian officials objected to someone travelling in their country under the name of the Bishop of the Falkland Islands.[29] Therefore in 1946 the two Dioceses were re-united, and Daniel Ivor Evans, who had been consecrated as an Assistant Bishop in the Diocese of Argentina in 1939 and at that time lived in Rio de Janeiro, became Bishop of Argentina and Eastern South America with the Falkland Islands. The title and the form of signature used by the Bishop was obviously a delicate matter.

Evans was succeeded in 1963 by Cyril James Tucker, Vicar of Holy Trinity, Cambridge. Like his predecessor, Bishop Tucker resided at Buenos Aires, but paid regular visits to the Falklands. Two of those visits coincided with important anniversaries. 1967 saw the 75th anniversary of the Consecration of the Cathedral. The Bishop exhorted the people of the Falklands that although they might now be a rather small and somewhat isolated part of the world-wide Anglican Communion, nevertheless they must 'think less about what can the Church in the world give to us and more about what we can do for the World Church.' 1969 was the Centenary of the Consecration of Bishop

Stirling. A commemorative brochure contains a life of Bishop Stirling,[30] and there was a special issue of postage stamps. Bishop Tucker wrote: 'I want the inspiration, the courage and the clear-cut Christian convictions of Bishop Stirling to become increasingly the character of the Church in the Falklands today.'

The senior Chaplain from 1966 to 1970 responsible for the anniversary arrangements was Peter John Millam,[31] who himself came from a 'kelper' family. His grandmother, Hannah Conisbee, in the 19th century was companion to the Duchess of Devonshire on a world cruise. Forced to stop off at the Falklands due to sea sickness, she stayed to marry the former light-house keeper, Christoph Bender, in 1888. Their daughters were educated by the Roman Catholic nuns and one, Beatrice, eventually married a Naval telegraphist whom she met on the Falklands. Peter Millam was their son.[32] In September 1966, soon after his arrival as Chaplain, he found himself, with the RC priest Fr Roel, negotiating with 18 armed guerillas who had hi-jacked an aeroplane, landed on the Stanley racecourse and taken hostage the complete force of six Marines together with the Chief of Police and several civilians. Fortunately the two priests persuaded them to release the hostages and eventually to surrender!

In 1974, Archbishop Michael Ramsey visited South America and inaugurated the Anglican Council of South America (CASA), which was later to become the Province of the Southern Cone of America. It was a time when feelings concerning the sovereignty of the Falklands were riding high, both in Argentina and the Falkland Islands. It was one thing for the Falklanders to belong to a Diocese which came directly under the Archbishop of Canterbury, as had been the case hitherto. It was quite another to be part of a Diocese whose Bishop was to be elected by Argentinians and which was to be part of an autonomous Province. The Falklands Chaplain, Patrick Helyer,[33] as one of the Diocesan clergy, went to Buenos Aires for the Archbishop's visit, but he and the Church Council on the Falklands, and indeed Bishop Tucker himself, understood that the Falklands were to be excluded from CASA. However, in the event – Professor Owen Chadwick suggests it was due to an error of drafting[34] – the Falklands were written into CASA as part of the Diocese of Argentina, and the Diocese of the Falklands lapsed. This caused consternation among the islanders who were prepared to petition the Queen to restore the Archbishop of Canterbury's jurisdiction, and the new Chaplain, Gerald Smith,[35] found himself in the middle of an ecclesiastical storm. Bishop Tucker resigned in 1976, and in 1977, Archbishop Donald Coggan resumed jurisdiction

of the Falklands but appointed the Bishop of Argentina as his
Episcopal Commissary. As can be imagined, this was not a popular
move and in 1982 the Falklands came directly under the Archbishop.

In spite of all the Diocesan changes, the clergy had maintained a
steady devoted ministry in a parish whose scattered nature created its
own problems. Patrick Helyer, Chaplain 1971-75, has kindly allowed
me access to the scrap books and diaries which he kept, and his
experiences are typical of many.

Visits to the many settlements in the Camp, and small islands, took
up about twelve visits a year, lasting anything from two to twelve days
each. Each Camp tour would cover many farms and include Holy
Communion, Baptisms, pastoral visits and slide shows, and very
occasionally a marriage. Canon Helyer – he was made a Canon in 1972
– would write up each tour, including historical notes. What days were
left would be spent in Stanley, where the Chaplain's house was still
known as the Deanery. Helyer was also Chaplain to the Missions to
Seamen, the Royal Navy and Royal Marines, the hospital and prison
and the Girl's Brigade. Hospitality was freely given, and every
Christmas Day Canon and Mrs Helyer would host members of the
crew of HMS *Endurance*. Special events were also recorded. In 1973, Mrs
Vi Robson celebrated 50 years as honorary organist to the Cathedral,
and in 1974 Mrs Harding left £2,000 to the Cathedral Trustees.

Helyer's successor, Gerald Smith, left in 1978 and the following year
the Intercontinental Church Society assumed responsibility for recruitment of the clergy, and appointed Harry Bagnall.[36] Harry had worked
in the wholesale meat trade before he was ordained, and he and his wife
Iris told me during my visit in 1984 that when they saw an advertisement for a priest on the Falklands with the requirement 'must be able
to butcher own beef and mutton' they thought it was meant for them.
He had to dig his own peat too! We have already referred to his and
Iris' splendid and courageous ministry during the invasion of 1982 and
it would be impertinent for me to presume to add to his own account in
Faith under Fire. He and Monsignor Spraggon were confined to Port
Stanley, where there was a curfew, and were not allowed to visit the
Camp, even for funerals. It is noticeable that by a judicious disregard of
the Argentinian regulations, they were able to exercise a full pastoral
ministry, visiting people in Hospital and in their homes. Indeed, Harry
Bagnall writes that as the Church administration became necessarily
less, the opportunities for pastoral care became greater, and very
important such care was. Harry Bagnall was made an Officer of the
Order of the British Empire in 1982. He and Iris served seven years on

the Falklands, and he was succeeded in 1987 by Canon 'Gerry' Murphy,[37] who had been Rector of Sandringham and Domestic Chaplain to the Queen. His successor, from autumn 1991, is Canon Stephen Palmer RNR.[38]

Christ Church Cathedral celebrates the centenary of its consecration on 21 February 1992. A hundred years of Falklands' weather takes its toll of a building, and 1990 saw the launch of an Appeal, with Her Royal Highness the Duchess of York as Patron, for funds for the restoration of the Cathedral. The immediate need is for £600,000, to replace defective brickwork, the roof, the organ and heating system and to refix the windows. To quote from the Appeal Brochure:

With other places of worship on the Islands, the Cathedral stands as a symbol of God in their midst and for the qualities of freedom, love, peace and justice which are greatly cherished.

THE UNITED FREE CHURCH – THE TABERNACLE

We have seen that a number of Scottish shepherds came to the Falklands in the nineteenth century. Mr Anthony Yeoman, a Minister of the Free Church of Scotland was ordained in 1871 for the Falklands. He and his wife lived some 70 miles from Port Stanley, at Darwin, where a prefabricated iron church was built in 1873. He resigned in 1882, and was succeeded by William H. Philip, who arrived with his family in that year. In his reports Philip speaks of travels on horseback of up to 2,000 miles a year, visiting especially, in order of frequency, Walker Creek, North Arm, Stanley, Douglas Station and Don Carlos. In 1886 he wished to move his Manse to Stanley but it was not possible. He resigned in 1890, because of his wife's ill health, but no replacement was available.[39]

However, in 1888, the famous Baptist Charles Spurgeon sent out a Baptist minister, George M. Harris, who based himself in Stanley. (It will be recalled that in 1885 the Baptists on St Helena had appealed to Spurgeon for a minister.) Under Harris' successor, C. E. Lawson Good, a prefabricated iron building was imported from England and erected in 1891 in Barrack Street, where it is known today as the Tabernacle.

The Reverend W. Forrest McWhan MBE, DD, a Scottish Presbyterian, was for 30 years the Nonconformist Minister at the Tabernacle. When he arrived, aged 21, in 1934, the Tabernacle had been without a Minister for 18 years. He played a full part not only in the Church but in the life of the community generally. He was a member of the Legislative Council and a number of Government Committees, and also Chaplain to the Boys' Brigade. He married a local girl, Miss Nellie

Ennega in 1940. He was Information Officer during the War, and from 1944 edited the *Falkland Islands Weekly News* until the appointment of a Government Information Officer four years later. In 1948 he was made a Member of the Order of the British Empire. In 1952 he published a book, *The Falkland Islands Today*. In it he notes that attendance at morning service in the Cathedral is small, but Sunday evening may 'bring out up to nearly 100 people'. Similarly at the Tabernacle evening congregations are larger than in the morning. Forrest McWhan died on 25 August 1965. A memorial plaque in the Tabernacle was unveiled by the Governor in May 1974, commemorating the renewal of the pulpit, the choir stalls and the interior panelling in his memory. The Government ship MV *Forrest* was also named in his honour, in 1968.

The Reverend Paul Charman, an independent free churchman, was Minister from 1967 to 1971. A good percentage of his time, like the other ministers of the Tabernacle, was spent visiting the farm settlements, occasionally on horseback.

The Reverend Robin W. Forrester, a Baptist, arrived in September 1971, resurrected the *Tabernacle Messenger* and took over the Editorship of the secular monthly *Falkland Island Times*.

In December 1976 a Home Council was formed in England to support the Tabernacle by prayer and finance. They launched the Penguin Project in July 1977 with the immediate aim of finding and financing a minister for the Tabernacle. They estimated the cost for a three year period to be over £12,000. The Project finally chose the Reverend Alex Queen, a Methodist from Canada, who had 24 years missionary experience in India, and latterly was Pastor of a Free Methodist Church in Ontario, Canada. Alex Queen and his wife arrived in 1978 for a three year tour. They were assisted by a layman, Mr Dennis Overton, a Presbyterian, who volunteered to serve for 10 months before going to Aberdeen University.

In August 1982 the Penguin Project sent the Reverend Paul Charman back to the Falklands for a four week visit to assess the post-conflict situation for the Church, and to express Christian solidarity. On his return he issued an account of his pastoral visit.

A Baptist, the Reverend Colin Frampton, came for three months, but from when he left in February 1984, up to the time of writing, the Tabernacle has been without a Minister, except for a visit for about six weeks towards the end of 1991 by the Reverend John Fraser, a retired Church of Scotland Minister.

THE ROMAN CATHOLIC CHURCH[40]

The expedition of de Bougainville which established the first French settlement at Port Louis on the East Falklands in 1764 carried a Benedictine monk Dom Antoine Joseph Pernety, who acted as botanist and wrote a *Historical Journal*. He and his successors screened off part of the dining room in their main building and used it as a church. The French settlement was handed over in 1767 to the Spanish whose first impressions were less than favourable.[41] 'I remain in this miserable desert suffering all for the love of God' wrote their Chaplain, the Franciscan Sebastian Villanueva. They renamed the place 'The Island of our Lady of Solitude' and Port Louis became known as Port Soledad. Within a year a church, just over 9 feet high, was built, mostly of sods. A wooden bell tower was added in 1774, to call the 80 settlers to worship. A pulpit and font were added to the church in the 1780s. In 1790 Fr Pius de Aguiar wrote to his Bishop in Buenos Aires that the church, which could only hold a hundred people, was too small for the increased size of the settlement. Work was begun on a new church of stone and brick in 1794 but progress was slow, due partly to a shortage of lime. It was finally consecrated on 4 November 1801. The Spanish settlement at Port Soledad was served by the Franciscans from 1767 to 1781, by the Mercedarians from 1779 to 1793, and by mostly secular priests from 1794 to 1811. The last priest was Fr Juan Canosa who left in February 1811, when the Spanish settlement came to an end.

The British settlement in the Falklands in the 1840s, as we have seen, included a proportion of Roman Catholics, but they had no priest. Thomas Havers, the Roman Catholic Colonial Manager of the Falkland Islands Company in the 1850s, rented a house in Stanley, where he held services on Sundays and gave religious instruction on some weekdays. He wrote to Cardinal Wiseman, Archbishop of Westminster, and also to Rome, in 1856, asking for a priest. As a result Monsignor Anthony Fahy in Buenos Aires sent Fr Laurence Kirwan in 1856/7 on a temporary mission. He was the first of several Irish priests from South America.

Governor Colonel A. K. D'Arcy arrived in 1870 and his wife became a staunch Roman Catholic. Stirling wrote to the Archbishop of Canterbury in November 1872 that 'since Mrs D'Arcy, the Governor's wife, joined the Roman Communion, Govt. House has become HQ of the Romish Propaganda in the Colony.'[42] His letter was evidently passed to Lord Kimberley who commented, 'I have heard of Mrs D'Arcy's proselytizing efforts, but I do not see how I can interfere with the Governor's wife in these matters.'[43] Possibly Stirling's real concern

St Mary's Roman Catholic Church

was the Governor's proposal to reduce the Colonial Chaplain's salary and to redistribute it to provide a subsidy to an RC priest and a Free Kirk minister. The Colonial Chaplain would be left with £150 p.a.[44]

The Roman Catholics had secured a grant of land on which to build a church in 1857, and had opened a subscription list to pay for the building but found it difficult to raise the money. Fr William Walsh visited from Montevideo in 1872 and used a Government building (the present Central Store) for worship. They then bought a quarter of an acre of land (Pump Green) on which a church was built with free Government labour. The church was opened in June 1873 by Fr Vincent de Vilas from Buenos Aires. So far the visits by priests had only been occasional, but in 1875 Fr James Foran of the Diocese of Hexham heard of Mr Havers' letter to Cardinal Wiseman and volunteered to come. He stayed until 1881, and then during the summer months until 1886. He started a school in 1880 'in Barry's old house, behind the court house'. In 1885, a new church was built on the site they had acquired in 1857, 'on the front road'. It was built in two months by Mr G. M. Dean, in part exchange for the old church and its land. Mass was first celebrated there on 28 February 1886.

Fr Patrick Dillon came in 1886 and Fr Felix M. Grisar in 1887.

Fr James Foran, had recommended that the RC Church on the

Falklands should be joined to the southern region of the mainland to form one Vicariate. In 1882, the Apostolic Prefecture of Patagonia Meridional was created, comprising the Santa Cruz area, the Falklands, Tierra del Fuego and the adjacent islands, with Mgr Jose Fagnano as the first Apostolic Prefect. Mgr Fagnano established himself at Punta Arenas in Tierra del Fuego, and wrote to Don Bosco, 'Soon I will send a priest to the Malvinas – someone who knows English well ... it is 2 years since they have had a priest.' In 1888 Mgr Fagnano accompanied the Irish born Fr Patrick Diamond to the Falklands, where they found a wooden chapel, 16 metres by 6 metres in good repair. Fr Diamond thus became the first Salesian Chaplain on the islands. For the next 64 years, until 1952, the Falklands were to be looked after by the Salesian Fathers of Don Bosco.[45] Mgr Fagnano returned, leaving a list of recommendations for Diamond:

(1) Keep a diary
(2) Note number of communicants each month
(3) Note number of baptized and converted
(4) Note hours of rest and work
(5) Clean the Chapel
(6) Renew the Host every 8 days
(7) Visit the Holy Sacrament every day.

Additional priests were sent to assist Fr Diamond and a school was begun, for about 60 boys and girls.

Diamond was succeeded in 1890 by another Irishman, Fr Patrick O'Grady. From 1892 the Mission received an annual grant of £60 from the Governor and £5 from the Falkland Islands Co. Mgr Fagnano visited and instructed that the priests should rise at 5 am and retire at 9.30 pm. In 1897 the school was too small for the growing number of pupils. A new prefabricated chapel was ordered from England and opened in 1899. Much of the cost had been donated by Luis Baillon, head of the Falkland Islands Co. The old chapel now became the school.

At the end of 1902, Diamond returned to succeed O'Grady. By 1904, the school had 41 boys and 34 girls, of whom half were non-Catholics.

Fr Mario Luis Migone, born in Montevideo in 1863 and who had already twice served as an assistant, returned to succeed Diamond in 1905.

In 1907, three Sisters of a teaching order, the Daughters of Maria Auxilladora, arrived to found a school for girls. Mgr Fagnano had instructed them 'to go and make our holy religion loved and respected in a population which is addicted to Anglicanism'. One hopes that the

Anglican Chaplain had the same opinion of the population! Classes began with 40 Catholic and 20 Protestant girls. The Sisters had no subsidy and lived on the school fees. Sister Maria Ussher came in 1909 to be Headmistress and stayed for 33 years. The Sisters grew in number.

Fr Migone died in 1937, after spending 33 years on the Falklands. At his own request he was the only RC priest there from 1905 until 1934. He had become the best known and best loved priest. 'He had never complained of the solitude or the climate but burned with the love of God and for the salvation of his brothers.'

Another Irishman, Fr Hugh Drumm came in 1934 to assist Migone and then succeeded him until 1947. He was there during a difficult time, with no Salesian visitors, and the more so when the Sisters left in 1942. He was succeeded in 1948 by a fellow countryman, Fr John Kelly who stayed until 1952. He was the last of the Salesian Fathers on the Falklands and later was to spend 15 years on St Helena.

In 1952 the Falkland Islands were made an Apostolic Prefecture, and the missionary order the Mill Hill Fathers were asked to accept responsibility for the Falklands, and Monsignor James Ireland arrived as Prefect Apostolic of the Falklands. Mgr Ireland was made an Officer of the Order of the British Empire in 1973. In that year he was succeeded by Mgr Daniel M. Spraggon, assisted by Fr Philip Bruggeman, who was later to spend some years on St Helena and Ascension.

Mgr Spraggon sadly died on the Falklands on 27 September 1985 and Fr Augustine Monaghan took responsibility until the appointment of Mgr Anton Agreiter in October 1986. When in August 1986 the islands of St Helena, Ascension and Tristan were designated a 'mission sui juris', they were placed under Mgr Agreiter, who was assisted by a succession of priests and Lay Brothers. At the time of writing Mgr Anton Agreiter is still the Apostolic Prefect of the Islands of the South Atlantic.

Notes and References

Abbreviations

EIC   East India Company
IOL   India Office Library
LPL   Lambeth Palace Library
       eg LPL BENSON65 f67 = Archbishop Benson's papers, Vol 65, folio 67
RHL   Rhodes House Library (USPG Archives)
       CLR = Copies of Letters Received
       CLS = Copies of Letters Sent
       Series D = Original Letters Received
SAMS   South American Missionary Society
SPG   Society for the Propagation of the Gospel united with the Universities'
       Mission to Central Africa (UMCA) to become
USPG   United Society for the Propagation of the Gospel
StHDA   St Helena Diocesan Archives
StHGA   St Helena Government Archives

In biographical details, b = born, p = ordained priest, d = died.

Introduction

1 RHL CLR1 16 f14
2 SPG Annual Report 1872
3 *cf* Tony Cross, *St Helena*. 1980 p44: 'Even the British Post Office, which for so long had used only string made from St Helena hemp, had turned to synthetic fibre.'
4 LPL MS3124 f67
5 Unpublished manuscript, kindly made available by Mrs Luard.
6 *Tristan Times* Dec. 1983.

Chapter One (pages 23 to 49)

1 Gosse, *St Helena 1502-1938*, 1990 p3, quoting Osorio da Fonseca, *Narrative of the Voyage of Joao da Nova Costella* in 1502.
2 It has been suggested that the chapel was built by a later expedition, on the grounds that there is no evidence that any of Castella's ships were unseaworthy, but this is an argument from silence.
3 Private letter to the author.
4 Gosse p12
5 Gosse pp15,16
6 A personal investigation, kindly undertaken for the writer, by Mr Trevor Hearl, into the British Library Cotton MSS, Appx XLVII (formerly Sloane 5008 – erroneously numbered in the Ayscough Catalogue '5007' for the *St Helena Journal*). See also (a) Elizabeth Story Donno (ed.) *An Elizabethan in 1582: the Diary of Richard Madox Fellow of All Souls*. Hakluyt Society 1976; and (b) E. G. R. Taylor (ed.) *The Troublesome Voyage of Captain Edward Fenton 1582-83*. Hakluyt Society 1957.

260   Notes and References

7 Kindly pointed out by the Reverend Gordon Taylor
8 J. H. van Linschoten. *Voyage to the East Indies.* Quoted in Gosse pp21,22
9 Gosse p27
10 Gosse p39
11 Gosse p32
12 Gosse pp28,29
13 Janisch. *St Helena Records.* 1885, 19/12/1673
14 Janisch 16/4/1701
15 Gosse p57
16 Norman Sykes, *Church and State in England in the 18th Century.* Cambridge 1934, p212. J. R. H. Moorman, *A History of the Church in England.* Black 1967, p286.
17 Janisch 19/12/1673
18 Janisch 1683
19 Janisch 21/12/1719
20 Cf John Keay, *The Honourable Company*, 1991, p250.
21 Janisch 7/9/1723
22 Janisch 4/1/1725
23 Gosse p76
24 Janisch 26/7/1732
25 Janisch 2/2/1774
26 Janisch 26/10/1691
27 Janisch 30/9/1732
28 Gosse pp140/141
29 When Gosse's *St Helena 1502-1938* was first published in 1938, Canon Walcott, Vicar of Jamestown and Editor of the Diocesan Magazine, felt that Gosse was too unsympathetic to the EIC Chaplains for this reason. Although he had already published a series of articles on the EIC Chaplains from December 1935 onwards, he repeated it at greater depth in an attempt to rehabilitate them.
30 Janisch 5/8/1684
31 Janisch 6/5/1685 & p31
32 Janisch 26/10/1691
33 Janisch 25/7/1692
34 Janisch 16/4/1701 (p69)
35 Janisch 10/2/1703
36 Janisch 21/12/1719. Jacks and Old Women are still names of fish on St Helena
37 Janisch 5/1/1720
38 Gosse pp318/9. Masham died on the island 30/4/1706
39 Janisch 26/12/1715
40 Janisch 28/8/1716
41 Janisch 8/10/1717
42 Jansich 29/9/1738
43 Janisch 16/9/1790
44 Janisch 29/8/1797
45 T. H. Brooke, *A History of the Island of St Helena :.. to the Year 1806.* 1808. See pp382-389
46 See Ernest Marshall Howse, *Saints in Politics, the Clapham Sect and the growth of freedom*, George Allen & Unwin 1973
47 Janisch 14/1/1811 and 23/8/1811
48 Janisch 27/1/1812 and 21/2/1812
49 Janisch 10/4/1812
50 Janisch 11/11/1701
51 Janisch 12/4/1813 (p233)

52 Janisch 23/1/1815
53 Janisch 10/4/1815
54 Janisch 15/4/1816 and 19/5/1816
55 G.C. Kitching *A Handbook and Gazetteer of the Island of St Helena*. p61
56 Chaplin *St Helena Who's Who*. pp227-231. Janisch 9/7/1821. See also Gosse pp285-287, quoting Chaplin.
57 Janisch 16/7/1821
58 Thomas Robson *St Helena Memoirs* Nisbet 1827. See also Chaplin, Chapter 'What happened at Mason's Stock House'
59 George Horsley Wood. b1796, son of Gen. Wood, 2nd Lt. 1813, d1874.
60 Born 1789 in Jamaica, son of ADC to the Governor.
61 Gosse pp277/9; 300
62 Kitching p60. Hearl points out that ironically it was a period of prosperity for many, especially tradesmen, and to some extent it was wealth which produced the squalor. See Hearl, *St Helena's Social Revolution 1834-1869*. St Helena Link 1991
63 I am indebted to Mrs A.M. Cunningham, Curator of Manuscripts at the Univ. of the Witwatersrand, and to the Reverend R. Cottingham, for checking that his last signature in the Church Registers is 12 February 1837 (St Paul's Baptism Register).
64 LPL BLOMFIELD59 f60. A letter from Bp. of London to Admiralty, asking for remuneration for Helps.
65 Max Warren, *Social History and Church Mission* SCM 1967 p55
66 Edwin Hatfield, *St Helena and the Cape of Good Hope* New York 1853. pp144/5; 161/2
67 LPLS BLOMFIELD43 f60
68 For Bishop's Gray's visits see:
   (a) Robert Gray, *Journal of Bishop's Visitation* 1859
   (b) Charles Gray, *Life of Robert Gray*, Rivingtons 1876
   (c) Audrey Brooke, *Robert Gray*, OUP 1947
69 Letter from STH 10/4/1849. *Journal* pp103-106
70 Gray summoned a public meeting, at which the Governor presided, to further the aims of the Society, 'the maintenance of the Ministry, the erection of Churches, Missions, and a fund for Bibles, Prayer books and other religious works approved by the Bishop and the foundation of a scholarship ... in connection with our Collegiate School at the Cape'. Gray's Journal pp110/1
71 See Chapter 5
72 Letter 10/4/1849. *Journal* pp108/9
73 StHDA
74 StHDA
75 Gutsche, *The Bishop's Lady*, 1970 p166
76 RHL CLRI15 f21. 19/12/1859 to SPG

Chapter Two (pages 50 to 96)
1 StHDA
2 StHDA 21/3/1866
3 RHL D Series 8 to SPG 19/12/1859
4 RHL CLRI15 f47 to SPG 27/6/1860
5 RHL CLRI15 f74 to SPG 21/11/1860
6 LPL MS1751 f88
7 RHL CLRI15 f47
8 RHL CLRI15 f24

9 SPG Annual Report 1860; *Mission Field* v 21
10 LPL MS1751 f69
11 RHL CLR115 f74
12 LPL TAIT121 ff50-55
13 LPL MS1751 f58 29/11/1861
14 LPL MS1751 f66 16/7/1861
15 LPL TAIT121 f60
16 stHDA But see Ch 1 – Jamestown and Bousfield 'whose district it was'.
17 stHDA
18 LPL TAIT159 f265
19 LPL TAIT194 f119 Col. Sec. Kimberley 30/8/1873
20 LPL TAIT83 f82 Col. Sec. Buckingham
21 RHL CLR116 ff47/9
22 RHL CLR116 f47
23 LPL TAIT201 f89 11/12/1873
24 LPL TAIT289 f167 15/5/1873
25 LPL TAIT289 f217 2/6/1873
26 RHL CLR116 ff291/2
27 The front page gives a useful summary of the Sunday services in all the churches.
28 SPG Annual Report 1895
29 RHL CLR117 f47 13/1/1899
30 LPL LANG105 f99
31 LPL MS3124 f57
32 LPL MS3124 f65
33 Taylor, *Sea Chaplains*, 1978 p438
34 Kotze, *St Helena Journal* p38
35 Mark Parker, Dio. of stH. Tour Report 1989. USPG
36 Private letter to author

Chapter Three (pages 97 to 114)

1 Janisch 30/9/1678
2 Janisch 26/10/1691
3 Janisch 7/4/1711
4 stHDA
5 Janisch 2/2/1774
6 See also (a) a print in the St Helena Museum of a drawing by J. S. Graham of the St Helena Artillery, made in the time of Brigadier General Dallas (Gov. 1828-36), and (b) a sketch by Ozias Humphry dated 1797, a print of which is reproduced in P. L. Teale's work on the artist.
7 stHDA
8 See account in *StH Guardian* 30/1/1862
9 Gosse p78
10 Janisch 26/10/1691
11 Janisch 20/4/1699
12 Janisch 30/9/1732
13 Illustrated in a thesis by Dr Percy Teale 1974.
14 *The Builder* Vol xi, No 541, 18 June 1853, p387, kindly supplied, with other information, by Mr Jonathan N. Mané, Lecturer in Art History, Univ. of Canterbury, New Zealand.
15 stHDA
16 stHDA

17 StHDA
18 StHGA
19 *The Builder* Vol XI, p387/8
20 StHDA
21 StHDA
22 Synod Report 1983

Chapter Four (pages 115 to 156)
1 SPG Annual Report 1867
2 RHL CLR116 f445
3 RHL CLR116 f483 18/11/1897
4 RHL CLR117 f36 22/11/1898
5 RHL CLR117 f47 13/1/1899
6 See Hearl, *The Rise and Fall of James Francis Homagee 1857-1917*, St Helena Link 1991.
7 b1856, Keble & Cuddesdon, p1880
8 St Aug. Coll. Cant.
9 Chancellors School Lincoln p1892
10 St Paul's Grahamstown, p1912
11 Keble MA, Leeds Clergy Sch. p1889
12 Lincoln Theol., p1928
13 USPG Annual Report 1954
14 b1903, Univ. of London, p1940, d1990
15 St Paul's Grahamstown, p1956
16 b1922, Lincoln Theol., p1955, d1991
17 b1912, Lichfield Theol., p1938
18 b1949, Lancaster BA, Durham PGCE, Chichester Theol. Coll. BTh, p1981
19 StHDA
20 RHL CLR116 f97
21 SPG Annual Report 1878
22 RHL CLR116 f255
23 SPG Annual Report 1891
24 SPG Annual Report 1892
25 StHDA, see also RHL CLR116 f423
26 RHL CLR116 f445
27 SPG Annual Report 1894
28 StHDA
29 RHL CLR116 f475-485
30 LPL F.TEMPLE60 f10
31 LPL F.TEMPLE60 f8,9
32 StHDA
33 Selwyn Coll. Camb. p1909
34 TCD MA Chancellors Sch. Linc. p1898
35 Lichfield Theol. p1917
36 b1914, Wycliffe Hall, p1964, d1991
37 b1914, Lincoln Coll MA, Wycliffe Hall, p1939
38 b1943, Stetson & Exeter Univ. MA, Cuddesdon, p1978
39 Univ of Rhodesia BA, St Paul's Grahamstown, p1975
40 b1942, K.Coll, London AKC, p1968
41 b1927, Brit. Columbia, p1962
42 *Kilvert's Diary* Ed. Plomer, Jonathan Cape 1938 Vol 1 p218
43 SPG Annual Report 1876

44 b1866, St Cath. Coll. Cam. p1895
45 RHL CLR118 f239a
46 St Aug. Coll. Cant., p1918
47 LPL MS3124 f65
48 Mirfield p1935
49 St Paul's Grahamstown
50 Univ. of Witwatersrand, KCL Warminster, p1976
51 b1927, Lampeter, p1955, d1975
52 b1918, Bp's Coll. Cheshunt, p1963
53 b1909, p1959, d1988
54 b1941, Kelham, p1973
55 p1983

Chapter Five (pages 157 to 178)
1 Janisch 19/12/1673
2 Janisch 1678
3 SPG Annual Report 1859
4 SPG Annual Report 1867
5 SPG Annual Report 1864
6 SPG Annual Report 1863/4
7 StHDA
8 RHL CLR116 f142/3
9 LPL MS3124 f65
10 Watkins, *Soldiers and Preachers Too*, 1906 and Trevor Hearl, 'An early Methodist on StH' 1988.
11 Kitching, p61
12 Kitching, p60
13 Hatfield, *St Helena and the Cape of Good Hope*, NY 1853; Ed Teale 1975, p134 & 159
14 RHL CLR115 f24
15 RHL CLR115 f47
16 LPL TAIT121 f60 letter to Canterbury 7/2/1861
17 LPL LONGLEY6 f257
18 South African Baptist Press 1957
19 R. Wiggins. *Hist. of Salvation Army*, Nelson 1964 especially Vol II p292, and Vol IV p135. Also article by Brigadier Young.
20 Born in Wiltshire in 1835, came to St Helena in July 1852
21 *The War Cry* (English) 23 July 1884
22 RHL CLR116 f270
23 'All the World' 1887
24 Trevor Hearl. *St Helena Salvationists in 1888.* July 1988 and Wiggins Vol IV p135
25 *The War Cry* (South African) 1989 p6,7

II Ascension (pages 179 to 197)
1 StHGA Misc papers relating to St Mary Ascension p4
2 StHGA Misc papers p7
3 SPG *Mission Field* Aug 1861
4 St Mary's Ascension Church records f1,2,3,4,38,39
5 SPG *Mission Field* Vol VI p169
6 Gill. *Six months on Ascension* 1878 p77
7 I regret I am unable to trace the originator of this phrase.
8 Asc. Ch. records f25

9 SPG *Mission Field* Vol VI p169
10 Asc. Ch. records f11,39
11 StHGA Misc papers p17
12 Asc. Ch. records f25
13 Ibid f26
14 Ibid f26
15 Asc. Marriage Register
16 Asc. Ch. records f40
17 Ibid f37
18 Ibid f67
19 Ibid f27,28,29
20 Ibid f12-24; f30-37
21 Ibid f31
22 StHGA Misc papers p19
23 RHL CLR116 f230 letter from Bp. 7/7/1882
24 RHL CLR116 f312
25 StHGA Misc papers p24,25,26
26 Asc. Ch. records f68-74
27 USPG Review of the year 1966 'paid for partly by a USPG grant and partly by a Government grant of £3,000'.
28 b1918, Edinburgh, p1951
29 b1926, Clifton, p1958
30 b1944, Kelham, p1969
31 b1942, St Chad's Durham BSC & Lincoln Theol. Coll., p1967
32 b1928, Wycliffe Hall, p1963
33 b1927, Bp's Coll. Cheshunt, p1959
34 b1951, Clare Coll MA & Keble BTh, Cuddesdon, p1979

III Tristan da Cunha (pages 199 to 233)

1 Augustus Earle. *Journal*. Longman 1832 p303 (OUP 1966 p211).
2 Tristan Marriage Register, quoted in *St Helena Journal* (p27) by Mrs Anne Kotze, to whom I am grateful for permission to quote.
3 SPG Annual Report 1856 p.lxxxvi
4 RHL CLR116 f142
5 Ibid f173
6 Ibid f174
7 Ibid f190
8 Ibid f231
9 Ibid f224
10 StHDA
11 RHL CLR116 f245
12 Ibid f270
13 Ibid f295
14 Ibid f401a
15 SPG Annual Report 1901
16 RHL CLR116 f408
17 Published as *Three years in Tristan da Cunha* Skeffington 1910
18 StHDA
19 Ibid
20 RHL CLR118 f147
21 Article in *Tristan da Cunha Newsletter* September 1990
22 issue 14/7/1922

23 RHL D Series 298 f62 7/1/1925
24 RHL CLR119 f15
25 RHL CLR118 f202 7/8/22
26 RHL CLR118 f235b 5/4/1923 see also CLR118 f144,147 & CLR119f12, 21a, 269.
27 RHL CLR119 f52 6/6/26
28 St Aidan's Durham, p1920, MC 1918, MBE 1937
29 See their books, *Crisis in Utopia* 1971 and *Tristan … and the Roaring Forties* 1982
30 RHL CLS230 31/5/1937
31 August and September 1950 issues
32 Univ. London BD, KCL, p1940
33 b1912, Lichfield Theol., p1938
34 b1919, Univ Leeds & Mirfield BA, p1945
35 b1915, Bp's Coll. Cheshunt, p1950
36 b1903, p1914, d1990
37 SPG Review of the Year 1964
38 b1927, Exeter Coll. Oxford, Llan. St Michael, p1956
39 SPG Review of the Year 1966
40 b1930, Trinity Coll. Camb. MA, St John's Durham, p1957
41 USPG *Tristan da Cunha Newsletter* 23. Spring 1973
42 b1908, Trinity Cambridge MA, Ridley Hall, p1934
43 *Home & Family* (MU Quarterly Magazine) March/May 1978
44 b1915, Wycliffe Hall ALCD, p1939
45 b1934, St Paul's Grahamstown, p1965
46 B.Soc.Sc. St Paul's Grahamstown p1983
47 *Home & Family* (MU) Dec 1985/Feb 1986
48 Vatican Newspaper, *L'Osservatione Romano* 12/3/1986
49 St Paul's & St Augustine's SA, p1946
50 b1930 St Paul's Grahamstown p1972
51 *Tristan da Cunha Newsletter* No9 Sept 1991. Pub. Tristan da Cunha Assoc.

IV Falkland Islands (pages 235 to 257)
 1 Cawkell etc, *Falkland Islands*, Macmillan 1960.
 2 LPL TAIT424 f220
 3 Wylie (Ed). *Life and Missionary Travels of the Rev. J. Ogle.*
 4 RHL CLR115 f38-40 15/3/1860
 5 Ibid f60 29/7/1860
 6 LPL TAIT171 f120
 7 Hardy, *Life of Stirling*, written for centenary of his consecration.
 8 RHL CLR115 f60
 9 LPL TAIT171 f135
10 Ibid f249
11 LPL TAIT170 f152-5
12 Ibid f156
13 LPL TAIT86 f266
14 LPL TAIT170 f156
15 LPL TAIT185 f191 27/5/1872
16 LPL TAIT202 25/9/1874
17 LPL TAIT214 f187
18 Ibid f191; TAIT225 f209
19 LPL TAIT93 f81 31/8/1874; BENSON19 f36
20 Cawkell etc, *Falkland Islands*, p133
21 LPL BENSON65 f67 17/11/1888

22 BENSON108 f1

23 A brochure compiled by the Rev. Peter Millam for the 75th anniversary in 1967 contains an account of the consecration in 1892 and subsequent history, including a useful record of gifts to the Cathedral

24 I am indebted to David B. Smith's article 'Church, State and Schooling in the Falkland Islands' in the *Journal of Educational Administration and History* Vol XXII No2, July 1990, Univ of Leeds.

25 LPL TAIT287 f337

26 LPL F.TEMPLE59 f364

27 RHL CLR115 f38,60

28 LPL FISHER10 f270

29 LPL FISHER1 f134-257

30 Hardy, *Life of Stirling*

31 b1936, Lampeter BA, Ridley Hall p1964

32 *Falkland Islands Newsletter* No49 Nov 1991. Pub. Falkland Islands Association. 'Art. Beartrice Orissa Millam 1899-1991'.

33 b1915, Wycliffe Hall ALCD, p1939

34 Owen Chadwick, *Michael Ramsey*, Oxford 1990 p233/4

35 b1936, Sarum Theol. p1964

36 b1930, Southwark Ord. p1968, OBE 1982

37 b1926, TCD MA, p1953, Domestic Chap. to Queen 1979-87, Chap. to Queen from 1987

38 b1947, Oak Hill p1975. See Art. in *Falkland Islands Newsletter* No47 May 1991.

39 *Proceedings of General Assembly of the Free Church of Scotland* 1872-1891. I am indebted to Miss Brenda Webster for her research on my behalf.

40 For the history of the RC Church in the Falklands I am indebted to Mgr Anton Agreiter, Apostolic Prefect, for a great deal of help. See his *Catholic Church on the Falkland Islands* August 1991.

41 Cawkell etc, *Falkland Islands*. For the Spanish period see Jose Brunet, *La Iglesia en las Islas Malvinas durante el periodo hispano*, 1969, kindly supplied by Mgr Agreiter.

42 LPL TAIT185 f196

43 LPL TAIT92 f123

44 LPL TAIT185 f196 14/11/1872 and f199 25/1/1873. See also TAIT194 f89 1/4/73

45 For the Salesian period see Baratta, *Prescentia Salesiana en las Islas Malvinas*, kindly supplied by the Father Archivist of the Salesian Fathers in Rome, and translated for me by Mrs Elizabeth Dooley, a missionary of the South American Missionary Society.

The Bishops of the Church of South Africa in the 1880s.
Back row: D. McKenzie, Zululand. H. B. Bousfield, Pretoria. A B. Webb, Bloemfontein &
Grahamstown. W. E. Macrorie, Natal. Front row: T. E. Welby, St Helena. W. W. Jones,
Cape Town. H. Callaway, St John's. (Courtesy Martha George, St Helena)

Appendix A

Part of Bishop's Charge
at St Helena Diocesan Synod 1983

CHURCH OF THE PROVINCE OF SOUTHERN AFRICA

... The Diocese of St Helena has been part of the Church of the Province of South Africa since 1859 ... In 1982, the Provincial Synod changed the name to 'The Church of the Province of Southern Africa', since a number of the Dioceses in the Province are outside the Republic of South Africa; St Helena, Lebombo and Niassa, Lesotho, Swaziland and Zululand.

We receive a great deal of help from the Province, especially towards paying our clergy stipends. In return they need the support of our prayers, especially in their continued struggles against the evils of racism, in consequence of which many have suffered detention and some have lost their lives ...

RECRUITMENT OF CLERGY

At the last Diocesan Synod in 1933 ... Ascension had not had a priest since 1905 ... and was not to get one until 1967, a gap of 62 years. The Bishop looked after the two Parishes of St Paul and St Matthew ... For 25 years of the last 50 years, either St Paul's and St Matthew's shared a priest, or the Bishop looked after St Paul's ... We cannot always rely on having a Vicar for each Parish.

VOCATIONS

But there is no reason why we should not have our own St Helenian priests. Two men, born on this island have returned to serve as priests – F.H. Baker 1884-94, and James Johnson ... 1966-71. I cannot believe that God will not call other St Helenians to serve Him as priests. Clergy, parents, teachers and friends must be continually alert to foster such vocations.

It may not necessarily be the full-time ministry. Many men, in England and Africa for example, who have a full-time job, as well as some retired men, are training in their spare time to be priests, and when they are ordained they continue with their normal jobs, but are able to minister the Word and Sacraments on Sundays, and it may be at other times. Why should we not have such men on St Helena, able to celebrate the Holy Communion for the people in the area where they live, and to lead them in worship?

And then there is the Lay Ministry. Men and women, not ordained and so not able to celebrate the Holy Communion, but who have had a sufficient training here on this island, to enable them to lead worship and to preach. Pray and consider well, whether God is calling you to some such form of ministry.

YOUTH WORK

Lay leadership is also needed in the field of Youth Work. Much is being done by the uniformed organizations, Scouts and Cubs, Guides and Brownies, Church Lads Brigade, and we are glad that men and women give their time and skills to the service of youth. But more leaders are needed. We need Youth Clubs to complement our uniformed groups, and there are some areas – Longwood springs to mind – where there is a gap to be filled. I urge Church Councils to consider what needs there are in their parish ... It occurs to me that this is an area in which the younger members of our Police Force may have much to offer.

ILLEGITIMACY

One fact which causes us sadness is the rise in the illegitimacy rate, now virtually 50 per cent of all births. You and I are aware that this figure does not have the same significance seen against the background of our island culture, as it might in other countries. It does not, I believe, indicate a high degree of promiscuity, as it might elsewhere. Account must also be taken, when making comparisons, of the fact that abortions are not permitted here on social grounds, for which we are thankful. Nevertheless the rise ... from 25 per cent in 1946, for example, must cause us all grave concern. We can no longer just say: 'that's the way it has always been'. We are also especially saddened by the alarming increase in the number of girls under 16 who become pregnant. It is no excuse for a man to say that the girl was a willing partner. The law exists to protect girls against their own youth and inexperience, and they are entitled to the protection which the law offers. They, and their babies are also entitled to our love and compassion. I urge all who have to do with youth, especially parents, but also teachers, clergy, youth leaders and others to consider well what guidance they should be giving and what example they should be setting.

EDUCATION

(The Bishop's points are dealt with in Chapter 5)

EMPLOYMENT

... Sadly our period under review saw the end of the flax industry in 1966, with nothing comparable in its place ... We deplore the continued refusal of the British Government to grant free access to UK for St Helenians, a disability under which this island has laboured since the Commonwealth Immigrants Act of 1962, and which was not helped by the British Nationality Act of 1981 ...

AGED AND HANDICAPPED

Our concern must be, not only for youth, but for the aged and for the handicapped of all ages ... I urge Church Councils to consider what more needs to be done. This is an area in which all the Churches can co-operate ...

CO-OPERATION BETWEEN CHURCHES

It has been a joy to see, over the last three years, a growing together of the Churches ... I am delighted to welcome this morning representatives of other Churches ...

FINANCE

... Over the years, the parishes have made great strides in their increased contributions, especially to clergy stipends and the maintenance of their buildings. But we are still heavily dependent on overseas help ... from the Province ... USPG ... Diocesan Association ... supporting parishes and individuals ... I am speaking of the Island of St Helena, for Ascension is largely self-supporting ... We are indeed grateful for all this help, without which we could not function as we do. But we cannot, and should not, rely on such help, nor assume that it can continue ...

STEWARDSHIP

But we in the Diocese cannot any longer consider ourselves a missionary area. We are the oldest Anglican Church south of the Equator. We cannot go on relying on outside help and it is high time that we stood on our own feet. It is, I believe, perfectly possible for us to pay our way, and have something left to give away. And so this Synod will be asked to consider a campaign for Stewardship. I would like to set ourselves a target of becoming self-supporting in 10 years time. I estimate we would need another £6,000 a year. This sounds formidable, but it is perfectly possible ... If every Easter communicant gave an extra 15p a week in the Church collections, we would be self-supporting in 1983, let alone 1993. Not everyone could do that, of course, but some would give less and some more, according to our ability.

I go to England in April, to talk to those parishes and people who support us, I ask this Synod to authorize me to say to them: 'Please go on supporting us for another 10 years, and by that time we will aim to support ourselves'.

When I was in South Africa a year ago. I came to understand that the reason why the Province can give us such financial support is because they take tithing seriously. Church people there are taught to follow the Biblical principle that all we have comes from God, and the first charge on our income should be to give one tenth back to God. True, tithing is interpreted in different ways ... Nor do I pretend that all Church members in the Province tithe. But many do ...

Now I have to ask this Diocese – Can we morally continue to accept help, unless we ourselves are giving at the same proportionate level as those who help us? ... It is not something which a Synod, or a Church Council, can demand of people. It is something which each individual, each family, must decide for themselves, for this is a family matter ...

There is another aspect to this. Parishes which take stewardship seriously all report a wonderful revival in parish life. It isn't that they now have enough money to pay the parson and repair the roof, and something to give away. The very commitment to Stewardship seems to bring a renewed commitment to the Church and a new vitality ... I believe that Stewardship is something which the people of St Helena can understand. I recall how generously and readily you gave for the restoration of St James', and the tiling of the Cathedral. Do you remember two years ago when I asked you for some money for the Algerian Earthquake Appeal? I thought we might raise about £300. Instead you gave £1,800, almost all in small amounts by several thousands of you, young and old. I said then that I felt humble and proud to be your Bishop. I also quoted a saying that Louisa George had taught me, before she died, 'Out of little, give a little, and God will make it up.' ...

Stewardship is not a gimmick for raising money. It springs from two things. First our belief that this is God's world, that it is good and that all we have comes from Him. And we are called to be good stewards of his gifts. It is not a case of giving to God what is ours, but of using His gifts to us responsibly. And secondly, stewardship springs from our commitment to Christ. Only if we have truly committed our lives to Him, can we begin to think of Stewardship. Do you turn to Christ? ... If so, and only if so, Stewardship follows as a natural consequence of our discipleship.

... Our continued commitment to Christ depends on our life of prayer. As with money, so with time. We are also to give a proportion of our time wholly back to God in prayer, so that the whole of our time may be sanctified.

My vision ... is that they should be islands, in the South Atlantic, from which prayer to God continually ascends. I would hope that Church Councils and individuals would demand of their clergy, and their Bishop, that they will teach them to pray. But this vision can only come true if Bishop, clergy and lay people continually grow in the life of prayer.

May God give us His grace that this may be so.

Appendix B

Memorials to Royal Marines and Royal Navy in St Mary's Church, Ascension Island 1836-1922

BY GRACE YE ARE SAVED
IN GRATEFUL REGARD FOR THE KINDNESS OF CAPTN.ROBT.CRAIGIE, AND
IN MEMORY OF
THE UNDER-NAMED OFFICERS AND MEN OF H.M.S. SCOUT,
WHO DIED, WHILST SERVING OFF THE WEST COAST OF AFRICA,
FROM THE YEAR 1836 TO THE YEAR 1839.

CHARLES BALDWIN DYKE ACLAND,
FIRST LIEUTENANT. MAY 10TH 1837, AGED 26;
THOMAS COLE, ASSISTANT SURGEON, MAY 6TH 1838, AGED 27;
JAMES NORRIS, GUNNER, AND JOHN CASS, CARPENTER'S MATE,
WERE BURIED AT COMFORT COVE, IN THE ISLAND OF ASCENSION.

HENRY MANSFIELD, COLLEGE MATE, MAY 6TH 1838 AGED 21;
RICHARD B. WEST, CAULKER; GEORGE JONES, CAPTAIN'S COXSWAIN
JAMES MORRIS, GUNNER'S CREW, HENRY ADAMS, JOHN AINON, A.B.
JAMES CULVERWELL, RICHARD BURTON, PRIVATE MARINES;
DAVID HOWIESON, GEORGE HAVARD, JOSEPH WESTCOMBE,
JOHN GILES, JAMES BRAY, JOHN BRISON, BOYS OF THE FIRST CLASS;
AND JOHN REED, BOY OF THE SECOND CLASS,
WERE BURIED AT SIERRA LEONE.

JAMES SMITH, PRIVATE MARINE, AND TOM ROSS, LANDSMAN,
WERE BURIED AT PRINCES ISLAND.

NELSON LOCKER, MATE, APRIL 22ND 1837, AGED 24;
JOHN SMITH, GUNNER, JAMES RICHARDSON, QUARTER-MASTER;
JOHN PEARSON, SHIP'S COOK, SAMUEL WEBB, CAPTN. MAIN TOP;
W.J.WATSON, CARPENTER'S MATE, MARK G.NOBLE, A.B.
JAMES FOSWELL, JOHN DISON, PRIVATE MARINES;
TOM FREEMAN, ORD. SEAMAN, JOHN CHAPMAN AND JOHN FURNAM, BOYS,
WERE ALL BURIED AT SEA.

"THE SEA GAVE UP THE DEAD WHICH WERE IN IT; AND DEATH AND THE GRAVE
DELIVERED UP THE DEAD WHICH WERE IN THEM; AND THEY WERE JUDGED
EVERY MAN ACCORDING TO THEIR WORKS." REVELATIONS, XX − 13.
"THE DEAD SHALL HEAR THE VOICE OF THE SON OF GOD: AND THEY THAT
HEAR SHALL LIVE." JOHN V − 25.
"FOR, AS IN ADAM ALL DIE, SO IN CHRIST SHALL ALL BE MADE ALIVE."
I COR XV − 22.

* * *

IN MEMORY OF

CAPTAIN EDWARD BATES, ROYAL MARINES,

FOR 10 YEARS, COMMANDANT OF THIS ISLAND.

WHO DIED OF FEVER AT NORTH EAST COTTAGE.

14TH APRIL 1838.

THIS TABLET WAS ERECTED, ON THE REDUCTION OF THE ISLAND

IN 1882 AS A TOKEN OF ADMIRATION FOR HIS ENERGY

AND SKILL IN CARRYING OUT MANY VALUABLE WORKS

TO WHICH THE ISLAND STILL OWES MUCH OF ITS COMFORT.

INTERRED IN THE GARRISON CEMETERY.

A.G.R.R.

(The name is incorrect, and should read Captain William Bate)

* * *

TO THE MEMORY OF

CAPTAIN ROGER SAWREY TINKLAR, R.M.

WHOSE REMAINS ARE INTERRED IN THE CEMETERY.

HE DEPARTED THIS LIFE SEPTEMBER 14TH 1840,

WHILST HOLDING THE COMMAND OF THIS ISLAND

IN THE 45TH YEAR OF HIS AGE.

THIS MONUMENT

IS ERECTED BY THE OFFICERS OF ASCENSION

AND THE SQUADRON ON THE WEST COAST OF AFRICA

AS A TESTIMONY OF THEIR ESTEEM FOR HIM IN LIFE

AND THEIR SORROW FOR HIS DEATH.

* * *

SACRED

TO THE MEMORY OF

JOHN STRUGNELL

LATE CAPTAIN OF THE FORE TOP

OF H.M.S. PHOENIX

WHO DIED AT ASCENSION

JULY 5TH 1850

AGED 37 YEARS

* * *

SACRED TO THE MEMORY OF

ARTHUR R. FOX

LIEUT.R.N. HER MAJESTY'S SHIP PROMETHEUS,

WHO DIED SUDDENLY ON HIS PASSAGE

FROM ST.HELENA TO ASCENSION

AUGUST 8TH 1852 AET 23 YEARS

THIS TABLET IS ERECTED

...PTAIN AND MESSMATES AS A TOKEN

.F RESPECT TO HIS MEMORY

(one corner of this marble tablet has fallen away)

* * *

IN MEMORY OF

THOMAS W. SHANKS

DIED AT BANANA ISLANDS

15TH SEPTEMBER 1852

AGED 29 YEARS

A BROTHER'S TRIBUTE

1873

* * *

IN MEMORY

OF

COMMANDER

ALEXANDER DUFF GORDON

THIRD SON OF

COLONEL GORDON OF PARK

BANFFSHIRE, WHO DIED ON THE 2ND OF DECR. 1856

WHILE IN COMMAND OF

H.M.S. "HECATE" ON THIS STATION

AGED 36 YEARS

THIS TESTIMONIAL WAS ERECTED BY

THE OFFICERS AND CREW OF H.M.S. "HECATE"

TO SHOW THE ESTEEM AND REGARD

ENTERTAINED BY THEM FOR THEIR WORTHY

AND KIND HEARTED COMMANDER

* * *

SACRED TO THE MEMORY OF

OLIVER T. LANG ESQRE R.N.

LIEUT. COMMANDING H.M.S. "LEE"

WHO WAS KILLED BY A FALL FROM THE BRIDGE

WHILE COMING TO AN ANCHOR OFF THIS ISLAND

NOVEMBER 2ND 1865 AGED 26 YEARS

ALSO MR PETERS ASSISTANT ENGINEER

WHO DIED AT SEA JANUARY 5TH 1863 AGED 27

ALSO GEORGE LEE, STOKER,

WHO DIED IN THIS ISLAND, 20TH MAY 1864 AGED 42 YEARS

STEPHEN AMBER, GUNNER R.M.A.

WHO DIED AT SEA. 21ST OCTOBER 1865 AGED 29 YEARS

THIS MONUMENT IS ERECTED BY THEIR SHIPMATES,

AND MANY NAVAL FRIENDS OF LIEUT. LANG

WHO MOURN HIS UNTIMELY DEATH.

"SO HE BRINGETH THEM TO THE HAVEN WHERE THEY WOULD BE"

* * *

IN MEMORY OF

JOHN COYLE, PTE. R.M.L.I.

WHO DEPARTED THIS LIFE 13TH FEBRY 1864,

AGED 33 YEARS.

THIS TABLET IS PLACED HERE BY HIS COMRADES

AS A LAST TRIBUTE TO HIS MANY ESTIMABLE

QUALITIES.

* * *

SACRED

TO THE MEMORY OF

JAMES GALLAWAY, PTE. R.M.L.I.

WHO WAS ACCIDENTALLY KILLED BY FALLING FROM NORTH EAST PATH

DOWN BLACK ROCK ON THE NIGHT OF THE 17TH NOVEMBER 1872

IN THE 31ST YEAR OF HIS AGE

ALSO

CHARLES STEVENS, PTE.

WHO DIED AT THE ROYAL NAVAL HOSPITAL ON 23RD NOV.

AGED 26 YEARS

THIS TABLET IS ERECTED BY THE NONCOMMISSIONED OFFICERS AND

MEN OF THE DETACHMENT, AS A TOKEN OF THEIR ESTEEM AND RESPECT.

* * *

IN LOVING REMEMBRANCE OF

LIEUT. EDWARD WILLIAM SAMPSON, R.M.L.I.

COMMANDING THE DETACHMENT

OF ROYAL MARINES ON THIS ISLAND

WHO DIED FEBRUARY 22ND 1875; AGED 32

LEAVING A WIDOW AND 2 CHILDREN.

HE WAS THE LAST SURVIVING SON OF THE LATE

REVD. THEOPHILUS SAMPSON

RECTOR OF EAKRING, NOTTS.

HE TOOK GREAT INTEREST IN THE WORKS UNDER

HIS CHARGE, PLANNING AND CARRYING OUT

MANY IMPROVEMENTS ON THE ISLAND,

& DIED DEEPLY REGRETTED BY EVERYONE.

HIS BODY IS INTERRED IN THE MOUNTAIN CEMETERY.

PSALM XXXIX, VII

* * *

JOHN DUNCAN EAST

DIED IN PEACE AUGUST 5TH

1878

AGED 17

BURIED IN THE MOUNTAIN CEMETRY

* * *

SACRED TO THE MEMORY OF THE
UNDERMENTIONED SEAMEN AND MARINES
WHO DEPARTED THIS LIFE BETWEEN
APRIL 1879 AND APRIL 1881 AT ASCENSION

W.A.NICHOLSON COOK 1STCLASS	AET 39 YEARS
D.R.HOIT ,, ,, ,,	,, 36 ,,
GEO. SCHUTTERLIN WD.RM.STEWD.	,, 26 ,,
W.J.PHILLIPS ACTG.SGT.MAJOR R.M.	,, 32 ,,
GEO. FENDICK CORPL.R.M.	,, 22 ,,
H.MUNRO PVTE.R.M.	,, 32 ,,
J.PROSSER ,, ,,	,, 26 ,,
W.DUFFIELD ,, ,,	,, 27 ,,
M.VICKERY ,, ,,	,, 35 ,,
C.LEMON ,, ,,	,, 32 ,,
W.BASSETT ,, ,,	,, 32 ,,
A.BRODICH MERCHT.SEAMAN	,, 40 ,,

* * *

IN AFFECTIONATE REMEMBRANCE OF THE UNDERMENTIONED
PETTY OFFICERS OF H.M.S. FLORA (TENDER) WHO WERE DROWNED
OFF PILLAR POINT BY THE BARGE STRIKING ON THE ROCKS
WHILST CRUISING ROUND THE ISLAND ON 30TH AUGUST 1879
MICHAEL PIGGOTT, CHIEF E.R.A. AGED 41 YEARS
WILLIAM B. COOK, WRITER AGED 23 YEARS
HENRY BLACKHURST, E.R.A. AGED 22 YEARS
HENRY GORING, GUNNERS MATE AGED 33 YEARS
WILLIAM JENKINS, CAULKER AGED 35 YEARS
THIS TABLET WAS ERECTED BY THE OFFICERS,
SEAMEN AND MARINES OF THIS ISLAND
AS A TOKEN OF THEIR ESTEEM.
"AND THE SEA GAVE UP THE DEAD WHICH WERE IN IT"

* * *

TO THE GLORY OF GOD
AND IN MEMORY OF
HENRY B. KEMP, R.M.L.I.
WHO WAS KILLED ON JULY 8TH 1885, WHILE BLASTING NEAR LONG BEACH
ALSO OF
WILLIAM RODEN, R.M.L.I.
WHO DIED IN THE ROYAL NAVAL HOSPITAL, ASCENSION, ON FEB 8TH 1888
FROM INJURIES RECEIVED WHILE BLASTING IN GARRISON
ALSO OF
RICHARD A. CORNELL, R.M.L.I.
WHO WAS DROWNED IN CRYSTAL BAY, ON NOV.24TH 1888
R.I.P.
THIS TABLET WAS ERECTED BY THE OFFICERS AND MEN OF THE ISLAND

* * *

SACRED

TO THE MEMORY OF

HENRY JAMES GORDON

SURGEON, ROYAL NAVY

(ELDEST SON OF THE LATE REVEREND THOMAS GORDON, D.D.)

WHO DIED SUDDENLY

AT THE MOUNTAIN HOSPITAL, ASCENSION

DECEMBER 15TH 1889

AET 31

ERECTED BY HIS SHIPMATES

THE OFFICERS AND MEN OF THE ISLAND

AS A TRIBUTE OF AFFECTION AND RESPECT

"EYE HATH NOT SEEN, NOR EAR HEARD, NEITHER HAVE ENTERED

INTO THE HEART OF MAN, THE THINGS WHICH GOD HATH PREPARED

FOR THEM THAT LOVE HIM"

* * *

SACRED TO THE MEMORY

OF

HUGH MCDOUGALL, A.B.

AGED 35 YEARS

WHO WAS ACCIDENTALLY DROWNED

NEAR ENGLISH BAY FEBRY 25TH 1902

THY WILL BE DONE

* * *

IN MEMORY OF

THOMAS JOHN JENNER

PRIVATE R.M.L.I.

WHO WAS ACCIDENTALLY KILLED

WHILE DRIVING THE DAILY CART

TO GREEN MOUNTAIN

17TH AUGUST 1908

AGED 38 YEARS

THIS TABLET WAS ERECTED BY

THE INHABITANTS OF THE ISLAND

* * *

IN MEMORY OF

EDWARD DINGLEY

1ST CLASS PETTY OFFICER ROYAL NAVY

WHO DIED AT ASCENSION

18TH JANUARY 1909

AGED 36

* * *

IN MEMORY OF
GEORGE BUCKWELL
AND
HENRY COLLINS
PRIVATES
ROYAL MARINES LIGHT INFTY
THIS TABLET IS PLACED HERE BY
THEIR COMRADES

* * *

IN MEMORIAM
ROYAL MARINES
WHO DIED ON THE ISLAND
1815-1922

(HMS PENZANCE *conveyed this*
memorial to Ascension in 1937)

IN LOVING MEMORY
OF THE FALLEN
IN THE ALLIED FORCES
OF TWO WORLD WARS
AND THE
FALKLANDS CONFLICT
IN GOD WE TRUST

* * *

The following memorial to Captain William Bate and others is on a
tombstone in the Georgetown cemetery:

This Monument
was erected by the Detachment of Royal Marines
serving on the Island of Ascension in the year 1838
IN MEMORY OF
their comrades who fell victims to a Malignant
Fever that visited this usually healthy Island & in
the space of 3 weeks removed from this life to eternity
twenty five individuals amongst whom was their
respected Commandant
Captain William Bate
and the undermentioned Non-commissioned Officers
and Privates etc.

Color Sergt John Cunningham
Corporal John Warren
,,   Thomas Hunt
,,   Arthur Madden
,,   George Cockerell
Private Samuel Barber
,,   John Blundell
,,   James Sears
,,   William Murray
,,   William Coleman
,,   William Whiley
,,   Stephen Murphy
,,   James Botting
,,   John Wright

Civilians
Robert Leonard   Master Cooper
Supernumeraries
Thomas Cole   Asst Surgeon
James Norris   Gunner
Walter Earle   Boy
Women
Martha Warren   Corpl's wife
Mary Dredge   Private's wife
Susan Knight   Private's wife
Children
John Leonard and Henry Whiley
Boys

James Cox Qtr.Master who was
accidentally drowned whilst securing spars near to
the boat shed belonging to the Victualling Department
on 31st May 1838

Appendix C
Island Postage Stamps with Local Church Interest

ST HELENA
1934
Centenary of Crown Rule
2*d*   The Quay. View of St James' Church from top of Ladder
2*s* 6*d*   St Helena and the Cross
The Picture taken from an Icon on the front of the Cathedral Pulpit (see Chapter 4)

1953
5*s*   Artist's impression of Jamestown (from Mundens?) shows St James' Church

1975
Bicentenary of visit by Captain Cook in 1775.
25p   Head of Captain Cook against background of Jamestown
St James' Church shown with tower over north porch and a spire. But Cook would have seen it with tower at west end and no spire. Tower was moved and spire built in 1834, 59 years after Cook's visit

1976
Definitive Issue. Old Pictures of St Helena
  8p   View from the Castle Terrace. G. H. Bellasis 1815
Shows St James' Church with tower at West end
  10p   Plantation House. J. Wathen 1821
Shows old Country Church with tower and spire
  18p   St Paul's Church. V. Brooks
  40p   St Matthew's Church. V. Brooks 1868
Date of picture incorrectly given on stamp as 1860. Cornerstone of church was not laid until December 1861

1979
Inclined Plane, Ladder Hill
  8p   Shows St James' Church in 1829, with tower at west end and no spire

1980
Centenary of visit by Empress Eugenie, widow of Napoleon III
  5p   Napoleon's tomb in 1848
  8p   Empress landing at St Helena
  62p   Empress at tomb of Napoleon
Also a 'mini' sheet. The scenes of the Empress landing and her visit to the tomb had been sketched by the Reverend J. C. Lambert, Vicar of Jamestown

1982
75th Anniversary of Scouts
29p   Canon Walcott, Founder of Boy Scouts on St Helena

1983
Christmas. Life of St Helena (first series)
From the late 15th-century glass in the Parish Church of St Michael & All
Angels, Ashton-under-Lyne
10p   The birth of St Helena
15p   St Helena goes to School
Unfortunately the picture in the 15p stamp was printed in reverse, to the
consternation of the parish

1984
150th Anniversary of St Helena Colony
7p   Reproduces 2d stamp of 1934
£1   Reproduces 2s 6d stamp of 1934

1984
Centenary of Salvation Army on St Helena
  7p   Mrs Rebecca Fuller OF 1883-1973 Former Corps Secretary
11p   Meals on Wheels. Captain Denis Strissel
25p   Salvation Army Hall, Jamestown
60p   Salvation Army Band at the Clock Tower, Jamestown

1984
Christmas. Life of St Helena (second series)
  6p   St Helena visits prisoners
10p   Betrothal of St Helena
15p   Marriage of St Helena and Constantius
33p   Birth of Constantine

1985
Christmas. Life of St Helena (third series)
  7p   St Helena journeys to the Holy Land
10p   Jambres slays the bull
15p   The bull restored to life: conversion of St Helena
60p   Resurrection of the corpse: the true Cross identified

1986
Friendly Society Banners
10p   Church Provident Society for Women
11p   Working Men's Christian Association
25p   Church Benefit Society for Children
29p   Mechanics Friendly Benefit Society
33p   Ancient Order of Foresters

1990

Christmas. St Helena Churches
10p   Baptist Church, Sandy Bay
13p   St Martin in the Hills
20p   St Helena and the Cross
38p   St James'
45p   St Paul's Cathedral

1985   On 30 July, the Baptist Church issued a Commemorative Envelope of 140 Years of Baptist Witness on St Helena, signed by the Pastor, the Reverend Garth Lahner and the Governor, His Excellency Francis Baker.

ASCENSION

1979

Ascension Day
8p   St Mary's Church from portico of old Royal Marines barracks

1981

Green Mountain Farm
12p   Farm in 1881
30p   Farm in 1981
Church Services have been held at the Farm since at least 1865. (Shown also on 1983 Island Views issue 15p)

1984

Island views
15p   St Mary's Church at night, illuminated

1988

150th Anniversary of death of Capt. Edward Bate
9p   Bate's Memorial in Georgetown Cemetery (not St Mary's Church)
See Appendix B for text of inscription

1991

Christmas. Ascension Churches
 8p   St Mary's Church Exterior
18p   St Mary's Church Interior
25p   Grotto Church (RC) Exterior
65p   Grotto Church Interior

TRISTAN DA CUNHA

1954
1s St Mary's Church

1969
United Society for the Propagation of the Gospel
4d   Sailing ship off Tristan
9d   Islanders going to Service
1s 6d   Landing of first Minister
2s 6d   Procession outside St Mary's Church

1971
50th Anniversary of Shackleton-Rowett Expedition
4p   Presentation of Scout Troop flag

1973
Golden Jubilee of St Mary's Church
25p   Interior of Church

1978
5p   St Mary's Church (painting by Roland Svensson)

1979
International Year of the Child. Children's drawings
5p   The Padre's House
15p   St Mary's Church

1981
Arrival of the Reverend Edwin Dodgson on Tristan 1881
10p   Youthful Edwin Dodgson in England
20p   Edwin Dodgson with Island in background
30p   Edwin Dodgson teaching a group
Also a 'mini' sheet with picture of Dodgson family, armed with croquet mallets,
outside Croft Rectory, circa 1860, including Archdeacon Dodgson and Charles
and Edwin Dodgson

1981
Flightless Rail
10p   Four se-tenant stamps, showing The Chicks; Atlantisia rogersi; The
Nest; The eggs
The Rail was named after the Reverend H. M. C. Rogers (1922-5)

1983
Definitive Issue
20p   The Reverend William F. Taylor with Mr Peter Green

1985
Shipwrecks (first series)
25p 1878 Mabel Clark. Aground by the Molly Gutch
Picture shows bell from the Mabel Clark in the belltower of St Mary's Church.
Designed by Mr Allan Crawford. Also a 'mini' sheet showing positions of
wrecks

1985
Centenary of loss of lifeboat and crew
20p Memorial plaque in church. Plaque and set of 3 stamps designed by Mr
Allan Crawford

1986
Shipwrecks (second series)
20p Font from wreck of Edward Vittery (1881), stamp designed by Mr Allan
Crawford

Mr Allan Crawford designed ten stamps in 1946, the first Tristan stamps. The
values were both in Sterling and, for local use, in potatoes. The 2s 6d stamp,
local value 120 potatoes, showed St Mary's Church. Unfortunately, only the 1d
stamp was printed, as a sticker.

FALKLAND ISLANDS

1969
Centenary of Bishop Stirling's Consecration
2d Holy Trinity Church
6d Christchurch Cathedral
1s Bishop Stirling
2s Mitre

1981
Early Settlements
33p Mission House, Keppel Island

Appendix D

Selected Annotated Bibliography

St Helena

GENERAL

Philip Gosse. *St Helena 1502-1938*. Anthony Nelson 1990 (first pub. Cassell 1938).
The standard history, which I have found invaluable for the secular background.

John Keay. *The Honourable Company*. HarperCollins 1991.
The most recent history of the East India Company.

The Laws and Constitution for the Island of St Helena 1682, with an introduction by Trevor W. Hearl. Pub. St Helena Link 1991.

Tony Cross. *St Helena*. David & Charles 1980.
A useful introduction to the Colony, written by a former Education Officer, with a short history and chapters on Ascension and Tristan.

Margaret Stewart Taylor. *St Helena Ocean Roadhouse*. Robert Hale 1969.
An account of a visit in 1967/68.

Oswell Blakeston. *Isle of St Helena*. Sidgwick & Jackson 1957
This account of a visit includes a long interview with Bishop Turner. The Bishopsholme library copy has Turner's pencilled comments in the margin.

Earlier works include:

J. Osorio da Fonseca. *Narrative of the Voyage of Joao da Nova Castella in 1502*, translated by J. Gibbs, 1752.

Thomas Henry Brooke. *A History of the Island of St Helena ... to the year 1806*. London 1808. 2nd Edition (to 1823) 1824.
The first history of the Colony, written from the Records by the Government Secretary and sometime Acting Governor.

Anon. *A Few Thoughts for the Stranger & Resident in St Helena*, with illustrations. London 1868.
Three of its eight chromolithographs by Vincent Brooks feature island churches. Also poems dedicated to churches and churchyards, including one to commemorate the reopening of St James' Church on its Patronal Festival 1866.

John Charles Melliss. *St Helena*. A Physical, Historical and Topographical Description of the Island, including its Geology, Fauna, Flora and Meteorology. L. Reeve & Co. 1875.
The classic Victorian volume on the history and natural history of St Helena, with comprehensive lists of flora and fauna, profusely illustrated with hand-coloured and chromolithographic plates.

Benjamin Grant. *A Few Notes on St Helena and Descriptive Guide*. St Helena 1883.
Written for tourists by the local newspaper editor and printer.

E. L. Jackson (Mrs). *St Helena: the Historic Island*. Ward Lock 1903.
Both historical and descriptive, with lists of plants and very useful list of officials and personalities around 1902, but no index.

Arnold Chaplin. *A St Helena Who's Who*. Arthur L. Humphreys 2nd Edition, revised and enlarged 1919.
Subtitled, A directory of the island during the captivity of Napoleon.

Hudson Ralph Janisch. *Extracts from the St Helena Records*. B. Grant St Helena 1885. 3rd Edition, edited by P. L. Teale and Pub. W. A. Thorpe & Sons St Helena 1980.
An interesting collection of extracts illustrating many facets of St Helena life from 1673 to 1835.

ANGLICAN CHURCH

S. J. MacNally. *The Chaplains of the East India Company*. 1971 Oriental and India Office Collections, British Library MSS Eur D 847.
A useful compilation of appointments etc. of all EIC Chaplains by a former official of the Accountant General's Dept. of the India Office.

Correspondence on Colonial Church Legislation. Colonial Office 1852. Part 1, pp54-74, relates to varied matters concerning the St Helena Churches, 1846-1851.

Robert Gray. *A Journal of the Bishop's Visitation*. 1849.

Charles Gray. *Life of Robert Gray*. Rivingtons 2 Vols. 1876.
Edited by his son. Contains accounts in his letters of Robert Gray's visits to St Helena.

Audrey Brooke. *Robert Gray*, First Bishop of Cape Town. OUP 1947.

Thelma Gutsche. *The Bishop's Lady*. Cape Town 1970.
A biography of Sophy Gray.

The Ecclesiologist. Volumes 1850 and 1851.
Comments on Benjamin Ferrey's designs for the new Country Church.

W. O. B. Allen & E. McClure. *History of the Society for Promoting Christian Knowledge*. SPCK 1898.
Accounts of grants to St Helena, Ascension and Tristan.

C. F. Pascoe. *Two Hundred Years of the SPG.* SPG 1901.
History and clergy lists for St Helena and Tristan.

St Helena (Diocesan) Magazine 1899-1951. Edited by Canon Porter 1899-1921;
Canon Walcott 1921-51. St Helena.
Invaluable, not only for contemporary Church news, but also for articles on
Church history researched from the Archives. See especially the series
December 1935 to April 1940.

Charles Christopher Watts. *In Mid Atlantic.* SPG 1936.
Based on the Bishop's lectures to ship's passengers visiting St Helena. Includes
Ascension and Tristan. The author admits it was written at sea and far from
books of reference.

Gordon Taylor. *The Sea Chaplains.* Oxford Illustrated Press 1978.
A monumental history of the Chaplains of the Royal Navy. The index has 13
references to St Helena, and three each to Ascension and Tristan. Includes an
account of Bishop Beardmore when he was a Royal Naval Chaplain. Also
Tristan during the second World War.

Anne R. Kotze. *St Helena Journal.* Cape Town 1990.
Limited edition. Delightful account by Provincial Archivist of visit to microfilm
Church Registers.

St Helena Diocesan Archives.
From 1814 onwards. St James' Registers date from 1680 (burials from 1767); St
Paul's Registers date from 1820, earlier ones having been destroyed in a fire.

ROMAN CATHOLIC

John Kelly SDB. 'The South Atlantic Islands of St Helena and Ascension'. 1974.
Two pages of notes.

Jarlath Gough OFM Cap. 'St Helena is my Parish', Pub in *The Word*, a magazine
of the SVD Fathers.

Philip Bruggeman MHM. 'Notes on the History of the Church'. 19 pages, 1985.

Brendan Sullivan MHM. 'History of the Roman Catholic Church on the Island
of St Helena'. *St Helena News*, issues May, June 1990.

NONCONFORMIST

Owen Spencer Watkins. *Soldiers and Preachers Too*, Being the Romantic story of
Methodism in the British Army. Charles H. Kelly 1906.

Trevor Hearl. *An Early Methodist on St Helena.* St Helena Link 1988.

G. Smith (Ed.). *Good News from Calcutta and St Helena.* London 1820.
An account of the introduction of the Baptist faith into St Helena during
Napoleon's exile by soldiers of the Royal Artillery.

Thomas Robson. *St Helena Memoirs*. 2nd Edit 1827. 'An account of a remarkable revival of religion that took place at St Helena during the last years of the exile of Napoleon Buonaparte'. There is an extract in Dr Chaplin's *A St Helena Who's Who*.

Edwin F. Hatfield. *St Helena and the Cape of Good Hope*. Edward H. Fletcher New York 1853.
Subtitled, Incidents in the missionary life of the Rev. James McGregor Bertram. The latter half of the book, dealing with his time on St Helena 1845-50 (Chapter 4 and Appendix), has been re-issued by Mr P. L. Teale.

Wilfred Edmunds. *An Isolated Family*. South African Baptist Press 1957. Contains history and list of ministers.

By Taking Heed, the history of the Baptists in Southern Africa 1820-1977. Baptist Publishing House 1983.

R. Wiggins. *History of the Salvation Army*. Thomas Nelson 1964. Vol IV 1886-1904. pp124-5.

Ascension

GENERAL

D. Hart-Davis. *Ascension*. Constable 1972.
A general history with bibliography.

John E. Packer. *Ascension Island*. 3rd Edition 1983.
A comprehensive handbook of 54 A4 pages, including history, topography with maps, geology, flora and fauna by a member of Cable & Wireless who spent many years on the island and was a Reader in the Church. Has a comprehensive bibliography. Obtainable from the Administrator's Office, Ascension Island, South Atlantic Ocean.

Mrs Gill. *Six Months in Ascension*. London 2nd Edit. 1878.
'An Unscientific Account of a Scientific Expedition.'
The wife of the astronomer David Gill relates the domestic hazards behind her husband's expedition in 1877. Charmingly written, it includes account of church services both in St Mary's and on Green Mountain.

James Avenell. 'Founding Fathers', Pub. in *The Sheet Anchor*, Journal of the Royal Marines Historical Society Vols IV and V.

CHURCH

Richard Davison. 'St Mary's 1843-1981', Pub. in *The Islander*, Ascension Island May 1981.

Michael Howes. *Notes on the History of St Mary's Church*. Ascension Island 1983. Revised and updated Michael Hawes 1984.

John Kelly SDB. 'The Grotto of Mary Help of Christians', Ascension Island. Single sheet.

Tristan da Cunha

GENERAL

Douglas M. Gane. *Tristan da Cunha.* George Allen & Unwin 1932
By the Founder and Secretary of the Tristan da Cunha Fund. Historical and
descriptive, with a consideration of the prospects for the island as seen in 1932.
Has a bibliography of 33 items.

Augustus Earle. *A Narrative of a Nine Month's Residence in New Zealand in 1827
together with a Journal of a Residence in Tristan D'Acunha.* Longman 1832. (OUP
1966.)
By the first artist of Tristan, stranded for eight months in 1824.

R. R. Langham Carter. 'Literature on Tristan da Cunha 1851-1889'. Pub. in
the *South Africa Library Bulletin* for March 1982.
By the Recorder of the Diocese of Cape Town.

Allan Crawford. *I Went to Tristan.* Hodder & Stoughton 1941.

Allan Crawford. *Tristan da Cunha and the Roaring Forties.* Charles Skilton 1982.
An excellent history, lavishly illustrated, by the Chairman of the Tristan da
Cunha Association, UK.

Margaret Mackay. *Angry Island.* The story of Tristan da Cunha (1506-1963).
Arthur Barker 1963.

D. M. Booy. *Rock of Exile.* Dent 1957.
Personal view by a Naval Telegraphist in HMS *Atlantic Isle.*

Peter A. Munch. *Crisis in Utopia.* Thomas Y. Crowell, New York. 1971.
By a sociologist who visited in 1938 and 1964.

J. H. Flint. *Fortunate Island,* a story of Tristan da Cunha. Typescript. By the first
teacher on Tristan after the eruption of 1961. No relation to Fr Keith Flint,
Chaplain at the same time.

George Crabb. *A History and Postal History of Tristan da Cunha.* Pub. by the
author. 1980.
Much of the history is based on research into USPG Archives and has many
letters and reports from the Chaplains.

Patrick Helyer. *A Mini Annotated Bibliography of Tristan da Cunha.* With
supplements. Pub. by the author, 1991.
Over 2,500 entries by a one-time Chaplain on the Island.

Nancy Hosegood. *The Glass Island.* Hodder & Stoughton 1964.
A history written as a historical novel.

Tristan da Cunha Newsletter. Pub. Tristan da Cunha Assoc., UK. First published
1987.

CHURCH

W. F. Taylor. *Some Account of the Settlement of Tristan D'Acunha.* SPG/SPCK 1856.
By the first resident priest.

Robert Gray. *Three Months Visitation by the Bishop of Capetown.* Bell and Daldy,
London 1856.
The Appendix reprints his letter of 5 April 1856 telling of his visit to Tristan in
Holy Week 1856.

K. M. Barrow. *Three Years in Tristan da Cunha.* Skeffington 1910.
The diary of her life on Tristan 1906-1909 by the wife of the resident Chaplain.

Rose Annie Rogers. *The Lonely Island.* George Allen & Unwin 1926.
Written by the widow of the resident Chaplain who went with him to Tristan at
the age of 19, and was there 1922 to 1925.

A. G. Partridge. *Tristan da Cunha: the Isle of Loneliness.* SPG 1934.
A booklet by a resident priest.

The Mission Field. SPG.

Tristan da Cunha Newsletter. USPG.
Contains a great deal of material on the life of the Church and the USPG
missionaries.

The Falkland Islands

GENERAL

V. F. Boyson. *The Falkland Islands.* Oxford 1924

M. B. R. Cawkell, D. H. Maling, E. M. Cawkell. *The Falkland Islands.* Macmillan
1960.
Sections on Church and School.

Ian J. Strange. *The Falkland Islands.* David & Charles 3rd Edit. 1983.
Section on Religious History.

W. Forrest McWhan. *The Falkland Islands Today.* Stirling Tract Enterprise 1952.
A general account by a Free Church Minister who had served 30 years on the
islands.

David B. Smith. 'Church, State and Schooling in the Falkland Islands', *Journal
of Educational Administration and History.* Vol XXII No.2. July 1990. Leeds
University.

Falkland Islands Newsletter. Pub. Falkland Islands Assoc.

ANGLICAN CHURCH

Robert Young. *From Cape Horn to Panama.* South American Missionary Society 1905.
The early part is a very moving account of Capt. Gardiner, Keppel Island, and the early Mission to Tierra del Fuego.

R.J. Hunt. *The Livingstone of South America.* Seeley Service 1932.
The life of W. Barbrooke Grubb, who was on Keppel 1886-9.

E. Lucas Bridges. *Uttermost Part of the Earth.* Century 1987.
The life of Thomas Bridges by his son, born at Ushuaia.

J. A. Wylie. *Life and Missionary Travels of the Rev. J. Furniss Ogle.* Longmans, Green 1873.

F. C. Macdonald. *Bishop Stirling of the Falklands.* Seeley, Service & Co. 1929.

P.J. Millam. *A Brief History of Christ Church Cathedral.*
7 pages written for the 75th Anniversary of the Consecration of the Cathedral. Contains useful list of gifts made and donated.

Winona Hardy. *A Short Life of Stirling.*
13 pages written for the Centenary of Stirling's Consecration.

Harry Bagnall. *Faith under Fire.* Marshalls 1983.
Church life during the Argentinian invasion by the resident Anglican Chaplain.

South American Missionary Society Annual Reports, 1869-73.

ROMAN CATHOLIC CHURCH

Jose Brunet O. de M. *La Iglesia en las Islas Malvinas durante el Periodo Hispano (1767-1810).* Madrid 1969.

Humberto Baratta SDB. *Presencia Salesiana en las Islas Malvinas.* Buenos Aires. (From Archives of Salesian Fathers in Rome.)
Covers period 1887-1952.

Anton Agreiter MHM. *The Catholic Church on the Falkland Islands.*
By the Apostolic Prefect on the Falklands. A brief survey, covering period 1764 to 1986.

NONCONFORMIST CHURCH

Proceedings of General Assembly of the Free Church of Scotland 1872-1890.

Appendix E
Clergy Lists

These are as complete as the author has been able to make them but neither completeness nor accuracy can be guaranteed.

St Helena

ANGLICAN: BISHOPS OF ST HELENA

1859-1862 Piers Calveley Claughton
1862-1899 Thomas Earle Welby
1899-1905 John Garraway Holmes
1905-1931 William Arthur Holbech
1931-1935 Charles Christopher Watts
1935-1939 Charles Arthur William Aylen
1939-1960 Gilbert Price Lloyd Turner
1960-1967 Harold Beardmore
1967-1973 Edmund Michael Hubert Capper
1973-1979 George Kenneth Giggall
1979-1985 Edward Alexander Capparis Cannan
1985-1991 James Nathaniel Johnson
1991-   John Harry Gerald Ruston OGS

ANGLICAN: HONORARY CANONS

1975 Derek Frederick Brown
1975 James Nathaniel Johnson
1981 William Richard Lindsay (died 1991)

ANGLICAN: ORDER OF SIMON OF CYRENE

A Provincial Order for Lay Churchpeople who have given distinguished service.
1963 James R. Bruce
1965 Charles Clingham (died 1987)
1968 John Field (died 1985)
1972 Matthew Crowie (died 1988)
1977 Reginald Victor Constantine (died 1980)
1989 Randolph Constantine

ANGLICAN: SUB-DEACONS & LAY MINISTERS

1951 Edward Frederick Constantine (died 1967)
1961 Arnold Flagg
1962 Kenneth Gough
1963 Matthew Crowie (died 1988)
1963 Kenneth Joshua (died 1974)
1986 Isaac Douglas Hudson
1990 Lily Crowie

ANGLICAN: ORDINATIONS

1849 April	DEACON	Ludwig Heinrich (Louis Henry) Frey
1860 March	PRIEST	Horatio Rees Webbe
1868 July	DEACON	John Compton Hands
1871 June	DEACON	Thomas Goodwin
1874 April	PRIEST	John Compton Hands
1874 April	PRIEST	Thomas Goodwin
1880 May	PRIEST	Joseph Christopher Lambert
1889	DEACON	George Mushet
1901 17 February	DEACON	Harry Gibbons
1902 11 June	PRIEST	Harry Gibbons
1935 24 February	PRIEST	Fenwick Hall
1961 20 August	PRIEST	Bryan Neville Bartleet
1963 5 May	PRIEST	Maurice Steadman Geen
1985 1 September	DEACON	Michael Crook
1986 7 September	PRIEST	Michael Crook

ANGLICAN: DIOCESAN SYNODS

First	September	1885	Bishop Welby
Second	September	1887	Bishop Welby
Third	September	1889	Bishop Welby
Fourth	September	1891	Bishop Welby
Fifth	September	1893	Bishop Welby
Sixth	December	1895	Bishop Welby
Seventh	September	1897	Bishop Welby
Eighth	September	1903	Bishop Holmes
Ninth	September	1906	Bishop Holbech
Tenth	August	1909	Bishop Holbech
Eleventh	May	1913	Bishop Holbech
Twelfth	October	1916	Bishop Holbech
Thirteenth	May	1933	Bishop Watts
Fourteenth	January	1983	Bishop Cannan

ANGLICAN: EAST INDIA COMPANY CHAPLAINS
(includes some visiting ship's Chaplains)
In this and in the following lists, date of death indicates that the person died on the island.

1671	Nathaniel William Noakes	1727	– Sawbridge
1673	William Swindle (Swindell)	1730	George White
1675	John Wynne	1734	John Coney
1681	Joseph Church	1736	Francis Fordyce
1683	John Cramond	1738	Francis Barlow (died 1738)
1684	Thomas Sault	1740	Edwin Alcock
1685	Robert Butler (visitor)	1746	William Field
1689	John Ovington (visitor)	1747	William Loveday
1691	– Willis	1750	William Lee
1692	William Rudsby	1764	John Thackeray
1693	Jethro Bridecake	1767	William Bearcroft
1695	Bartholomew Harwood	1774	Robartes Carr
1697	– Simons (visitor)	1781	John Wilson (died 1802)
1699	John Humphreys	1785	Edward Sewel
1701	Jethro Bradock (visitor)	1797	John Fletcher Wilkinson
1702	John Kerr		(schoolmaster from 1788)
1705	Charles Masham (died 1706)	1808-1815	Samuel Jones
1706	Laurence Hackett	1811-1830	Richard Boys
1707	Joshua Thomlinson	1816-1834	Bowater James Vernon
1719	John Jones	1829	James Boys (from Madras
1722	– Long		during furlough of R. Boys)
1723	Estcourt Giles	1831-1834	Robert Parkinson Brooke

In 1834 St Helena became a Crown Colony

ANGLICAN: COLONIAL CHAPLAINS

1834-1837 R. P. Brooke (Acting)
1837-1839 W. Helps
1839-1861 Richard Kempthorne. Rural Dean from 1852, Archdeacon from 1857

ANGLICAN: SPG MISSIONARIES

1847-1851 William Bousfield
1849-1870 Ludwig Heinrich (Louis Henry) Frey. Deacon & Master of Government Country School (not SPG) (died 1870)
1852 J. Chambers
1852-1854 Matthew Hale Estcourt (died 1858 aged 39)
1857 H. Rees Webbe
1858 George Bennett
1858 Edward Bennett

ANGLICAN: JAMESTOWN

ST JAMES

1861-1863 George Bennett
1863-1866 Henry Whitehead
1866-1871 George Bennett
1874-1876 Lister Smith
1877-1878 Peter Frank Cadman
1879-1886 Joseph Christopher
         Lambert
1886-1891 Stephen John Ellis
1891-1895 Edwin Hughes
1895-1896 Stephen John Ellis (died
         1896)
1896-1899 Edwin Heron Dodgson
1899   M. H. M. Wood
1899-1904 Alfred Porter
1904-1908 Harry Gibbons
1908-1909 F. M. Lane
1909-1917 Laurence Chase Walcott

ST JOHN

1867-1870 Henry Whitehead
1872-1874 Thomas Goodwin,
         Schoolmaster
1885-1887 John Compton Hands

1889   George Mushet
1893-1900 John Compton Hands

1901-1904 Harry Gibbons

1913   St James' and St John's combined into one parish

1917-1918 Robert John James Garrod
1919-1921 Gerard C. Day
1921-1950 Laurence Chase Walcott (died 1951)
1950-1952 Douglas Humphrey Cumming
1952-1954 Edgar James Mitchell
1954-1963 John Edgar Keith Flint
(1959   William Thomas Walter Samuel – licensed to officiate)
1963-1964 Fenwick Hall
1964-1966 Eric William Kleb
1966-1968 Leonard Albert Smith
1968-1981 William Richard Lindsay, Archdeacon
1981-1984 David Neaum, Archdeacon
1984-1989 Michael Alan Houghton
1990   Louis Donald Ilett
1990-   Ronald Frederick Cottingham

THE COUNTRY PARISHES

ST PAUL'S		ST MATTHEW'S	
1861-1862	Edward Bennett		
1863-1870	George Barrow Pennell	1862-1867	Henry James Bodily
1870-1884	Henry Whitehead (died 1884)	1868-1911	John Compton Hands
1885-1894	Frederick Henry Baker		
1894-1899	Edwin Arthur Barraclough		
1899-1904	Bishop Holmes		
1904-1921	Alfred Porter	1911-1919	Christopher Fenn Streeter Wood
		1919-1920	John Compton Hands
		1920	Sydney Wilson Ruscoe
	1921-1922 Frederick L. Ashworth		
	1922-1924 Gilbert Price Lloyd Turner		
	1924-1926 Harold Alfred Lewty		
	1927-1932 Frank Oxley		
	1932-1934 Bishop Watts		
	1934-1935 Basic H. Warner		
1935-1937	Bishop Aylen	1934-1937	Fenwick Hall
	1937-1938 Bishop Aylen		
	1938-1939 Gilbert Price Lloyd Turner		
1939-1959	Bishop Turner	1939-1944	Percy Clark
		1945-1956	Fenwick Hall
		1957-1961	Fenwick Hall
1960-1962	Bishop Beardmore	1961-1964	Bryan Neville Bartleet
1962-1965	Maurice Steadman Geen	1964-1965	Fenwick Hall
1966-1971	James Nathaniel Johnson	1954-1967	Maurice Steadman Geen
	1968-1970 James Nathaniel Johnson		
1972-1976	Charles Henry Milton-Smith	1970-1975	Gerwyn James Jones
1976-1979	Angus Greer Macintyre	1975-1978	Dennis Stanley Mander
1979	Bishop Giggall	1978-1983	John Diseworth Harvey
1980-1982	Melvin Clay Knowles		
1982-1985	Andrew David Irwin Neaum (Archdeacon from 1984)	1984-1986	Hermon John Crowie
1985-	Michael Crook (NSM)		
1985-1986	Peter Stewart Cowen	1986-1988	Peter Stewart Cowen
1988-1990	Peter Charles Price	1988-1991	John Merrick Ryder

ROMAN CATHOLIC

1852   Fr McCarthy (first of about 20 Military Chaplains)
1891-1906 J. H. Daine (last Military Chaplain)
1957-1963 Jarlath Gough OFM Cap
1963-1978 John Kelly SDB
1979-1980 Peter Paul Feeney OP
1981-1985 Philip Bruggeman MHM
1986   Mgr Anton Agreiter MHM, Apostolic Prefect
1988-1989 Joseph Holzknecht MHM
1989-   Brendan Sullivan MHM

BAPTIST

1845-1871	J. McGregor Bertram	1938-1958	W. C. Benjamin
1848-1852	Hudson Ralph Janisch	1958-1960	Eric Hayward
1865-1868	W. J. Clother	1960-1963	P. J. Visser
1868-1870	Robert Kerr	1963-1966	L. Ressell
1885-1886	F. R. Bateman	1967-1969	R. de Wet
1887-1888	J. W. Setchfield	1970-1973	P. J. Visser
1889-1892	Joseph Young	1973-1976	Findlay Austin
1893-1896	John R. Way	1976-1980	J. M. Longstaff
1897-1905	Thomas Aitken	1980	J. Hayes
1905-1910	W. J. Buchanan	1981-1983	J. D. Smith
1911-1915	N. G. Wood	1984-1988	G. Lahner
1916-1918	W. D. Morris	1988	R. C. Lennox
1918-1938	Alfred Nicholls	1989-	A. P. Coats

SALVATION ARMY

1886-1887 Capt. and Mrs Harris
1887-1888 Capt. and Mrs Gale
1888-1889 Capt. Wilcox and Lieut. Evans (Women Officers)
1889-1890 Capt and Mrs Jack
1890-1891 Capt. and Mrs Hancox
1891-1892 Capt. and Mrs Evans
1892-1893 Capt. and Mrs Jordan
1893-1894 Capt. and Mrs Pagett
1894-1895 Capt. and Mrs Gilroy
1895-1896 Ensign and Mrs Meyers
1896-1897 Ensign and Mrs Holt
1897-1898 Adjutant and Mrs A. G. Cunningham
1898-1899 Capt. and Mrs Bainbridge
1899-1900 Adjutant and Mrs Foster
1900-1903 Adjutant and Mrs C. Widdowson

1903-1905 Adjutant and Mrs Richardson
1905-1907 Adjutant and Mrs Craig
1907-1909 Ensign and Mrs Gillingham
1909-1912 Adjutant and Mrs Frank Robinson
1913-1915 Ensign and Mrs Jonas
1915-1920 Adjutant and Mrs Thomas Bunting
1920-1922 Capt. and Mrs Richard Southall
1922-1924 Capt. Wright and Lieut. Alfred Eritson
1924-1926 Capt. and Mrs Woodhouse
1926-1927 Ensign Fred Harrison
1927-1929 Capt. and Mrs Charles Hoskins
1929-1932 Ensign and Mrs Sydney Mannouch
1932-1934 Ensign and Mrs George A. P. Spencer
1934-1936 Adjutant and Mrs Townsend
1936-1938 Adjutant and Mrs J. Wilson-Hebden
1938-1941 Capt. and Mrs Rich
1941-1944 Adjutant and Mrs A. L. Jansen
1944-1947 Capt and Mrs James Campbell
1947-1948 Major and Mrs Wellard
1948-1950 Capt. and Mrs Constable. Mrs Constable 'promoted to Glory'
1952-1956 Major and Mrs J. S. Brewin
1956-1959 Capt. and Mrs J. Malins
1959-1964 Capt. and Mrs William du Plessis
1964-1968 Capt. and Mrs Colin Fairclough (Lt. Col. Whittermore)
1968-1970 Capt. and Mrs Dennis W. Norgate
1970-1973 Capt. and Mrs Graeme Harding
1973-1980 Capt. and Mrs Howard Sercombe (Lt. Col. Skjoldham)
1980-1984 Capt. and Mrs Dennis Strissel
1984-1985 Brigadier Keith Anderson
1985   Capt. and Mrs K. Harvey
1985-1986 Major and Mrs L. Cooper
1986-1987 Brigadier and Mrs Keith Anderson
1987   Brigadier and Mrs G. Young
1987-1990 Lieut. and Mrs Harry Fillies
1990-   Lieut. and Mrs L Pinner

Wives have been included, since they are normally Officers in their own right.
Names in brackets indicate Officers 'holding the Citadel' during furlough.

SEVENTH DAY ADVENTIST

1949-1955 H. Camphor
1955-1958 G. Beyers
1958-1963 W. Philips
1963-1970 W. Philmore
1970-1972 A. DuPreez

1972-1976 G. Baxin
1976-1978 W. Turner
1980-1989 B. Kriel
1989-   C. Chalmers

Ascension

ROYAL NAVAL CHAPLAINS
*indicates a mention in Taylor's *The Sea Chaplains*

1844	George Bellamy	1876	Hamlet Wm. Millett*
1847	William Bell	1878	John McG. Ward
1849	W. H. Pilcher	1881	George M. Sutton*
1853	Hugh McSorley	1884	John Cavanagh*
1856	Henry Glasson	1887	Arthur Price Hill*
1859	Arthur George Berry	1890	Thomas Austin*
1862	Douglas J. Bentflower	1893	Alwyne C. H. Rice
1862	Robert Hind	1896	William V. Rainier
1865	James Robinson	1899	Henry P. Dawson
1870	John T. Westroff	1902	Dallas Brooks*
1872	George C. Waller		

The Naval Chaplains were withdrawn in 1905.
Readers conducted the services until 1966.

VICARS

1966-1969 John Archibald Leitch Thomson Crawford
1969-1973 Thomas Patrick Duffy
1975-1977 David Anthony Bowles
1978   John Diseworth Harvey (P. in charge)
1980-1982 Richard Ireland Davison

ROYAL AIR FORCE CHAPLAINS

1982   Noel Beddoe Walters James (July-September)
1982-1983 David Stuart Mackenzie (Sept.-January)
1983   Kenneth R. Brown (January-April)
1983   Michael John Norton Howes (April-August)
1983   Geoffrey Roger Huddleston (August-December)
1983-1984 Michael Rowell Hawes (December-April)

VICARS

1984-1985 George Henry Bradshaw
1986-1990 Ronald Frederick Cottingham
1991-   Nicholas Anthony Turner
1991-   Ann Turner (Non Stipendiary Deacon)

LAY PEOPLE AUTHORIZED TO TAKE SERVICES
Date first licensed

1905 Captain Reginald Morgan, Asst. Paymaster Oswald Carter
1927 McGrath, R. C. Saxby, Ford-Smith, Brown
1928 Warden, Kent, Knight
1929 Robertson, Macey, Keilor, Blythman, Maclachlan
1931 N. T. Bramble, W. C. Gare
1932 E. A. Willmott, G. C. A. Williamson, H. B. Challoner
1934 W. Norman Barnes
1937 J. R. Bruce
1939 H. J. Howell
1940 J. W. Sawyer
1945 K. Finney, S. Biron
1947 F. K. Duncan
1948 H. S. Phipps
1950 J. S. Innes, P. H. Straw
1952 R. J. M. Perring
1954 F. B. Stephens, W. L. Heard, G. Govan
1955 Dr M. Lockie
1956 G. R. A. Heath
1957 M. A. Page, J. E. Packer
1958 N. D. Grant Davie, R. G. Allan
1959 G. V. Lewis, E. G. Elkerton
1963 J. W. Parsons
1964 P. R. Keslake, R. F. J. Mann
1965 E. E. Pierce, G. N. Bayley
1969 R. H. B. Smith
1972 J. F. W. Proctor, J. K. Donald
1974 G. C. Guy
1978 Mrs Valerie Allen
1983 D. Bendall
1985 S/Ldr M. Watkins, F. Lyndon Moore
1989 N. Shacklady
1990 J. Nex

Tristan da Cunha

1851-1856 William Frederick Taylor
1881-1885 Edwin Heron Dodgson
1886-1889 Edwin Heron Dodgson
1906-1909 John Graham Barrow
1922-1925 Henry Martyn Cheselden Rogers
1927-1929 Robert Alexander Chernside Pooley
1929-1932 Augustus George Partridge
1933 Augustus George Partridge

1934-1941 Harold Wilde
1942-1944 Cyril Percy Lawrence RN
1944-1946 David Ingles Luard RN
1946-1948 Alec Edward Handley (died 1948)
1949 David Ingles Luard
1949-1952 Dennis Wilkinson
1952-1956 David Neaum
1956-1961 Philip Harold Bell
1961 Charles John Jewell
[Evacuation of Island]
1963-1966 John Edgar Keith Flint
1966-1968 William Paul Seymour Davies
1968-1971 Angus Alexander Welsh
1975-1978 Edmund Digby Buxton
1978-1980 Patrick Joseph Peter Helyer
1981-1983 Michael Norman William Edwards
1984-1987 James David Pearson
1988-1989 Philip Drew Jourdan
1989- William Stanley Skipper

READERS AND LAY PREACHERS

1817	(William Glass)	1962	Lars Repetto
?	(Mrs Cotton)	1964	(Peter Day)
?	(Peter Green)	1974?	Edward Rogers
1927	Philip Lindsay	1979	Alfred Rogers
1959	(Miss R. M. Downer)		

ROMAN CATHOLIC LAY MINISTERS

1932?	Agnes Rogers	1982?	Dereck Rogers
1970	Cyril Rogers	?	(Anne Green)

Falkland Islands

ANGLICAN: BISHOPS OF THE FALKLANDS

1869-1900 Waite Hockin Stirling
1902-1910 Edward F. Every
1910-1914 Lawrence Frederick D. Blair
1919-1934 Norman Stewart de Jersey
1934-1946 John Reginald Weller
1946-1963 Daniel Ivor Evans
1963-1976 Cyril James Tucker
1977 The Archbishop of Canterbury resumed jurisdiction of the Falkland Islands.

ANGLICAN CLERGY

Colonial Chaplains
1845-1855 James Leith Moody
1855-1859 Henry Martyn Faulkner (died 1859)
1859-1873 Charles Bull
1872-1875 Henry Coulson Lory (Acting)
1877-1907 Lowther E. Brandon
Deans
1892-1907 Lowther E. Brandon
1907   C. H. Golding-Bird
1911   E. J. Seymour
1915   J. S. Smith
1926   F. S. Vaughan
1931   H. E. Lumsdale
Senior Chaplains
1935-1936 Robert Thompson Wade
1937-   G. K. Lowe
1945-   R. G. R. Calvert
1950-1951 Maldwyn Lloyd Jones
1951-1953 John Durno Steele
1953-1957 Jack Gould
1957-1961 John Ozanne Vere-Stead
1962-1966 Eric Thornley
1966-1970 Peter John Millam
1971-1975 Patrick Joseph Peter Helyer
1975-1978 Gerald Smith
1979-1986 Harry Bagnall OBE
1987-1991 John Gervase Maurice Walker Murphy
1991-   Stephen Palmer
Readers
1954-1984 Stanley Bennett

ROMAN CATHOLIC CLERGY OF ENGLISH SETTLEMENT

1856-1857 Laurence Kirwan
1872   William Walsh
1873   Vincent de Vilas
1875-1886 James Foran
1886   Patrick Dillon
1887   Felix M. Grisar
Salesian Fathers of Don Bosco
1888-1890 Patrick Diamond
1890-1902 Patrick O'Grady
1902-1905 Patrick Diamond

1905-1937 Mario Luis Migone (died 1937). Fr Migone had served as
          assistant priest 1889-91 and 1895.
1934-1947 Hugh Drumm
1948-1952 John Kelly
Mill Hill Missionaries
1952-1973 MGR. JAMES IRELAND, first Apostolic Prefect
1952-1954 Fr Edward Callen
1953-1954 Br Leo Kaanders
1954-1959 Fr Cornelius Landman
1954-1973 Br Arnold Roozendaal
1959-1963 Fr Norbert Prior
1963-1965 Fr John Pacey
1965-1971 Fr Rudolph Roel
1967-1969 Br Frederick Rainer
1971-1973 Fr Daniel Spraggon
1973-1985 MGR DANIEL SPRAGGON, Apostolic Prefect (d.1985)
1972-1977 Fr Philip Bruggeman
1977-1987 Fr Augustine Monaghan (1985-6 Pro-Prefect)
1985-1986 Fr Patrick Littlewood
1986-   MGR ANTON AGREITER, Apostolic Prefect
1987-1991 Fr John Doran
1987   Fr Theodore Beemster
1989-1990 Br Joseph Priller
1991   Fr Joseph Haas

FREE CHURCH MINISTERS

1871-1882 Anthony Yeoman. Free Church of Scotland
1882-1890 William H. Philip. Free Church of Scotland
1888- ?   George M. Harris. Baptist
1890-1892 C. E. Lawson Good (died 1892). Baptist
?   ?
1934-1965 W. Forrest McWhan (died 1965). Church of Scotland
1967-1971 Paul Charman. Independent Free Churchman
1971- ?   Robin W. Forrester. Baptist
1978-1981 Alex Queen. Methodist. He was assisted by Dennis Overton, Lay
          Presbyterian
1984   Colin Frampton. Baptist
There have been no Free Church Pastors since 1984 except for a six-week visit
in Nov/Dec 1991 by John Fraser, a Minister of the Church of Scotland.

Index

The index relates only to the general text, and not to the Appendices.

Church, Rev J. 29, 32
Church Society 46, 161
Cilicia, HMS 219
City of Cairo 135
Civil, Dr 34
Clapham Sect 35-6
Clark, Rev Percy 152
Claughton, Alan O. 55
Claughton, Bishop Piers 49-55, 71-2, 103,
   114-5, 128, 147, 171-2, 182, 188
Claughton, Piers Edward 55
Clayton, Archbishop Geoffrey 71, 222
Cleopatra, HMS 246
Clergy
  Stipends 57, 65-6, 74, 87, 119, 148-9,
    151, 244-5, 247, 255
  Endowment Fund 76, 78, 82, 87
  Provincial Augmentation of Stipends 78
  Provincial Clergy Pensions Fund 65
  Provincial Common Fund 65
  Provincial Parity of Stipends 78, 87-8
Clifford, Edward 175
Clifton, William 33, 157
Clingham, Charles 138
Clother, Rev W. J. 172
Clough, Rev P. H. 224
Coggan, Archbishop 250
Coats, Andrew 172
Colchester 24, 137
Cole, Old King 24
Colenso, Bishop 54
Collins, Ven Arthur 81
Colonial Bishoprics Fund 50
Colonial Chaplains 41-9, 51, 57-8
Comfortless Cove 182, 190
Conisbee, Hannah 250
Constantine, Edward 142
Constantine, Michael 126
Constantine, Randolph 142, 145, 147
Constantine, Reginald 82, 142
Constantine, R.S. 71, 134, 141, 146
Constantine the Great, Emperor 24
Constantius Chlorus, Emperor 24
Conway 73
Cook, Captain James 98
Corker, William Newton 102
Corona 219
Corpus Christi College, Cambridge 66
Cottingham, Rev Ronald 92, 94, 96, 128,
   195-6
Cotton, Mrs 203
Cotton growing 166
Couch, Rev Andrew 194
Cowdry, Bishop Roy 224-5

Cowen, Dr 183
Cowen, Rev Peter 92, 143-4, 154-5, 164
Cracker, HMS 244
Cranmer Farm 242
Crawford, Allan 217-18, 220-1, 232
Crawford, Rev John 74, 192-3
Cronje, General 63
Cronk, Quentin 85
Crook, Rev Michael 89, 92, 143
Cross Hill 196
Crowie, Rev H. J. 154-5
Crowie, Lily 145, 155
Crowie, Matthew 154
Cuddesdon College 66, 68, 96
Cumming, Rev D. H. 123, 125, 136
Curacao, HMS 205

da Costa, Rev John 77
Daine, Fr J. H. 160, 166
Dakers, Lionel 141
d'Albuquerque, Alphonse 181
Daley, William 201
da Nova Castella, Admiral Joao 23, 181
Darbyshire, Archbishop John 69
d'Arcy, Colonel 254
Darwin, Charles 239
Davies, Rev P. 226-7
Davies, Idris 140, 154
Davis, John 237
Davis, Sir Spencer, Governor 137
Davis, Admiral Sir William 73
Davison, Rev R. I. 85, 194
Dawson, Rev H. P. 186, 189
Day, Rev Gerard 120
Dean, G. M. 246, 255
de Aguiar, Fr Pius 254
de Blank, Archbishop Joost 72
de Bougainville 237, 254
Dee, Rev Dr John 25
de Grook, J. 176
de Jersey, Bishop N. S. 249
Denstone College 232
Derby, Lord 245
Desire 25, 237
Despard, Rev P. 239
de Vilas, Fr Vincent 255
Diamond, Fr P. 256
Diamond, HMS 204
Dillon, Fr P. 255
Dinizulu, Prince 94, 130-1
Diocese of
  Cape Town 19, 43, 50, 71, 221
  Dunwich 71
  Falklands 51, 244-9